THE RHETORIC OF
POPE JOHN PAUL II

THE RHETORIC OF POPE JOHN PAUL II

The Pastoral Visit As a New Vocabulary of the Sacred

Margaret B. Melady

 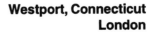

PRAEGER

Westport, Connecticut
London

Library of Congress Cataloging-in-Publication Data

Melady, Margaret Badum.
  The rhetoric of Pope John Paul II : the pastoral visit as a new
vocabulary of the sacred / Margaret B. Melady.
     p. cm.
  Includes bibliographical references and index.
  ISBN 0–275–96298–9 (alk. paper)
     1. John Paul II, Pope, 1920– —Journeys. 2. Communication—
Religious aspects—Catholic Church. I. Title.
  BX1378.5.M45 1999
  282′.092—dc21   98–44672

British Library Cataloguing in Publication Data is available.

Library of Congress Catalog Card Number: 98–44672
ISBN: 0–275–96298–9

First published in 1999

Praeger Publishers, 88 Post Road West, Westport, CT 06881
An imprint of Greenwood Publishing Group, Inc.
www.praeger.com

Printed in the United States of America

The paper used in this book complies with the
Permanent Paper Standard issued by the National
Information Standards Organization (Z39.48–1984).

10 9 8 7 6 5 4 3 2 1

Copyright Acknowledgments

The editor and publisher gratefully acknowledge permission to use the following
material:

Selected excerpts totalling about 1840 words from *The Pope Speaks to the American
Church* by Pope John Paul II. Copyright © 1992 by the Cambridge Center for the Study
of Faith and Culture. Reprinted by permission of HarperCollins Publishers, Inc.

Every reasonable effort has been made to trace the owners of copyright materials in this
book, but in some instances this has proven impossible. The author and publisher will
be glad to receive information leading to more complete acknowledgments in subsequent
printings of the book and in the meantime extend their apologies for any omissions.

To my three grandchildren,
Alexandra, Nicolas, and the one about to be born.

Contents

Acknowledgments   ix

1. Introduction   1

2. Between the Sacred and Chaos   17

3. Background to the Visits   31

4. Sensing the Faithful   53

5. Textual Address: Audience Identification and
   Characterization   99

6. Textual Analysis: Symbol Choice   139

7. Visits as Performance   175

8. Push and Pull of Sacred and Secular   203

Appendix   235

Selected Bibliography   237

Index   251

Acknowledgments

When I arrived in Rome, anxious to begin another chapter in my life, the Pontifical Gregorian University welcomed me and offered me a challenge. I thank the university for the opportunity, especially for the guidance of Father Sergio Bernal, dean of the social science faculty when I entered. I am grateful to all my professors, and also the staff, whose dedication, professionalism, and kindness gave me enormous support in this venture.

Most of all, I owe a great deal to my director, Father Robert White, S.J. First, he agreed immediately to take me under his direction in a program that he was just beginning to develop at the university. For the nearly four years I was in Rome, the Center for Social Communications grew, and so did its students. Our small group of graduate students was in the forefront of an exciting and stimulating program. When Father White and I first talked about my dissertation topic, we explored a number of areas, but we kept returning to Pope John Paul II. To write about a living pope can be intimidating. However, throughout the entire period, even when I had returned to the United States, Father White was patient, but always prodding.

There were many friends and associates at the Vatican who were willing to answer my questions or lead me to some pertinent information. Members of the church's hierarchy and others who had closely worked on or observed papal visits were especially helpful in my research. Monsignor (now Bishop) Robert Lynch and Russell Shaw provided me with invaluable material, including drafts of papal speeches.

Of course, my family, especially my husband Tom, has been at my side throughout my work on this dissertation. Achieving this goal has been as much Tom's dream as mine. After all, we two have been one for thirty-five years.

Finally, the long and sometimes arduous task of analyzing Pope John Paul II as a communicator has been more than an intellectual challenge; it has been a spiritual journey.

CHAPTER 1

Introduction

Pope John Paul II's image has appeared repeatedly in print and electronic media throughout the world during the twenty years of his papacy. Largely because of his travels and their extensive media coverage, John Paul II is probably better known than any other pope in modern times. His forceful and captivating personality has facilitated the creation of a high media profile, but personal appeal alone cannot sustain the public interest and recognition that John Paul II has continually received year after year. When Pope John Paul II was chosen *Time* magazine's Man of the Year for 1994, *Time* correspondents explained their choice by pointing to the pope's "mass proselytizing," in which he used well and often the "world's bully-est pulpit" to make the world listen to his message.[1] Consequently, John Paul II's high media profile is due not to one or several single acts, but to his multiple, sustained, and purposeful efforts to construct meaning for the church in the public forum of the world. Certainly, John Paul II is not the first pope to preach to the world on moral issues, nor is he the first pope to venture outside the Vatican. However, he is the first pope to use the international visit as a new form of communicating with the far reaches of the Catholic Church, contributing a unique character to the development of the modern rhetorical papacy.

EMERGENCE OF THE RHETORICAL PAPACY

John Paul II's use of communicative tactics is an outgrowth of social and political changes that have led to an emergence of a rhetorical papacy. During the last one hundred years, as the Catholic Church gradually became disengaged from its reliance on territorial claims, direct political support, and massive networks of confessional social structures, the papacy adopted strategies to enhance its spiritual and moral leadership.[2] These strategies included symbolic and communicative tactics that became increasingly a part of a rhetorical papacy.

The industrialization of the nineteenth century produced enormous changes in the world to which the Catholic Church had been intimately tied. In Europe and North America, increased urbanization required more systematized forms of organizing regional and national life. These developments, coupled with the incorporation of liberal democratic principles into emerging forms of government, gave birth to a new concept of tolerance that posed both problems and promise for the Catholic Church. For example, Catholicism would no longer be punished as a crime in England, but Catholics would eventually have to live beside atheists, anticlerics, and free masons.

The new, more pluralistic societies were serviced and enhanced by popular and cheap newspapers aimed at reaching the masses with their neutral and nonconfessional message. A press, free of state and church influence, was considered an objective presenter of the decision-forming information needed in a democratic society. Consequently, the public became less and less dependent on the pulpit for the type of information that would guide their everyday decisions.

These growing democratic aspirations were met with staunch resistance by the popes of the mid–nineteenth century, who denounced the new freedoms of conscience and the press and held fiercely to their political control of the papal states. In the 1860s, Pius IX denounced liberalism, centralized church authority in the Holy See, and called the First Vatican Council to confirm papal infallibility in matters of faith and morals. However, before his papacy ended, Rome was occupied by Italian armies, and the papacy was effectively stripped of its temporal dominion. In a reluctant turnabout, Pope Leo XIII recognized democracy and relocated the church as a custodian of liberty. His encyclical, *Rerum Novarum*, written in collaboration with a team of specialists, reflected the church's social activity and thinking at that time regarding the misery of the working class.[3] Employing a new approach, Pope Leo XIII no longer appealed to civil authorities alone, but addressed a much wider audience of rich and poor, capital and labor, and warned that it would be a mistake to "leave out the Church" in this public discussion.[4]

Rerum Novarum was the first of a now one hundred-year tradition of the Catholic Church to survey, reflect upon, and respond to the opinion of the times by adding a critical moral voice to discussions on social issues such as labor policy, economic development, arms control, trade, and ecology. From the beginning, social teaching documents remained sensitive to the polarities of ideologies and partisan positions, while trying not to compromise the church's moral leadership.

The outbreak of World War I greatly challenged the emerging importance of the church's moral leadership. Vatican support was solicited by each of the opposing sides. However, a decision was made to follow a neutral policy in which the church subordinated any potential political advantage to moral condemnation of war.[5] In a sense, the policy of neutrality was part of a sequence of decisions that stimulated what Vallier called "structural differentiation between the Church and major secular spheres."[6] However, this process of extricating the church from territorial claims was not easy. Even though Benedict XV pleaded unrelentingly for peace during World War I, papal representation was excluded from the final peace conference, ostensibly because of the Vatican's unresolved territorial claims to Rome. In 1929, Benedict's successor, Pius XI, resolved the Roman question by renouncing the church's territorial claims in exchange for a sovereign and independent Vatican. This firmly established a territorial neutral base from which Pius XII could appeal for peace when war once again tore Europe apart.

During World War II, Pope Pius XII's Christmas radio broadcast, devoted to themes of peace and international order, became a media event throughout the world. Following the war, he continued to use this communication tool, extending concepts of social justice to South American landowners and Southern Rhodesian colonialists. Pius XII's discourses touched on a wide range of subjects, even dental science and nuclear physics, reflecting the tendency of the Thomistic revival in the church to present a systematized Catholic opinion about everything.[7]

When Pope John XXIII followed Pius XII, he was determined to give his pontificate the special markings of his simple personal character. Immediately, he instructed the official news organ, *L'Osservatore Romano*, to drop the pompous phrases such as "Illuminated Holy Father" and use only "the pope," "Pope John," or simply "John." At his coronation, John XXIII announced that he would not be a diplomat, a statesman, a scholar, or an organizer, but rather a good shepherd of his flock.[8] Emphasizing this role, he left the Vatican frequently to visit hospitals, churches, and prisons. During each visit he would slowly wind through the streets smiling and waving at crowds, even stopping to walk and mingle informally with the masses. Unstructured and seemingly unplanned, John XXIII's populist style was decidedly in contrast to his predecessors.

John XXIII's simplicity was revolutionary, but the most significant achievement of his pontificate was the calling of the Second Vatican Council. When the Council began in 1962, television cameras and newspaper journalists gathered to cover the deliberations of twenty-five hundred Catholic prelates and numerous observers from all corners of the world. Pope John's opening remarks admonished the prophets of doom and called upon the church to take a leap forward in its renewal effort. Debate began, and news reporters, barred from the official Council sessions, sought out stories by piecing together information dramatizing the controversies that pitted the more liberal theologians against a waning conservative minority. The break in the Roman Catholic Church's apparent monolithic authoritarian image became news.

John XXIII's death occurred in the midst of Vatican Council II, but his optimism had unleashed a progressive spirit that eventually carried out a far-reaching renewal. When the Council ended in 1965, its documents reflected a transformation and broadening of thought among the leadership within the church. Instead of a triumphalist proclamation of the one true church, Vatican Council II characterized the church's relationship to the modern world as an open dialogue in which the church "experiences the same earthly lot which the world does."[9] Pluralism was accepted and freedom of religion was defended as a human right. Furthermore, the Council declared the church's independence from the state by relinquishing the privileges and protections that had tied the church so closely to civil authorities. In principle, the church had completed its disengagement from the state, freeing it to further develop its moral leadership role.

During the Council's four years, bishops from all over the world experienced a new sense of power, deliberating together and working in close collaboration with the pope. This spirit of open debate and consultative process began to filter down to the local levels where not only theologians, but also laity expected to be included in the church's future decision-making process. A euphoria of change permeated the church and led many to expect even more radical interpretations of church doctrine than were actually promulgated in the Council's documents.[10]

From the beginning of his pontificate, Pope Paul VI enthusiastically embraced the Council's mandate to discern "the signs of the times."[11] Many of his writings and actions emphasized that the church's mission was to bring about peace and justice in the world in very concrete ways. Paul VI, grasping that the world had changed radically from the times of Pius XII, understood the global imperatives of the church. His written teachings examined large-scale international solutions to development problems, sometimes criticizing those political and economic structures that hampered justice. To underscore his global vision, Paul VI began a new era of international papal travel, pleading the case of the poor before the United Nations, and learning firsthand about the depth of poverty in India, South America, and Africa.

Paul VI's trips also underscored his intense desire to remove the barriers that separated the church from other Christians. In the Holy Land and in Istanbul, he embraced the patriarch of the Eastern Orthodox Church. In Geneva, he addressed the World Council of Churches. In Rome, he welcomed the Anglican archbishop of Canterbury and formed permanent secretariats to work towards unity between people of all religions. In this regard, Paul VI transformed the vocabulary of righteous excommunication to humble apology and forgiveness for past recriminations.

Paul VI was intent on casting off the symbols that he felt impeded the church from effectively working in the world. He sold his tiara and used the funds for the poor, reduced some of the ceremonial pomp, and abolished papal noble titles, transforming the monarchical court into a papal household. The Vatican had freed itself from the binding interests of temporal political power; now it had to overcome the vestiges of its autocratic pride in order for the pope to be a humble "servant of the servants of God."[12] Pope Paul VI had wanted the papacy to be accessible and thus demystified it, allowing himself to be seen as a human being.[13] This obsession with shedding his papal role in order to be more available to his priests and bishops had its drawbacks. In private audiences, he was known to read prepared denunciations against unorthodox actions and then, sensing that his duty was fulfilled, he would abandon his authoritative posture for a more conciliatory tone.[14] That same conciliatory posture was apparent in other areas affecting internal church discipline. Believing it futile to hold defecting priests and religious to their commitments, Paul VI allowed the granting of laicization to 97 percent of the growing numbers of priests asking to be released from their vows.[15]

The implementation of the Vatican Council II reforms became a primary focus of Paul VI's papacy. However, the enormous reforms of the Council became the center of controversy. The Council documents contained some ambiguities reflecting the compromises made to achieve reform while preserving certain traditional teachings. Conservatives resisted implementation of reforms; liberals reinterpreted the documents to justify even further reforms. The conflicts between the two groups were carried out in the public forum under norms of open debate and free discussion. Pope Paul VI called for an end to these perpetual discussions of already clarified truths, but the conflicts continued. Intent that one must convince rather than conquer, Paul VI was reluctant to use forceful action against those obstructing the reforms. After his personal meeting failed to persuade Archbishop Marcel Lefebvre to abandon his defiant opposition to the Council reforms, Paul VI refused to resort to excommunication, and instead submitted the issue to a commission of cardinals. Likewise, investigations of other "erring" theologians were begun, but no conclusions were ever reached. As journalist Wilton Wynn noted, "The 'suffering pope' projected the image of servant more than chief."[16]

By the end of Pope Paul VI's papacy, it became more apparent that papal leadership had been transformed. In many ways, this transformation followed a path similar to the leadership of other institutions. Rather than governing an institution through the inner workings of the system, dominant personalities such as presidents of democratic governments now conduct the affairs of governance largely through direct address of the people.[17] Thus, like presidential leadership, papal strategies rely more and more on public discourse and symbol making to articulate meaning. The use of these persuasive techniques to gain acceptance and cooperation among audiences demonstrates the emergence of a rhetorical papacy.

NORMATIVE CRISIS FACED BY
NEW POPE JOHN PAUL II

In 1978, Polish Cardinal Karol Wojtyla, chosen to succeed the short-lived John Paul I, faced a church and a society in crisis. Amidst both enthusiasm and doubt, church leaders were committed to implementing the theological and liturgical reforms of the Council despite the threats of resistance and radical experimentation. The liturgical reforms renewed interest in scripture and preaching, but abolished forms of devotions which had nourished spiritual life for generations. Shaken by the loss of Latin and Gregorian chant, groups such as those led by Archbishop Marcel Lefebvre publicly defied Rome by refusing to change the liturgy. In Holland, an experimental catechism aimed at reformulating Catholic beliefs for adults began a turbulent period of conflicts over authority between the Dutch hierarchy and the papacy.

Claiming a mandate had been given to them by the Dutch "People of God," Dutch bishops openly criticized papal teaching on contraception and recommended that celibacy be optional for Dutch priests. These threats of schism, one representing a resistance to modern reform and the other a radical movement toward increased democratization in the church, required the immediate attention of the new pope. To deal with these issues, Pope John Paul II followed the advice of his bishops and utilized the pressure of collegial opinion to produce an uneasy truce.[18]

These two examples of threats of schism presented tangible targets that could be approached through concrete strategies. In a sense, they were easier to confront than the more subtle evidence of crisis. For example, church officials had begun to note the fall in regular church attendance among populations who had previously been known for their steadfast practice of the faith. In the United States, the percentage of Catholics attending Sunday Mass dropped from 74 percent in 1958 to 52 percent in 1978.[19] The lines outside of confessionals practically disappeared. Men and women were leaving the religious orders and the priesthood. During Paul VI's fifteen-year papacy, more than thirty thousand priests were released from their vows.[20] Priests who remained were finding it very difficult to attract replacements. Family attitudes toward supporting the priesthood had definitely changed, and the statistics on seminarians showed severe drops. In the United States, the losses in religious orders had a devastating effect on the maintenance of Catholic schools, whose enrollment numbers declined significantly. This decline was alarming because there is a strong correlation between Catholic education and adult religious behavior.[21] In Italy, the statistical measures of baptisms and marriages also indicated a decline in the strength of Catholicism. The percent of Roman babies being baptized fell from 89 percent in 1960 to 81 percent in 1977. More than a quarter of Romans married in civil ceremonies in 1978, whereas in 1963 only 3.2 percent shunned a church marriage.[22]

The crisis in the church reflected a transformed society. The countercultural movements in Western society of the sixties and their fanatical onslaught on institutions and values produced widespread changes that incorporated elements of the expressive revolution into the mainstream of the seventies culture. The vocabulary and perception of fulfillment became private and personal, separated and opposed to former social structures based on tradition and custom. Institutions and their bureaucracies that limited individual freedom became suspect. The large voluntary organizations that were dependent on membership watched their numbers dwindle. Within institutions, egalitarian principles weakened the customs of authority. Students demanded to be consulted in major decisions of the universities. Schools became open and exams gradeless. Distinctions were erased between teacher and pupil, leader and follower, parent and child. The ideal was total egalitarianism, and any barriers that remained had to be torn down. With the traditional communal bonds severed, people tended to form enclaves only with those who shared their personal interests.

The sexual revolution was also in many ways an attack against the boundaries between the private sphere and the public. Sexual activity that had been secret and taboo outside the institution of marriage was now publicly admitted. Increased divorce, single parenting, rejection of formal marriage, and homosexual household arrangements became more acceptable in modern society, threatening the concept of the traditional family unit.

The church, once thought to be resistant of these modernizing tendencies, was not immune to the normative crisis of the expressive culture. The forces of democratization demanded that distinctions be erased within the church's authoritative structure, as well as between church and the rest of the world. The laity pressured for more responsibilities in parish and diocesan decisions. Women demanded an equal role in the ministry. Priests and religious, now in secular dress, raised their proposals and complaints about bishops and superiors in public. Among Catholics, the divorce rate and sexual behavior were found to match those of the non-Catholic population. Studies of religious attitudes in the U.S. church showed more and more Catholics had a "pick and choose" mentality about their religious beliefs and practices, ranging from their choice of parish, to their disregard for the church's teachings on birth control.[23]

The centralizing elements so firmly established by Pius XI and the First Vatican Council were being loosened by intense centrifugal forces of the modern age. The use of the vernacular in the liturgy encouraged more decision-making in regional and language-similar groups. Church missionaries, armed with anthropological data, became more aware of the church's own ethnocentric past and urged local churches to make Catholicism relevant to the diverse cultural conditioning of their populations. Moreover, demographic trends, especially the declining birth rates in Western Europe and North America, encouraged church leaders to turn their attention to the importance of growing areas in the Third World and their diverse ethnic populations.

In the latter days of Pope Paul VI's papacy, it became clear that the church was facing a crisis. It was difficult for Paul VI to mobilize any efforts to stem the tide. He had faithfully continued church renewal, transforming the authoritative papal image into that of a humble servant which, in the end, seriously hampered his ability to restore authority and discipline. The election of Pope John Paul I, whose papacy lasted only thirty-three days, did little to address the multitude of problems. However, during his short papacy, he made several lasting innovations. He inaugurated the first hyphenated name, choosing to join the John and the Paul of the last two papacies. He also was the first to shun coronation for a more simple ceremony, and was the first to replace the corporate "we" with a familiar "I."

AGAINST ODDS, JOHN PAUL II IS "GREAT COMMUNICATOR"

In October 1978, Karol Wojtyla, the first non-Italian pope since 1523, acknowledged to the cheering crowd that he came from a "far country." Although only a few hours by plane from Rome, Poland had been far away from the recent mainstream of events in Western society. Ravaged by war and foreign occupation, the nation had turned inward to protect and guard its national culture, which from the formation of the Polish state in 966 was strongly linked to its Catholic faith. Having very few periods of freedom, Polish messianic poets characterized the sufferings of the nation as an imitation of the sufferings of Christ that were necessary for eventual redemption.[24] This suffering during the period of Communist occupation of Poland not only disestablished the church from any formal political ties, but forced much of its activities underground.

Soon after the Polish pope's election, the radical liberal factions began suggesting that, based on his Polish background, the new pope would restore an authoritarian church. Democracy and diversity, according to these observers, were alien to the Polish mentality.[25] Furthermore, the totalitarian, godless regime in Poland allowed neither linkage nor compromise. It is this all-or-nothing, either-or world of the Polish church that some have said has influenced the absolutist thinking of Karol Wojtyla.[26]

Despite the supposed personal and historic shortcomings attributed to the new pope, John Paul II quickly established himself as a "great communicator" and an important moral leader. The secular media soon began to portray him as a "superstar" and an "icon for our age."[27] He was the subject of twelve *Time* magazine cover stories in seventeen years,[28] far more than Paul VI who was featured only three times in his fifteen years. National polls in the United States indicated favorable ratings, naming John Paul II the most important man of the year in 1979, and among the top three in 1981.[29] During a 1981 inquiry on religious leaders, those who said their views were similar to the pope's led those with dissimilar views by six percentage points, with more than a third of the respondents unable to make a judgment.[30] In 1995, polls demonstrated that the pope continued to be popular. John Paul II had a 64 percent approval rating among all Americans. Among those identifying themselves as Catholics, 83 percent had a favorable opinion of the pope.[31]

John Paul II's popularity has been linked by some researchers to a modest religious revival in the church. The dramatic declines in U.S. Catholic mass attendance ceased and numbers stabilized after 1978. Furthermore, surveys indicated an increase in the number of participants of religious activity outside of mass attendance between 1977 and 1986.[32] Church statistics also began to show improvement. The numbers of ordinations of diocesan priests and the numbers of diocesan seminarians reached a low point in 1976 and increased modestly in the next few years. In the year 1981, more substantial increases began appearing in both areas. By 1985, diocesan seminarians had increased 39 percent and diocesan ordinations 26 percent over the numbers in 1978, the year when John Paul II became pope.[33] Reports for 1993 demonstrated that the numbers of ordinations and seminarians had increased at an even greater rate. However, the increases were not consistent geographically because parts of North America and Western Europe were still in decline or experiencing modest rebounds.[34]

The restored interest and confidence in the papacy, and the lifting of morale in many areas of the church coincided with an increase not only in media coverage by the press, but in the amount of communications from the papacy. The printed record of papal audiences and messages in the first few years of John Paul II's pontificate almost doubled compared to the first few years of Paul VI.[35] The church has always given high priority to communications, but as is the case with many other institutions, the church is discovering the importance of skillful practice of communications in a vastly more complex and technically mediated world.

A NEW WAY TO COMMUNICATE THE SACRED

When Pope John Paul II began his papacy in 1978, he encountered a normative crisis in the church and society. In an enormously diverse world of competing messages and value systems, religious institutions, once the primary means of anchoring common meaning, were in disarray. With the old vocabularies of the sacred having been deemed irrelevant, experimentation shook the fabric of these churches and split many apart into what Wuthnow called "deep fissures."[36] These divisions, which some have called liberal and conservative, were based on how far churches and groups within churches accommodated to or resisted the increased trends toward secularization. Like many of its Protestant counterparts, the Catholic church embarked on an effort to make the church more relevant to modern society's political, social, and economic changes. In the process, old vocabularies of the sacred were abandoned, unleashing experiments that expressed the new sacred-secular synergy. However, change confused members and weakened the institutional church. As Jay Dolan noted, "For Catholics, the anchor appeared to have disappeared; disappointed and disillusioned, many stopped going to church."[37]

During stressful periods when a society perceives that its cultural system is in such disarray that people lose their bearings, leaders emerge with new vocabularies and symbols to help reorient and revive common understandings of core moral and religious beliefs that provide continuity and sustain a culture.[38] During the current crisis, Protestant televangelists and other fundamentalist preachers have sought communicative ways to reconstruct common meaning about the sacred. Scholars of culture and communication have examined these and other Protestant Church responses to secularization and the accommodating-resistance dilemma, but there have been few studies of the Catholic Church's response, specifically through the communicative strategy of Pope John Paul II.

In this modern era, popes and presidents can rarely command, but must rely heavily on tactics of persuasion. Because he has traveled more frequently and extensively than any other modern pope, John Paul II's overseas visits, their techniques, forms, and practices are a "style" of communicating that the pope has stamped on his papacy, and consequently on the organizational and institutional practice of a growing rhetorical papacy. Since the international pastoral visit is the pope's distinct way of communicating to the church during these unsettled times, the overseas pastoral visit constitutes a new form of papal communication that is specifically designed to meet the crisis posed by increased secularization. Consequently, it is a new way of speaking about the sacred.

Similar to other religious renewals and awakenings, the communicative task of the papal visit is to sort out the relationship of the church to the world. Unlike the fundamentalist branch of Protestantism, the Catholic Church is not inclined to withdraw completely from worldly concerns. Furthermore, John Paul II, like other popes, is limited by previous doctrinal decisions and is obliged to adhere to the dogmatic teachings of the councils.[39] Therefore, he is necessarily committed to the "opening to the modern world" that Vatican Council II set in motion. More importantly, cultural change is very pervasive. The tide of modernization is impossible to resist. The more extreme elements might be checked and reined in, but today's cultural fabric is so intimately woven by the spirit of the expressive revolution that any vocabulary of the sacred has to recognize these changes. However, the problems caused by close association with a secularized society have to be addressed. As leaders of religious revival movements found, restoring connections with the old tradition was not enough. These connections had to be reformulated from a new perspective. Therefore, the papal rhetorical style has to reconnect with past vocabularies, and at the same time, give definition to these vocabularies through a new and fresh outlook, recognizing that today's cultural fabric is intimately woven by the spirit of the expressive revolution.

Using the categories of liberal and conservative, most accounts in the popular media admit that John Paul II is difficult to classify. They acknowledge his conservative image, but observe how he opens the church to the ways of the postmodern world. This profound ambiguity confounds many who wonder why John Paul II can be so popular even among many Catholics who seemingly are in disagreement with the church's moral teachings. The problem is that the popular media examine the pope's discourse based on logical and systematic rules where argument follows a path toward one narrow and explicable conclusion. A vocabulary of the sacred cannot follow these logical and systematic rules. Perhaps this is why John Paul II has resisted the political classifications of liberal and conservative, even in treating these tendencies within the church. When André Frossard began speaking of a "Christian Right and Left," the pope answered that he did not know what these terms meant or to whom they alluded.[40]

On the other hand, by approaching John Paul II's rhetorical strategy as a discourse of symbols which is designed to evoke deep experiential feeling about the sacred and the human relationship with the sacred, the pope's ambiguity ceases to be an absence or obscurity of definition and, instead, becomes an acceptance of multiple tension-filled relationships as a means of expressing the sacred. As religion's primary subject matter, the sacred is both known and unknown. It can only be expressed in relation to human experience, and yet it signifies an entity that is outside of human experience. Religious language is caught in a constant interplay of opposites because there is always tension between what is human and what is above and beyond the human. Furthermore, the church as an extension of the sacred on earth is always dealing with its relationship to the contextual world. It adjusts and accommodates; then it pulls back and resists worldly influence. Wuthnow, in discussing the deep divide between the resistance mode of evangelical churches and the accommodating posture of liberal churches, admitted that the tensions between the two perspectives perform positive functions because they each help define one's position more clearly, strengthening the overall place of religion.[41]

By examining the pope's dominant form of communicating with the church, namely the international pastoral visit in relation to the sacred-secular dilemma, I aim to explain John Paul II's enigmatic style. I expect his vocabulary of the sacred to keep the tension-filled relationship between the church and the world alive, thereby helping people to understand and feel boundaries between their sacred and secular selves. Therefore, my first probe is to determine how John Paul II's visits interpret the relationship between the sacred and the secular. Does the papal visit allow the pope to speak about the sacred in more accommodating terms, or is the visit designed to recall the sacred by resisting the secular world?

Secondly, an enigmatic style is related to the audience's postmodern experience. In a fast-paced world of instantaneous communication, humans swing incessantly back and forth in their striving for identification with both the sacred and secular. How does the papal visit articulate a persuasive and plausible church whose members are steeped in the fluidity of a postmodern experience?

Thirdly, I contend that John Paul II's rhetorical strategy appears so enigmatic because it must deal with the chasms developing between the personal moral pragmatism of church members and the normative ideals of the church. Secular culture's thrust toward absolute independence loosened the bonds that once held individuals to the normative structures of society. Obligations of any sort are not easily sustained in a society of self-interested individuals. The pope cannot fail to preach the sacred norms that distinguish the church from exclusively human enterprises. Nevertheless, he cannot disregard the fact that these norms present sometimes impossible dilemmas to many in today's church. A new vocabulary of the sacred has to make sense out of these contradictions. Is the papal visit a new vocabulary of the sacred and in what does this reframing consists?

Finally, John Paul II's use of overseas visits to local churches as a new form of communicating about the sacred is rooted in the pastoral practice of the Catholic Church. Bishops have regularly visited the parishes in their dioceses. Itinerant religious priests were often invited into local parishes to revive people's faith through a parish mission, a practice popular in the nineteenth and early twentieth centuries in the United States. The papal visit as a communication strategy is also a continuation of papal historical experience of the last one hundred years. As Leo XXIII led the church into public discussion of the rights of the worker, John Paul II leads the church into a public discussion of the problems associated with today's secularized world. Because this public discussion takes place in a pluralistic society, the papal visit competes with and relates to other vocabularies of the sacred. Specifically, how does the papal visit relate to other religious responses to the accommodation-resistance dialectic?

My study is organized in the following way: In chapter 2, I present the theoretical and methodological assumptions upon which my study is based. To operationalize my rhetorical study, I outline the categories used to systematize my interpretative analysis of symbols and discuss how a prototype visit is chosen. Chapter 3 provides background on John Paul II as a communicator and on the communicative functions of the Catholic Church as they are organized at the Vatican. In chapters 4 through 7, I examine the prototype visit in-depth. First, I consider the preparation of the trip as a negotiation of symbols, then examine how John Paul II addresses diverse audiences and utilizes textual imagery. I also consider the performative aspects of the visit, that is, the nonverbal elements of presentation, the actual contextual elements, and the media coverage of the events. Finally, in chapter 8, I consider my findings in relation to the operational categories of sacred and secular and present my conclusions.

NOTES

1. Paul Gray, "Empire of the Spirit," *Time*, 26 December 1994/2 January 1995, 53.

2. The relationship between church disengagement from temporal control strategies with enhanced moral prestige is developed by Ivan Vallier, *Catholicism, Social Control, and Modernization in Latin America* (Santa Cruz: University of California, 1970).

3. Hervé Carrier, *The Social Doctrine of the Church Revisited* (Vatican City: Pontifical Council for Justice and Peace, 1990), 20–23.

4. Leo XIII, *Rerum Novarum* in *The Papal Encyclicals 1878–1903,* vol. II, ed. Claudia Carlen (Wilmington, North Carolina: McGrath Publishing Company, 1981), no. 24, p. 245.

5. J. Derek Holmes, *The Papacy in the Modern World* (New York: Crossroad Publishing Co., 1981), 3.

6. Vallier, *Catholicism, Social Control, and Modernization in Latin America, 149.*

7. Holmes, *The Papacy in the Modern World,* 197.

8. Peter Hebblethwaite, *John XXIII, Pope of the Council* (London: Geoffrey Chapman, 1984), 294–295.

9. Vatican Council II, *Gaudium et Spes in Vatican Council II: The Conciliar and Post Conciliar Documents,* ed. Austin Flannery (Wilmington, Delaware: Scholarly Resources, 1975), no. 40.

10. Avery Dulles, *The Reshaping of Catholicism* (San Francisco: Harper and Row, 1988), 11–16.

11. Vatican Council II, *Gaudium et Spes,* no. 5.

12. Holmes, *The Papacy in the Modern World,* 254.

13. Peter Hebblethwaite, *The Year of Three Popes* (London: William Collins, 1978), 10–11.

14. Ibid., 12.

15. Wilton Wynn, *Keepers of the Keys* (New York: Random House, 1988), 248.

16. Ibid., 247.

17. Jeffrey K. Tulis, *The Rhetorical Presidency* (New Jersey: Princeton University Press, 1987), 173–182.

18. See John Coleman, *The Evolution of Dutch Catholicism, 1958–1974* (California: University of California Press, 1978), 102–120; Peter Hebblethwaite, *In the Vatican* (Oxford: Oxford University Press, 1986), 123–124, 184; Jan Grootaers, *De Vatican II à Jean-Paul II: le grand tournant de l'Eglise catholique* (Paris: Le Centurion, 1981), 208–210.

19. George Gallup Jr. and Jim Castelli, *The American Catholic People: Their Beliefs, Practices, and Values* (Garden City, New York: Doubleday, 1987), 26.

20. Francis X. Murphy, *The Papacy Today* (London: Weidenfeld and Nicolson, 1981), 195.

21. Andrew M. Greeley, *The Catholic Myth* (New York: Charles Scribner's Sons, 1990), 169.

22. Peter Hebblethwaite, *In the Vatican,* 20.

23. Gallup and Castelli, *The American Catholic People,* 178.

24. George Huntston Williams, *The Mind of John Paul II* (New York: The Seabury Press, 1981), 42–44.

25. Penny Lernoux, *People of God* (New York: Viking, 1989), 29–33.

26. Peter Hebblethwaite, *In the Vatican*, 47–48.

27. David Sanford, "The Pope's Groupies," *Harpers*, December 1979, 86–89.

28. David Shaw, "Activist Pope Puts Catholics at Front of Media Attention," *Los Angeles Times*, 18 April 1995, sec. A, p. 1.

29. Roper Center for Public Opinion Research, University of Connecticut, December 1979 and October 1981.

30. Roper Center for Public Opinion Research, *Survey on Sex, Profanity, and Violence*, Storrs: University of Connecticut, 20 April–3 May 1981.

31. Washington Post-ABC News National Survey, *Washington Post*, 4 October 1995.

32. Gallup and Castelli, *The American Catholic People*, 26–31.

33. *L'Osservatore Romano* (English edition), 31 August 1987, 4.

34. *Statistical Yearbook of the Church* (Vatican City: Vatican Polyglot Press, 1995).

35. *L'Attivitá della Santa Sede* (Vatican City: Libreria Editrice Vaticana, 1966, 1981).

36. Robert Wuthnow, *The Struggle for America's Soul: Evangelicals, Liberals, and Secularism* (Grand Rapids, Michigan: William B. Eerdmans, 1989), 32–33.

37. Jay P. Dolan, *The American Catholic Experience: A History from Colonial Times to the Present* (Garden City, New York: Doubleday, 1985), 433.

38. William McLoughlin, *Revivals, Awakenings, and Reform* (Chicago: University of Chicago, 1978), 10, 211.

39. Patrick Granfield, *The Limits of the Papacy: Authority and Autonomy in the Church* (New York: Crossroad Publishing, 1987), 70.

40. André Frossard, *"Be Not Afraid!"* (New York: St. Martin's Press, 1984), 79.

41. Robert Wuthnow, *The Struggle for America's Soul*, 182–184.

CHAPTER 2

Between the Sacred and Chaos

Secularization and pluralism have shaken the institutional foundations of established religions, including the Catholic Church. Once directly involved in territorial rule, churches now struggle to be heard in the public forum. Similarly, in the cultural and ideational areas, the rise of science and rational thinking has pushed aside religion's mystical interpretations, relegating expressions of the sacred to a narrow portion of modern life. Moreover, pluralistic living which demands that all religions and expressions of religions be treated with equal respect tends to dislodge automatic acceptance of the superiority of Christianity, making all religious belief relative. As a consequence, in this postmodern era, a papal rhetorical strategy must acknowledge the diminished and relative standing of religious vocabularies. However, as Dobbelaere has observed, when the secularization and pluralistic process is considered to be dependent on social constructs that are not simply given facts but defined and constructed through human interaction and engagement, the outcome of the process is far from inevitable, leaving open the possibility of religion's persistence.[1] The emergence over the last one hundred years of a rhetorical papacy, that is, a papacy that relies on persuasive discourse to lead the church, demonstrates how Christianity has adjusted to the competition of secular ideologies. This papal discourse, as part of a shared vocabulary constructed by the Catholic Church, is what Wuthnow deems an important consideration in learning about how humans order their worlds.[2]

SYMBOL SYSTEM TO INTERPRET THE SACRED
AND THE SECULAR

The first task is to examine John Paul II's visit for the kind of symbolic system he uses to interpret the relationship between the sacred and the secular. For a definition of the system itself, the study relies on Peter Berger's treatment of religious meaning as a humanly constructed sacred cosmos that acts to order a fragmented world. For Berger, humans order their worlds by constructing an immensely powerful sacred "other" as an effective defense against anomie and meaninglessness. However, this shield against anomie becomes an agency for alienating humans from their human profane world.[3] As a result, humans adjust the relationship between the sacred cosmos and human or secular worlds by desacralizing meaning systems to accommodate the secular world. When meanings become too dependent on the precariousness of the everyday secular world, humans remystify the sacred to resist secularization and the onslaught of chaos. Therefore, meanings are constantly being constructed and reconstructed, adjusting the relationship between the sacred cosmos and human or secular worlds. Historically, the Catholic Church has participated in this bargaining process with secular thought through periods of resisting and accommodating to the modern world. During the period of Vatican Council II, many church leaders advocated an open dialogue and close union of the church and the times.[4] This process of accommodation that merges the sacred and secular tends to remove the sacred from its dominating position. Without the sacred's powerful presence, humans try to depend on their own efforts to confront their uncertainties, but doubt and disorder return. The task facing the church at the time of Pope John Paul II's elevation to the papacy was to restore a sense of the sacred, thus halting the accommodating process.

Berger's definition of religious meaning also pertains to the second question, which examines how a symbolic framework of the sacred can remain plausible and still make sense to people coping with an intensely diverse and pluralistic world. For Berger, religious meaning systems, whether or not they are in a resisting or accommodating mode, depend on how religious institutions maintain their plausibility. Today's church members experience a very fluid world in which identities and allegiances shift, overlap, and disconnect depending on time, circumstance, and personal experience. As the social world becomes more and more diverse and pluralistic, the possibilities of symbol adaptation and cross-fertilization become so much more complex and multidimensional.[5] This presents enormous problems in terms of how the symbol system can be maintained. For Berger, religious institutions remain plausible when religious structures are perceived as massive and durably real. As these structures weaken, religious reality becomes faint in human consciousness.[6]

To correct Catholicism's growing alienation from the modern world, the church reversed its strategy of separating its members from opposing ideologies. The parallel institutions such as schools and professional organizations that acted as plausibility structures reinforcing Catholic notions of the sacred were no longer considered necessary in open dialogic relationship with others. With the disappearance and weakening of these parallel institutions, the Catholic Church and other established churches began losing their massivity and hence the appearance of durability. Dulles noted that Catholicism with its strong visible signs of unity bestowed on its members a very powerful sense of belonging to a single religious community. When its style became more and more unrelated to the diverse cultural conditions of modern life, the church embraced an inculturation policy in which local cultures and identities were preserved and appropriated.[7] The emphasis on local diversity, especially in liturgical reforms, together with an ecumenical spirit that acknowledged the presence of diverse churches, mitigated against the Catholic Church's massivity and durability that had previously supported a taken-for-granted reality of the sacred. It is impossible for the church to return to the former strategies of a complex of external institutions that separated and protected its members. However, without some type of plausibility structure, either externally present or internally experienced, it becomes difficult, if not impossible, to determine what is authentically Catholic or Christian.

Papal communication strategies have to include ways to enhance the perceived massivity and durability of the church, and at the same time, construct a symbol system that is related to the sociocultural world in which we live. Bernice Martin and Bellah et al. observed how symbol systems adjusted to the increased fluidity of human experience that resulted from an intense period of social change in the latter part of the twentieth century. According to Martin, extreme elements on both sides of the accommodating-resistance spectrum tore down structures and seized the ecstatic to give new believability to the sacred. This state of constant pursuit of flux and chaos may be "madness,"[8] but the liminal experience of being on the threshold between one realm and the other, as between the profane and the sacred, is an important element of religious ritual.[9] During this brief period of liminality, one leaves the

categories and boundaries of past identities to enter the realm of anomie that encompasses every possibility and potential. Bernice Martin
believes that the extreme experiments with constant flux have faded,
but the expressive revolution has left lasting marks. The seizing of the
mystical and ecstatic by "fringe" religious groups caused the symbol
systems of middle mainstream churches to appear "banal" by comparison. During previous times of cultural stress, religious institutions suc-
cessfully revitalized regular communication with the sacred by closing
the gap between this world and the next.[10] A new sacred vocabulary has
to consider this taste for the mystical as an antidote to contemporary
skepticism.

In today's society, the symbols of institutions—organization, structure, bureaucracy—are suspect. This wariness of communal structures
has produced a fulfillment vocabulary trapped in the personal and private sphere. There is a lack of language to mediate between the self and
any other reality such as society, the world, and most importantly the
Ultimate Being. As Bellah et al. discovered, Americans are very at-
tached to their language of self-cultivation, but they are also apprehen-
sive about the consequences of their radical individualism.[11] Hoover
and Peck have studied how fundamentalist televangelism links its viewers to a loose parachurch community that does not necessarily alienate
its members from the self-fulfillment vocabulary of modern consumer
culture.[12] A religious rhetoric has to address audiences whose vocabularies contain the lasting marks of the expressive revolution, namely, a
disillusionment with the structures of the rational and material world,
and a fear of the lonely consequences of a radical individualism that has
broken traditional communal ties.

Finally, how a religious rhetoric deals with chasms that have developed between the sacred ideals and the pragmatic decisions made in
everyday life will require a new vocabulary of the sacred. This vocabulary must retain the essential features of the sacred which David Martin
proclaimed as necessarily paradoxical and ambiguous. Since the sacred
is both known and unknown, sacred symbol systems are filled with tension.[13] At the same time, the vocabulary's new character has to appeal
to those characteristics of the expressive revolution that Bernice Martin
concluded were deeply embedded in our contemporary culture. Both
Martin and Bellah et al. described how today's distrust of institutions
leads to a populist imperative.[14] Believing in their own self-sufficiency,
individuals insist on direct participation and control of decisions concerning their lives. In religious symbolism, this populist need for direct
participation is related to a more immanently real God, increasing the

possibilities for humans to experience direct contact with the sacred. In their study of pilgrimages, Turner and Turner observed the characteristics of this populist spirit. Not only does the pilgrimage offer "a route to the liminal world" where the sacred is touched and experienced as real, but the pilgrimage itself is developed and supported by the often spontaneous actions of ordinary people of the church.[15] In other words, ordinary people participate in shaping the church's symbol system.

Bernice Martin also observed that the language of self is contemporary culture's preferred way of speaking. As Bellah et al. confirmed, Americans no longer see themselves as connected in morally meaningful ways to a larger common life, and thus there is no other way of relating to one another or to the Ultimate Being except in very self-descriptive ways.[16] Many scholars, particularly those of the electronic media, have concluded that this intimate style of interpersonal conversation, which is more open, spontaneous, and self-revealing, is now being mimicked by public discourse.[17] As Bellah et al. found, the language of the self-reliant individual is the first language, and talk of communal tradition and commitments is a second language.[18]

The question is how to reconnect these two ways of speaking. The second language of tradition often involves commitments, and these social ties that limit individual expression and action are often suspect for their authoritarian possibilities. Above all, the individual guards one's freedom as a protection from any type of coercion. As a consequence, the language of belonging becomes possible when characterized by a voluntariness that is not only respectful of individual freedom, but also cognizant of the fact that voluntary social relationships, as Bellah et al. discovered, may now be driven largely by self-interests.[19] Jay Dolan pointed out that prior to the mid–twentieth century, the Catholic Church, in stressing external rubrics as duties, de-emphasized the role of the individual conscience in sorting out the way to salvation.[20] In today's language of self, a return to this type of church definition is impossible. However, there are other church traditions that become more amenable for reformulation. In the Middle Ages, as Turner and Turner observed, the thrill of the pilgrim adventure was related to a taste of freedom. Withdrawing from the obligatoriness of their everyday lives, the pilgrims freely left their tightly structured lives to pursue voluntary activities and associations.[21] This voluntariness was a sign of growing self-determination which today is an accepted code of all discourse, even that of sacred symbols.

The countercultural movements of the sixties experimented with pure ecstasy. As Bernice Martin observed, even though these experi-

ments have faded, youth culture and rock music carried expanded liminal possibilities to the adult world, even to mainstream churches which
appropriated more emotional and affective expressions.[22] According to
Stewart Hoover, evangelical Christian churches have capitalized on this
new mood for ecstasy by reviving a religion of the heart.[23] In his work,
God in Popular Culture, Andrew Greeley counseled the church to recall its former traditions of devotional imagery and narrative that appealed to the senses.[24] Turner and Turner described how the church
"fleshed out" abstractions by retelling stories of saintly apparitions,
miracles, and communion with the dead.[25] However, contemporary
appeal to the emotive and imaginative, according to Jamieson and
Peck, has become feminized. Rather than a hot, passionate style, public
discourse has become warmly congenial and nurturing, largely because
this type of emotional talk is less threatening to the rationally based
secular culture.[26]

EXPECTATIONS

Peck and Witten have examined sermonic and oral communicative
forms of Protestant religious leaders for signs of accommodating and
resistance preaching.[27] Some of the same questions raised by these rhetorical studies of Protestant responses to the sacred-secular dilemma are
asked in this study. Does the papal visit allow the pope to speak about
the sacred in more accommodating terms, or is the visit's purpose to
strictly recall the sacred in resistance to the secular?

Moreover, the problem with categorizing the symbolic system as either accommodation or resistance is that preachers and popes have to
construct symbols that resonate and make sense to their audiences. In
today's intensely diverse and pluralistic world, these audiences experience an enormous amount of fluidity in their everyday lives. With constant change an accepted way of life, people exhibit a "deafness and
blindness" with regard to custom and tradition.[28] Because the church's
plausibility structures which support and maintain meaning construction have been weakened, it is difficult to reach a "middle" or "common" ground. As a result, the church and its members are more
susceptible to the constantly fluctuating, overlapping, and sometimes
competing systems of symbols. To determine if the papal visit meets the
challenges of this age of fluidity, it is important to examine the visit's
symbol system as it relates to the church's ability to build massivity and
durability in ways that make sense to people whose self-cultivation
tends to foster diversity rather than communal ties.

The third area which poses a problem for religious rhetoric is the developing chasms between the normative ideal and the pragmatic decisions of everyday life. If what the religious leader is communicating about the sacred remains unconnected to everyday behavior, doubts arise about the church and its ability to construct sacred symbols. Religious discourse has to restore a sense of the sacred which can only be imaged through time-tested techniques of double meanings, inversion, and paradox. However, connecting with past vocabularies is not enough. There needs to be a new vocabulary of the sacred that incorporates elements into its style to allow the sacred to resonate with postmodern audiences.

Because the plausibility of the church "competes" with diverse ideologies and beliefs, this new vocabulary of the sacred necessarily relates to other religious discourses as they cope with the accommodating-resistance dialectic. Hoover's study of neoevangelical traditions of the electronic church indicated that televangelists seem to be successful in building a shared community that can serve as a plausibility structure to sustain religious consciousness.[29] Peck discovered differences in symbol construction, pointing out how televangelists have countered modernity with popular style or with certain concessions to modern conceptions of self.[30] Culturally, the evangelical Christian tradition differs markedly from that of the Catholic Church, and therefore, one expects differences in the construction of a symbol system. However, the successes that televangelism and the papal visits have had as new vocabularies of the sacred may also be related.

To examine how the overseas pastoral visit of John Paul II is a new vocabulary of the sacred to meet these problems, the following questions need to be answered:

- Does the visit delineate well the differences between the sacred and the secular without severely disrupting the relationship of church and world?

- Does the visit recognize the limits of our culture of fluidity, and how does it develop a plausibility that may sustain religious consciousness in the face of this fluidity?

- To what extent does the visit appropriate elements of our expressive culture into the paradoxical nature and multileveled meaning structure of the sacred so as to help us understand the discrepancies between normative ideals and everyday practice?

- How does this new vocabulary of the sacred relate to other religious responses to the accommodating-resisting dialectic, and are there any weaknesses and failings in relation to meeting the test of these questions?

I propose that the visits themselves, the way they are planned, the speeches that are written and delivered, the manner in which John Paul II moves through his itinerary—sometimes highly scripted, at other times refreshingly spontaneous—unites a disparate church in maintaining some sense of sacred Other. By observing his rhetorical strategy in terms of Berger's accommodation-resistance continuum, I expect more "resistance talk" to restore the boundaries that were torn down by those accommodation strategies seeking relevance in a secularized world. At the same time, in steering a course for the church in the postmodern era, I believe that John Paul II's rhetorical strategy moves outward to the world and inward toward the church in relation to the audiences he addresses. There is no one midpoint of balance. In fact, John Paul II's style demonstrates that any new vocabulary of the sacred is not constructed by seeking a middle ground through compromise. Since reconciliation of the two polar opposites of church and world, sacred and secular is constantly concerned with preserving the diversity of each entity, John Paul II's symbolic construction of the sacred expresses that paradoxical frustration of tension. Using David Martin's words, the visits are designed to code the tension between limit and possibility, between wholeness and brokenness. John Paul II does this, not in private settings, but in massive public events whose mediated images are carried to millions of viewers. In its public dimension, the papal visit aims to invite church members to associate together in recalling the sacred; these visits appear to be John Paul II's way of holding the church together.

METHODOLOGY AND IMPLICATIONS

In defining religion, Geertz wrote that it is a system of symbols that "establish powerful, pervasive, and long-lasting moods and motivations."[31] Employing a phenomenological approach, I have considered the papal visits as cultural forms that manifest the intentionality of John Paul II and those who assist him in planning and executing these visits to build shared meanings with his audiences. Like Peter Berger, Mary Douglas, David Martin, Bernice Martin, Victor and Edith Turner who, immersed in the culture that they are studying, recognize the nuances and multiplicity of common meanings from within that culture, I study John Paul II's visits from within my Catholic faith, drawing upon firsthand observation of the papal visits and an inside view of the relationship between the visit's text and the social worlds of church members.[32] A critical analysis of the papal visits, for example, using media coverage or audience response as data, is a valid method of studying the pope as an important moral spokesman. However, choosing to forego this type of analysis, I concentrate on a qualitative study that systematically treats discourse, symbols, their contexts and arrangements as discrete and observable data of shared meaning. From these shared meanings, I move to deeper levels of analysis, constructing ideal types and relating the shared meanings to these constructs to illuminate and diagnose how the symbol system of the papal visit intends to order the church and the world.

Specifically, papal speech text and the interpretations of papal discourse given by readers, listeners, journalists, discourse planners, speech writers, and the speaker himself are my empirical evidence. In selecting the data for observation, I classified the papal visits outside of Italy by purpose, duration, and type of invitation extended, and concentrated on the "pastoral visit" in which John Paul II's rhetorical strategy is directed largely to the local Catholic Church. To determine further if typical patterns exist in a pastoral visit's preparation, type and size of audiences addressed, places visited, types of ceremonies, textual themes, level of planning, and spontaneous variations, I examined closely four papal pastoral visits that represent different time periods and continents.[33] For the data on the preparatory aspects of a visit, I rely primarily on personal interviews, and secondarily on journalistic and scholarly writings on the decision-making procedures. Textual data consists of official texts of the twenty-nine to sixty speeches in each of the four visits. For the performance of the speeches, I examined videotapes, photographs, and journalistic accounts. In several cases, I personally observed the event. From this group of four pastoral visits, I chose the visit to the United States in 1987 to analyze in-depth as a case study, mainly because the United States is a society in which the secularization tendencies have been identified and studied. Additionally, I had access to considerable original data and secondary material on the 1987 visit, which was planned and constructed based on eight years of papal visits and one previous visit to the United States, increasing the likelihood for purposeful rhetorical choices. Undoubtedly, my study of the visit as a new vocabulary of the sacred concentrates on meaning construction within the American culture. Nevertheless, as the 1987 papal visit demonstrates, American audiences are very diverse.

Similar to historical studies, my methodology draws upon the classical rhetorical principles of invention, arrangement, style, and delivery.[34] I examine the purposeful choices in planning and arranging themes and audiences for the visit, in creating a style through managing form and imagery, and in performing or delivering the visit. Although I focus on

the discourses of a dominant personality as interpretations of the struggles of a community during crisis, I do not follow an exclusively speaker
orientation because my methodology is influenced by the interactive
process of communication that involves a reciprocal movement between audience and speaker. To examine textual style, I rely on Kenneth Burke to guide my probes of symbolic clusters in the modes of
address and in the rhetor's metaphoric and other uses of imagery. Following Burke, I assume that these clusters of terms work cumulatively
to build an interpretative system that can make sense to audiences who,
steeped in modern fragmentariness, are still hungry for some sense of
order and community. Burke's insistence on attention to difference and
strangeness in goading us humans toward identification suits the theoretical dialectic framework of sacred and secular.[35]

In delving into the thick webs of complex cultural meaning, I use
three levels of symbol systems to develop sacred and secular indicators
as ideal types, which when arranged as end points on a continuum, delineate accommodating-resistance movement of the church with relation to the secular world.[36] I observe the patterns of symbolic
construction in the planning, the symbolic formulation in the textual
address and imagery of the speeches, and the symbolic production in
the performance of the papal visit. Matching these observed patterns of
variables to the categories on the continuum, I can determine if the papal visit as a symbol system exhibits accommodating or resistance tendencies, and under what contextual conditions. In my second probe, I
search the theoretical literature for the problems of plausibility posed
by the current sociocultural condition. After categorizing these weaknesses into three areas—loss of massivity, distrust of the material world,
and solitude—I observe and test the antidotes to these plausibility
problems in the papal visit's symbol system. My third probe consists of
observing and locating John Paul II's predominant rhetorical strategies, and then relating them to the theoretical literature with regard to
the process of creating new symbols and vocabularies of the sacred. Returning to the data, I test these strategies, observing their strengths and
weaknesses in relation to audiences and contexts. Finally, I conclude by
relating my findings on the papal visit with other religious responses to
the accommodating-resisting dialectic.

The study's theoretical progression has followed a sociology of culture approach through which the subtle symbolic patterns of boundaries and connections are unraveled for the purpose of analyzing how
these patterns build and shape a social world. As Wuthnow pointed out,
sociologists have borrowed from language studies in order to advance

an understanding of how public life functions. However, there is no single theoretical or methodological perspective.[37] Since there have been studies using the accommodating and resistance dialectic to examine Protestant rhetorical response to the crisis of secularization, I expect that my study may provide data and conclusions which could be compared to these other studies in an overall evaluation of the communicative strategies and the plausibility of religion as a whole.

Sociology and rhetorical criticism also overlap in studies employing the generic approach in which the power of prior rhetorical conventions and traditions mold and constrain subsequent rhetorical acts. Jamieson argued that genre can play a more decisive role than the time-bound situation in shaping the rhetorical act. She contended that the papal encyclical as a genre impedes the introduction of radical change.[38] Jablonski suggested in her study of U.S. Catholic bishops' messages that established genres function to preserve institutional order, especially in times of change.[39] In this study, I contend that the papal international pastoral visit to local churches is a newly developing rhetorical strategy that lies outside the framework of the more established rhetorical genres employed in previous papacies. In this sense, the papal visit is less constraining than the encyclical or other formal methods of papal communication. It allows for innovation and adaptation to time-bound situational demands. During the papacy of John Paul II, the papal visits have emerged to form certain patterns, establishing precedents that create expectations among audiences. These patterns and forms already place constraints on current papal rhetorical strategies and, I imagine, could affect the communicative strategies of future popes.

NOTES

1. Karel Dobbelaere, "Secularization Theories and Sociological Paradigms: A Reformulation of the Private-Public Dichotomy and the Problem of Societal Integration," *Sociological Analysis*, 46 (1985): 377–379 and K. Dobbelaere, "Some Trends in European Sociology of Religion: The Secularization Debate," *Sociological Analysis* 48, no. 2 (1987): 116.

2. Robert Wuthnow, "New Directions in the Empirical Study of Cultural Codes" in *Vocabularies of Public Life*, ed. Robert Wuthnow (London: Routledge, 1992), 13.

3. Peter L. Berger, *The Sacred Canopy: Elements of a Sociological Theory of Religion* (Garden City, New York: Doubleday, 1969), 26, 86–89.

4. Avery Dulles, *Models of the Church* (New York: Doubleday, 1987), 91–92.

5. Robert Wuthnow, *Rediscovering the Sacred: Perspectives on Religion in Contemporary Society* (Grand Rapids, Michigan: William B. Eerdmans, 1992), 86–87.

6. Berger, *The Sacred Canopy*, 45–49, 150.

7. Avery Dulles, *The Reshaping of Catholicism: Current Challenges in the Theology of Church* (San Francisco: Harper and Row, 1988), 69–70.

8. Bernice Martin, *A Sociology of Contemporary Cultural Change* (New York: St. Martin's Press, 1981), 10.

9. Victor Turner, *The Ritual Process: Structure and Anti-Structure* (Chicago: Aldine, 1969), 94–95.

10. Bernice Martin, *A Sociology*, 15–16, 20, 231.

11. Robert N. Bellah, Richard Madsen, William M. Sullivan, Ann Swidler, and Steven M. Tipton, *Habits of the Heart: Individualism and Commitment in American Life* (Berkeley: University of California Press, 1985; reprint New York: Harper and Row, 1986), 285–291.

12. Stewart M Hoover, *Mass Media Religion: The Social Sources of the Electronic Church* (Newbury Park, California: Sage Publications, 1988), 218; Janice Peck, *The Gods of Televangelism: The Crisis of Meaning and Appeal of Religious Television* (Cresskill, New Jersey: Hampton Press, 1993), 228–230.

13. David Martin, *The Breaking of the Image: A Sociology of Christian Theory and Practice* (Oxford: Basil Blackwell, 1980), 126–127.

14. Bernice Martin, *A Sociology*, 226–228; Bellah et al., *Habits of the Heart*, 247–248.

15. Victor Turner and Edith Turner, *Image and Pilgrimage in Christian Culture: Anthropological Perspectives* (New York: Columbia University Press, 1978), 30–32.

16. Bellah et al., *Habits of the Heart*, 50.

17. Kathleen Hall Jamieson, *Eloquence in an Electronic Age: The Transformation of Political Speechmaking* (New York: Oxford University Press, 1988), 165–166, 182–183.

18. Bellah et al., *Habits of the Heart*, 154.

19. Ibid., 167–187.

20. Jay P. Dolan, *The American Catholic Experience: A History from Colonial Times to the Present* (Garden City, New York: Doubleday, 1985), 225–231.

21. Turner and Turner, *Image and Pilgrimage*, 8–13.

22. Bernice Martin, *A Sociology*, 149–152, 225.

23. Hoover, *Mass Media Religion*, 45.

24. Andrew Greeley, *God in Popular Culture* (Chicago, Illinois: The Thomas More Press, 1988), 91.

25. Turner and Turner, *Image and Pilgrimage*, 204–211.

26. Jamieson, *Eloquence in an Electronic Age*, 67–89; Peck, *The Gods of Televangelism*, 177–182.

27. Peck, *The Gods of Televangelism*; Marsha Witten, *All Is Forgiven: The Secular Message in American Protestantism* (Princeton: Princeton University Press, 1993).

28. Bernice Martin, *A Sociology*, 16–18.

29. Hoover, *Mass Media Religion*, 210.

30. Peck, *The Gods of Televangelism*, 228–231.

31. Clifford Geertz, *The Interpretation of Cultures* (New York: Basic Books, 1973), 90.

32. Robert Wuthnow, James Davidson Hunter, Albert Bergesen, and Edith Kurzweil, *Cultural Analysis: The Work of Peter L. Berger, Mary Douglas, Michel Foucault, and Jürgen Habermas* (Boston: Routledge & Kegan Paul, 1984), 77–132; David Martin, *The Breaking of the Image*; Bernice Martin, *A Sociology of Contemporary Cultural Change*; and Victor Turner and Edith Turner, *Image and Pilgrimage in Christian Culture*.

33. France 1980, Africa 1985, The United States 1987, and Brazil 1991.

34. Halford R. Ryan, *Franklin D. Roosevelt's Rhetorical Presidency* (Westport, Connecticut: Greenwood Press, 1988), 5–6. Ryan also considers the fifth classical canon, memoria. He admits that Roosevelt saw no need to memorize a speech, but argued that Roosevelt's familiarity with the speech aided his delivery.

35. Kenneth Burke, *On Symbols and Society*, ed. Joseph R. Gusfield (Chicago: University of Chicago Press, 1989), 135; Kenneth Burke, *A Rhetoric of Motives* (New York: Prentice-Hall, 1950), 19–29, 43–46.

36. See Appendix.

37. Wuthnow, "New Directions in the Empirical Study of Cultural Codes," 12.

38. Kathleen Jamieson, "A Rhetorical-Critical Analysis of the Conflict over *Humanae Vitae*," Ph. D. dissertation, University of Wisconsin, 1972, 37–40, 230–236. Also see Kathleen Jamieson, "Antecedent Genre As Rhetorical Constraint," *Quarterly Journal of Speech* 61 (December 1975): 406–415.

39. Carol J. Jablonski, "*Aggiornamento* and the American Catholic Bishops: A Rhetoric of Institutional Continuity and Change," *Quarterly Journal of Speech* 75 (1989): 416–432.

CHAPTER 3

Background to the Visits

COMMUNICATIVE TRADITION OF VISIT

Christianity is intimately linked to communications because at the heart of its mission is Jesus Christ as the self-communication of the Father on earth. Catholic theology has always used communication themes and symbols: prayer, preaching, communion, revelation, evangelization. Since Vatican Council II, the church has changed its mode of communication. Instead of using images that convey a transmitting or transporting of information, the church of Vatican Council II employs language and symbols to signal a more participatory, dialogical, and interactive mode of communicating about the church.[1] When describing the functions of the church, theologians refer to the way individuals and God communicate with each other, and how the church is the means for all humanity to communicate and unite as one. God speaks to humans and humans speak to God. Christ is the Word; this Word of God, found through sacred scripture and tradition, is constantly being understood and shared with others.[2] A key church document on communications calls Christ the "Perfect Communicator," because, in having become a human, Christ identified himself with whom he was communicating. He used words to communicate about God's love, but more importantly, his whole manner of life demonstrated that love.[3] In this manner, the church has applied updated communication theory to elaborate on its own meaning.

One of the communication themes expanded upon by Vatican Council II was the work of evangelization and the duty of the whole church, as the People of God, to do this work. Today, the church speaks also of reevangelization for those Christians who have forgotten or who have never received instruction in the faith. Bishops, who have a primary role in proclaiming the Gospel, teach in communion with the pope, the bishop of Rome, who is pastor to the whole church. Prior to Vatican Council II, the teaching role and authority of the church was often concentrated on the pope and the ability of Peter's successor to teach infallibly. Vatican Council II stressed that the bishops, under the leadership of the pope, form a collegial body of teachers and pastors. The Council referred often to the *sensus fidei*, or mind of the church, in order to convey the supernatural gift through which the whole church together can understand God's revelation. In this way, the pope and bishops are not acting separately from the rest of the church when they teach or proclaim an understanding of truth, but rather they articulate what the whole church understands through the church's experience. Therefore, the communicative role of the pope is viewed as closely connected to the bishops and the entire people of the church. For a pope to function in this role, he must communicate in ways that visibly demonstrate this close communion with bishops and the universal church. The overseas visits of John Paul II represent movement toward the local churches. Carefully balanced to include all parts of the world, they are specifically designed to communicate the universality or all-embracing nature of the church from the point of view of geography and cultures.

The term pastoral, used to describe the visits of the pope to local churches, can be viewed from several perspectives. From a juridical point of view, a pastor is a member of the clergy who has been chosen by the bishop to be responsible for a parish, the primary unit of the Catholic Church at the local level. He is charged with the spiritual care and guidance of the congregation. Like a herdsman caring for the flock of sheep or goats, a metaphor often used in scriptural passages, the pastor leads his congregation, shows them the way, and tends to their needs. The pastor must be able to provide for the sacramental life as well as the spiritual education of the people. It is assumed that a pastor will know the local parishioners so well that he will be able to anticipate their needs. In the organization of the Catholic Church, parishes are congregated into a diocese of which the bishop is the head. Parishes are not autonomous units which operate on their own; they are united to the universal church through their bishop. Therefore, the bishop, who is responsible for all in his diocese, will periodically make pastoral visits to the parishes of the diocese.

Avery Dulles outlined five types of communication that correspond to the five models of ecclesiology: hierarchical, herald, sacramental, communion, and dialogue. In a sense, the pastoral visit can be described using those five models. In the first two, called the hierarchical and herald, scripture and tradition are entrusted to the magisterium, that is, the bishops together with the pope, to safeguard, interpret, and proclaim the divine teachings. The bishop visits the parish to preach to the people and make sure that they are receiving "authentic" authoritative teaching from their pastors. The third model is the sacramental church; on a pastoral visit, the bishop will usually preside at a Eucharistic celebration or the Sacrament of Confirmation. This is a special event for which the people in the parish carefully prepare because the presence of a bishop, as a successor to the apostles, is a special sign of Christ's presence in this particular local parish of the church. The fourth model is community or communion; when the bishop makes a pastoral visit, all in the parish are invited to join in the celebration so that the pastor can present his entire congregation to the bishop. Groups within the parish often have an opportunity to report to the bishop on their programs and to express their needs. Coming together, the people of the parish demonstrate their existence as a community, united to each other, their pastor, and to their bishop. Finally, Dulles described his fifth model: a church which is in dialogue with the secular world. In this model, the laity, working with their pastors, are involved in interpreting and influencing the secular realm. Being actively engaged in human institutions, lay people can provide concrete and technical solutions to everyday problems within their specific competencies. On a pastoral visit, the bishop will look to the local church to learn of these specific local issues. As Dulles noted, in the first two models, communication tends to flow in one direction, requiring the congregation to respond with submission and faith. In the other models, the congregation participates, witnesses, and dialogues.[4] No matter what theory of communication prevails, the true spirit of a pastoral visit is oriented toward the flock or religious community. The pastor is in regular contact with the bishop through written reports and face-to-face meetings at the diocesan center. The visit of the bishop to the local church is an opportunity for the bishop to communicate directly with the people in the congregation.

Leaving the diocesan center and traveling outward to the parish to visit the local congregation's holy site, the bishop aims to assess how the local congregation is faring in its spiritual journey. The parish interrupts its normal habits to receive the bishop as a special occasion. During the visit, the bishop's goal is to praise, prod, motivate, and recommit the parish. It is also an opportunity for the people of the parish to see themselves as connected and in union with a larger identity of church, that of diocese. Because the parish community is reconstituted and oriented toward remembered or new goals, the pastoral visit is a type of pilgrimage.

Pope John XXIII used his prerogative as bishop of Rome to make visits outside of the Vatican, but he did not travel very far, nor did he venture outside of Italy. Pope Paul VI startled the world when, only six months after his election to the papacy, he announced that he planned a trip to the Holy Land in January of 1964. Because an overseas visit was so novel, Vatican officials had no precedents. They had to organize technicalities, invent diplomatic explanations, and most of all, interpret the meaning of the trip. For Paul VI, his purpose was "to show the world that the pope cares about people no matter how far away they are, no matter how isolated and lonely they may be."[5] As Peter Hebblethwaite observed, Pope Paul VI wanted his papacy to be accessible and demystified.[6] In explaining the reasons for Paul VI's first international voyage, the Vatican stressed that the trip to the Holy Land symbolized the church's return to its roots as humble disciple of Christ. Indeed, Paul VI projected the image of humble pilgrim when he set out on foot to walk the Via Dolorosa in Jerusalem, but he was nearly mobbed by an overenthusiastic crowd. The Vatican soon learned that future journeys needed tighter planning and more attention to security.[7]

These first papal international visits of Pope Paul VI were largely organized as single events: the Eucharistic Congress in Bombay and Bogota, the fiftieth anniversary of the Fatima apparitions, the meeting with the Eastern Orthodox patriarch in Istanbul, the United Nations General Assembly in New York, and the symposium of African bishops in Uganda. All of Paul VI's trips after the Jerusalem visit were organized by Archbishop Paul Marcinkus from Chicago who is known for his tough and candid approach. Under Marcinkus, the papal trips of Paul VI began to incorporate elements that are standard features in the international travels of John Paul II. When Paul VI arrived in Bombay, he greeted the crowd in typical Hindu fashion, saying "I bow to you." While in Bombay, he met with orphaned children, ordained bishops, and blessed the sick and lame who were given a special seating at one of the masses he celebrated. Members of the press accompanied Paul VI on his plane from Rome to Bombay. In New York, after he had addressed the United Nations, Paul VI went to Yankee Stadium, and before ascending the altar, he circled the field in an open limousine, blessing the cheering crowd.

Paul VI's ninth and last visit was unlike all previous visits because it included several stops in six Asian countries. Scholars have noted how this trip prefigured John Paul II's pastoral visits.[8] It had a missionary character, aiming to consolidate the Catholic communities and expand the church's mission in populous Asia. Throughout the ten-day trip, Pope Paul VI touched on what would be a major theme for John Paul II: the need to combat the Western model of materialism. While in the Philippines, Paul VI was the subject of an assassination attempt when a Bolivian, dressed as a cleric, threatened Paul VI with a knife, but was quickly overpowered. In a number of ways, Paul VI's last visit was a precursor of John Paul II's major thrust to develop a new form of papal communication.

THE VATICAN'S SYSTEM OF COMMUNICATIONS

No one can deny that the Vatican has a reputation for secrecy. When the cardinals enter into the conclave to elect a pope, they are locked within the Sistine Chapel until a pope is chosen. No direct account is ever given of the deliberations. Vatican Council II, an ecumenical council to update the Catholic Church, was essentially held in closed sessions. The bishops and cardinals who participated in the Council were obligated to keep secret the discussions and the opinions of individuals. Some observers attribute the Vatican's closed communicative style to its imperial and monarchical culture. In exchange for the privilege to be included in the royal court, one has to remain loyal, especially in guarding the royal secrets. Defending a decision to bar the press from attending the Dutch Synod held in the Vatican in 1980, Pope John Paul II described the "certain occasions" when the church "like all families" needs moments of "intimacy and discretion."[9]

The "family" at the Vatican is relatively small. There are approximately four thousand people working at the Vatican; about half of them are in the executive level, and most of these are clerics. Those who assist the pope in governing the universal church are part of the Roman Curia. The most influential position in the Curia is the secretariat of state, whose head holds an office similar to that of prime minister. Besides handling the official relations with other countries, the secretariat of state is responsible for all documents and correspondence to and from the pope, and as a result, is the intermediary between the pope and others in the Curia. In addition to the secretariat of state, the major divisions of the Curia include nine congregations which would be equivalent to cabinet-level government departments or ministries, three tribunals or courts, and eleven councils. The congregations and councils are structured as committees who, acting like boards of trustees, are responsible for the policy and overall governance of the area. All of the congregations and most of the councils are headed by cardinals. These Curia cardinals often serve on two or three boards outside of their own congregation or council, producing a close-knit interlocking form of governance. The manageable numbers, and the interlocking nature of the Vatican's organizational chart, make direct communication among the controlling executives the norm. Working in this interrelated fashion, individual cardinals know what is happening in several other areas of the Vatican Curia in addition to their own departments. Therefore, Vatican governance has a better chance of grasping the multifaceted "big picture" of the church. Some believe that this leads to an efficient, yet autocratic governance since power resides in a handful of cardinals. Others maintain that although Curia cardinals, because of their committee assignments, may know what is happening in other departments, they do not share this information beyond their ranks.[10]

The Vatican maintains two regular means of distributing information externally—its official newspaper and its radio station. Critics like to point out that the Vatican newspaper, *L'Osservatore Romano*, is not really a newspaper, and the news on Vatican Radio is not really news in the sense that news reports seek out independent viewpoints.[11] Despite the intent of the Vatican's newspaper and radio to present a prescribed viewpoint, both established their reputations in historical periods and geographic areas that were characterized by totalitarian control of information. Actually, *L'Osservatore Romano* was founded in 1861 by four laymen as an independent complement to the official newspaper of the government of the Papal States. When the Papal States disappeared, Pope Leo XIII purchased the *L'Osservatore Romano*. Later, during World War I, the newspaper, reflecting the Vatican's policy of neutrality, attempted to steer a moral course independent of the partisan positions of the warring nations, and its circulation increased to 120,000. During the rise of fascism in Italy, the *L'Osservatore Romano* became a popular source of independent news, and was frequently seized from Roman news dealers and burned by Mussolini supporters. After World War II erupted, the *L'Osservatore Romano* was more cautious, concentrating on religious matters.[12] Today, the daily version of the newspaper is in Italian, and contains texts and reports from the pope and Vatican organizations, as well as editorial comments on religious and international political issues of interest to the church. In the years following World War II, *L'Osservatore Romano* started printing weekly editions in other major European languages. Under Pope John Paul II, a Polish edition was started.

On February 12, 1931, Pope Pius XI broadcast Vatican Radio's first message over transmitters built by its inventor, Guglielmo Marconi. By the outbreak of World War II, the radio was broadcasting regularly on an international scale. When Mussolini led Italy into collaboration with Hitler, the Vatican became a neutral haven in the midst of a war-torn Europe. Maintaining diplomatic representatives, as well as ecclesiastical contact on both sides of the conflict, the Vatican's intelligence networks were vast and complex. The Vatican set up an information center for prisoners of war, refugees and missing persons, and used its radio to broadcast over a million and a quarter inquiries.[13] People from all over the world tuned into Vatican Radio to learn of their loved ones, and listen to unfiltered news of the war. Historical accounts of the war years have pointed out how radio became an enormously influential means of communication. Along with Edward R. Morrow's wartime radio broadcasts were the special addresses of Pope Pius XII, particularly his Christmas messages, which became important rhetorical milestones in the war years. After the war, Vatican Radio became a vital link with those local churches that had been forced underground by communist atheistic governments in the Soviet Union and Eastern Europe. In fact, Vatican Radio and the Voice of America were considered the only means of independent news and information in communist controlled countries. Currently, Vatican Radio, broadcasting to over 170 countries in thirty-four languages, includes news, music, spiritual reflections, liturgies, and talk about current events and culture in its programming. Its purpose is to inform its more than ten million listeners of ethical and moral issues behind the day's headlines, as well as to instruct and inspire people with regard to the Catholic faith.

Dealing with the secular press as an ongoing activity is a relatively new area for the Vatican. In the preparatory stage of Vatican Council II, John XXIII set up a press office to meet the demand for information. Under Paul VI, the Vatican began to take press relations seriously. When Paul VI started traveling, he was aware of the value of the press in covering the event and thus invited its members to accompany him on his plane. John Paul II has continued this practice, but his increased travel has also increased reporting on factual information about Catholicism.[14] In this way, his trips cause news and promote discussion and commentary about religion and morality. Journalists who accompany the pope on the plane have access to John Paul II when he walks through the journalist section to greet them. Valentina Alazraki, a Mexican journalist, recalls that during Paul VI's trips, journalists (all male) dressed formally in jackets and ties, resisted asking questions of Paul VI as he passed through the cabin to greet them. With John Paul II, journalists, both men and women, dress more casually on the plane and often take the opportunity to ask the pope questions about the trip.[15] On the plane to the United States in 1995, a journalist asked John Paul II his opinion of the O. J. Simpson trial. The pope deftly avoided a direct answer, but took the occasion to comment about justice.

In 1965, Pope Paul VI met privately with a journalist from a well-known secular newspaper, thus granting the papacy's first interview to a journalist. Strategically, it occurred after a *Time* magazine cover story that had contained some unfavorable comments of Paul VI's personality. The result was a story which disputed some of the previous analysis of his manner and ability.[16] The practice of granting interviews is still rare, but occasionally John Paul II decides to speak personally with a writer or journalist. Wilton Wynn, correspondent for *Time* magazine, recalled being invited to dinner with the pope at Castel Gandolfo only three days after the Vatican made public its letter telling American theologian Charles Curran that he could no longer teach theology at Catholic University. As Wynn described, the pope wasted no time on insignificant issues. They immediately launched into an intense discussion of the affair. When Wynn reminded the pope that there seemed to be a strong negative reaction in the United States over the Vatican action, the pope stated, "It is a mistake to apply American democratic procedures to the faith and to the truth. You cannot take a vote on truth. They must not confuse 'sensus fidei' with 'consensus.' "[17] Obviously, the pope had strategically chosen his time and forum to enunciate his point of view on the Curran issue.

Pope John Paul II made two significant appointments that have influenced the direction of the Vatican's relationships with the media. He appointed Archbishop John J. Foley, a former editor of the Philadelphia archdiocesan newspaper, to head the Pontifical Council on Social Communications. After Foley took charge, Dr. Joaquin Navarro-Valls, an experienced journalist, became the first lay person to head the Vatican's press office, and soon began to interpret the pope's words to the media. Navarro-Valls has been surprised at how much confidence the pope has invested in him.[18] At the United Nations Conference on Population and Development in Cairo in September 1994, and again at the UN sponsored Conference on Women in China in 1995, Navarro-

Valls, rather than the head of the delegation, was quoted by journalists as giving the pope's interpretation on the events.

Some journalists still complain about lack of access, filtered news, and abstract language. Nevertheless, when the pope entered the hospital for intestinal surgery, Navarro-Valls gave a detailed explanation of the medical problem and the pope's condition. This obviously had been a strategy that the pope approved in advance, and a far cry from the secrecy and mystery that have surrounded the physical condition of other popes. Journalists have also noted that information flows both downward and upward to the pope, who receives a packet of international news coverage every morning. This packet has increased enormously during the papacy of John Paul II.

The workday of John Paul II is filled with opportunities to communicate. Rising between 5 and 6 A.M. every day, his first semipublic appearance begins with 7 A.M. mass in his private chapel. A small number of guests are invited to join in his celebration of the Eucharist. Afterwards he greets these guests and occasionally invites a few of them to breakfast with him. He then spends a few hours doing official paperwork, reading reports, and editing speeches. He is briefed on the day's schedule and major diplomatic developments. At midmorning he moves to his more official office in the papal apartments for private audiences and diplomatic formalities. Once a week, on Wednesdays, John Paul II appears at public audiences in a large, modern conference hall constructed adjacent to St. Peter's Basilica. At lunch, he continues working, often with a visiting cardinal or bishop, or members of the Vatican staff. After a short nap, and a walk in the roof garden, there are more meetings and paperwork, and sometimes a visit to a church or religious institution in Rome. Dinner consists of a relaxing hour or two with a few old friends, or it is an opportunity for the pope to meet and talk with clerical or lay scholars. Very often a guest will receive short notice of the pope's invitation, sometimes in the morning for dinner that night. The pope, who rarely engages in small talk, invites people to his luncheon or dinner table to discuss issues. People at the Vatican call his table his "executive desk" because they often come away from the meal loaded with a list of things the pope wants done.[19]

Both Peter Hebblethwaite and Kathleen Jamieson consider the art of written documentation to be a major activity at the Vatican. Hebblethwaite defends the "paperwork" criticism of the Roman Curia, explaining that written judgments of the Vatican courts, replies to the many letters from diocesan officials throughout the world, and preparation of draft documents on current issues require that words be written down on paper, or at least, on word processors.[20] Jamieson claimed that the Roman Catholic Church is known to the world as "that which issues bulls, addresses, allocations, encyclicals and *ex cathedra* pronouncements."[21] The preparation of papal speeches, as well as the translation of speeches, documents, news, and other items into many other languages has increased the volume of words being crafted in the Vatican offices. Communicating in written form has long been the special work of the church. From its handcrafted manuscripts to the first samples of printed scripture, the Vatican library and archives are the guardians of a long historical past of words. Today, Vatican officials are keenly aware of their obligation to preserve a record for history. After John Paul II's first visit to the United Nations, Archbishop Rigali, while cleaning up his desk, discovered that he had the handwritten text of the pope's original draft of his speech. He quickly gathered it and other items, and sent them to the archives where they will remain locked up until a future pope decides it is appropriate for historians to study them.[22]

The pageantry of Vatican ritual is another preoccupation of the Vatican. For centuries, the ceremonial splendor of popes captured the attention of Christian adherents. In the nineteenth century, newly built railroads made pilgrimage to Rome easier and a wide variety of people from all over Europe came to the Vatican to attend papal ceremonies, hoping to catch a glimpse of the pope. Large numbers of people still come to Rome, especially for the Easter week liturgies and periodic ceremonies that elevate candidates to sainthood. Now, these solemn and intricate rites are broadcast on television throughout the world.

Handling of crowds has always been an art form for Vatican officials. The practice of holding audiences was prevalent in the royal courts and was adopted by pontiffs in both their religious and civic roles. When their temporal power ended, popes continued the practice, using the papal palace halls as well as the open courtyards. Today, every Wednesday, thousands of visitors descend from buses with audience tickets in hand. They take their seats in the huge audience hall built during Paul VI's papacy to accommodate 7,700 people seated, and wait anxiously for the moment when the pope arrives. John Paul II usually walks down the aisle extending his hand to people fortunate enough to have aisle seats. The audience ceremony itself is like a pep rally. Organized according to language, the program includes the introduction of special groups in the audience who will often stand and break out in song. The pope then acknowledges them, speaking their particular language. The crowds clap, cheer, and chant their enthusiastic approval of papal attention. They unfurl banners and display their group identity by some sort of matching garb. The Wednesday audience has fulfilled an important function of communicating with the thousands of Catholics and others who want to have some personal face-to-face experience with the pope. When very large pilgrim groups are in Rome, the Vatican sometimes schedules a second Wednesday audience in St. Peter's Basilica, which holds 7,000 to 8,000 people, or in St. Peter's Square, which has accommodated up to 150,000 people.

HISTORICAL RHETORICAL PERSONA OF JOHN PAUL II

John Paul II's Prepapal Background

Many observers acknowledge the pope's ability to project a personal presence. They often connect this ability to John Paul II's experience as an actor. His ability to project his voice, his timing, and his confidence before a large audience are all traits that are often learned through study and training. John Paul II, then Karol Wojtyla, began playing leading roles in local plays during his high school years. As a university student in Krakow, he became involved in the Rhapsodic Theater when both the university and the theater were forced underground by the Nazi occupation of Poland. The productions of this "theater of the word" were presented in the limited space of Krakow's apartments where there were few stage props, giving only a suggestion of character. Emphasis was placed on the delivery of the rhymed verses through voice, precise pronunciation, emotion, and expression. The Rhapsodic Theater's emphasis on words was a reaction to the "overtheatricality" of theater spectacles. Instead of watching drama unfold, audiences listened to the word so that inner thoughts and imagination could be expressed without being influenced by the externals of theatrical production.[23] During his involvement with the theater, Wojtyla began writing poetry and plays, which he continued to compose after he was ordained a priest.[24] He even published poems, under several pseudonyms, when he was a bishop. As the biographer Williams claimed, the pope's way of speaking is very much influenced by his poetic and dramatic leanings.[25] He often uses poetic expressions, particularly those which are closely connected to patriotic and national traditions. His facility in using facial expressions to develop communication with a crowd and his deeply resonant voice reveal his former life as an actor.

John Paul II spent many years in the university community, as a doctoral student, a professor, and as chaplain to university students. It is widely thought that the pope's ease with young people is largely due to his experience as a teacher when he was a young priest. Tad Szulc recounted stories of Wojtyla taking students on mountain excursions kayaking, skiing, and spending long hours with students discussing topics way into the night. Even as a professor, he is remembered by students for acting in an unusual and extraordinary fashion. His clothing included a mixture of frayed clerical garb, aviator caps, green overcoats, and trousers. Shunning kneelers in the chapel, he chose the hard floor for his hours of reflection. He also was willing to try novel approaches, calling for medical doctors to give premarital courses in areas where the priests were not competent.[26]

During these university years, particularly at the faculty of Christian philosophy of the University of Lublin, John Paul II formulated many of his philosophic positions on the human person. Like his fellow professors at Lublin, he engaged the trends of modern philosophical thinking, such as existentialism and phenomenology, and sought to frame them within a Thomistic tradition. This Thomist personalism was an attempt to stress the dignity of the human person in opposition to the determinism of Marxism and other modern philosophic trends.[27] However, critics reviewing Wojtyla's work in philosophy contend that to classify his work as a reaction to modern determinism does not do justice to the contributions he has made to Christian philosophy. His originality consists first in his use of a phenomenological method through which he added a subjective dimension to scholastic thought by intimately consulting each person's concrete experience. This included viewing the human self through its corporeality and temporality. He was quite aware of the tendency of the new self-consciousness to remain trapped in solitude, but he was convinced that this modern view of self could be used positively if consciousness were placed as an important aspect of the whole person who is situated within a community of persons and a universal community of being.[28] Thus, John Paul II's intellectual formation as a student and professor, particularly his work on the philosophy of the human person, is reflected in his papal writings and indeed, as this study confirms, in his rhetorical style.

In comparison to other modern popes, John Paul II's youthful background was quite unique. He also followed a very unusual path to become bishop. He had only a few years of pastoral experience and no administrative background. However, as a scholar and popular university professor, he was singled out to become an auxiliary bishop of Krakow in 1958. By the time Vatican Council II opened, the Archbishop of Krakow had died, and Wojtyla, then the vicar for the diocese, was chosen to be part of the Polish delegation to the Council's first session in

Rome. It was not until the end of the second session of Vatican Council II in December 1963 that Wojtyla was elevated to archbishop of Krakow. When Wojtyla returned to the third and fourth sessions of the Council, he became actively involved in drafting points and spoke on issues of religious liberty and the church in the world. Even during the Council, he continued his writing, including a series of poems, one entitled "The Negro," obviously addressed to one of his bishop colleagues from Africa.[29]

As archbishop and later when he was elevated to cardinal in 1967, Wojtyla's activities can be grouped under two categories: teacher and pastor. As a teacher, he continued his intellectual writings. In 1969, he published the first version of *The Acting Person* in Krakow and in the years that followed, he continued to refine his work, delivering papers on the subject and discussing concepts during his regular Thursday evening gatherings of intellectuals at his residence.[30] Part of his ministry was preaching "meditation days" to specific professional groups, such as doctors, lawyers, teachers, and youth. The communist government's political organization in Poland sometimes criticized and challenged Wojtyla on these practices, which they called divisive, but according to Tad Szulc, who cited documents of the Polish communist secret police, Wojtyla's intellectual reputation made him less threatening to the communist government than his overtly anticommunist colleagues. The secret police concluded that he was "overintellectualized," and therefore was not a political leader. Furthermore, they saw him as being open to coexistence with communism and referred to his leisure activities with students as evidence of a "secular lifestyle."[31]

Far from being exclusively involved in intellectual activities, the Polish Cardinal Wojtyla engaged in other pastoral activities that were clearly aimed at communicating in a more popular style. After preventing the communist government from completely taking over his seminary, he led the seminarians on a silent march to dedicate the building to the Virgin Mary. When the communist government refused to grant him permits to build new churches, he held mass in the open lots, and complained to the government that parishioners were forced to stand in the cold and rain to worship.[32] In 1969, Wojtyla launched the "Sacrosong Movement," an attempt to use modern "beat" music with religious lyrics to appeal to youth and bypass the government's restrictions on religious education. He helped organize annual Sacrosong festivals like soccer matches, awarding a championship cup to the winner of the religious music contest.[33]

By 1978, Wojtyla had gained a reputation among fellow philosophers, particularly among phenomenologists. He delivered a paper at a conference under the auspices of Harvard in 1976, and several of his papers derived from the original Polish version of *The Acting Person* were published in an American philosophical journal. He was known also among the Polish community in Canada and the United States, and his diocese was a popular stopover for bishops traveling to Poland. Through his participation in the Council, his travels, and contacts with church officials in Europe and North America, he was known and respected among certain intellectual and church circles. He had, of course, made a name for himself in Poland, but he was relatively unknown outside of those circles. When his election to the papacy was announced, it was clear that he was, in a sense, a stranger to most in the church.

Key Rhetorical Moments in Early Papacy

First impressions are very lasting. As the ballot in the Sistine Chapel reached the two-thirds plus one number necessary to elect a pope, Cardinal Wojtyla was seen writing furiously. He had barely a few minutes before he would be swept into the ceremony of greeting his colleagues and the waiting public as Pope John Paul II. As he stepped out onto the balcony over St. Peter's Square to give his first blessing, he departed from the prescribed ceremony to address the crowd in Italian. He described himself as coming from a distant country that was, on the other hand, so close in its communion of faith and tradition. He jokingly asked the crowd to correct his Italian and then proceeded to pledge himself to start anew on the church's path of history, asking the help of both God and man.

Immediately, in the first days of his papacy, he showed his sensitivity to symbol. Like his predecessor, he refused the tiara or papal crown, but he worked its three-pronged symbolism into his inaugural remarks. Rather than receiving the cardinals seated on a throne, he stood to give them bear-like hugs, causing many to forget to even attempt to kiss his ring. As the aging Polish Primate Cardinal Wyszynski came forward, John Paul II knelt before him, and the two men emotionally embraced. Instead of blessing the cardinals, he asked them to bless each other and himself, setting in motion a new symbol of collegiality.

Observers of the papacy have remarked that the inauguration of a new pope is often marked with solemnity, revealing a loneliness on the part of those who are chosen to fill the shoes of Peter. However, these same observers noted how different John Paul II approached these moments. First, his speech delivered the morning of his election appeared to be truly his own writing, reflecting many of the themes he often preached in Krakow. In hindsight, those remarks, together with his inaugural homily are also the core themes and symbols to which he has so often returned during his papacy. Rather than proceeding carefully, with almost trepidation, John Paul II looked ahead "to the year 2000" and told the crowd "do not be afraid," but "open wide the doors for Christ." At the close of his homily, he switched from Italian to greet the crowd in many different languages. The Poles were the first group, and in a brief paragraph he signaled his intention to use words and much more than words to communicate. He told them that the meaning of words would fade when compared to "what my heart feels, and your hearts feel," and that it would be best to simply leave words aside and be silent before God.[34]

On the afternoon of his first day, John Paul II emerged from the Vatican walls in an open car to visit Bishop André-Marie Deskur, the Polish head of the Commission for Social Communications, who lay unconscious in a Roman hospital. For John Paul II, leaving the Vatican walls (although not in an open car) would become a common occurrence. Only three months after his election, John Paul II embarked on his first overseas trip to participate in a conference of Latin American bishops in Puebla, Mexico. It would be his first encounter with "Liberation Theology," whose extreme adherents were identified with a militant social justice that sometimes flirted with Marxist philosophy and tactics. With firm gentleness, he upheld the church's concern for the poor, but reined in what he believed to be dangerous tendencies of identifying the church with overly political and confrontational movements. During the same visit, John Paul II directly dealt with the issue of land reform, claiming that it is inconceivable to have peasants without land.[35]

John Paul II's next trip was to Poland, which Tad Szulc called a study in "creative political friction." The communist government in Poland attempted to control and contain the pope's visit. They instructed the television cameras to use only tight shots of the pope so Polish viewers could not see the crowds. Likewise, newspapers could use photos no wider than one column. Nevertheless, the enthusiasm of the people won out. It was estimated that ten million of the thirty-five million Poles saw the pope in person at one of nine locations on his itinerary. If the pope intended to boost the moral of the Polish church as it struggled to keep faith alive in the face of constant harassment by the communist government, he succeeded. However, historians believe that this first trip achieved even more; as Poles walked for miles and assembled in disciplined and peaceful crowds to demonstrate their faith, they began to see how powerful they could be in withstanding communist control of their religion and their lives. During the visit, John Paul II employed images of Polish history to evoke a religious patriotism of the past. Observers described a moving moment of the trip: a lone voice starting singing a Polish patriotic hymn, the crowd followed, and soon the Pope, in tears, had joined them.[36]

The energy with which John Paul II began his papacy was astounding. Even while planning his first overseas visits, the pope immediately set to writing his first encyclical which was finished and issued less than five months after he took office, faster than his five immediate predecessors. Furthermore, the encyclical, *Redemptor Hominis*, was not a simple treatise. In it, John Paul II expressed a comprehensive vision of the whole created order and the history of mankind. Redemption achieved through Christ is understood not only as eternal salvation in afterlife, but as a wholeness in the present, enhancing the dignity and preciousness of the human being in this world.

Peter Hebblethwaite noticed that shortly after a pope takes office, a mythologization of his background begins.[37] It is not that history is rewritten, but it is interpreted to show that the man must have been destined for the office. For John Paul II, the first non-Italian pope in 450 years and the first Slavic pope in the history of the papacy, his Polish background became a fascinating tale of human tragedy and triumph. By age twenty, he was alone, having lost his mother, father, and brother. He had lived as a young boy in a town near the site of one of the worst Jewish death camps. During the German occupation, he worked in a factory and studied in the underground seminary. Woven into the emerging persona of the pope were deeds of heroic proportion. In probing the origins of Pope John Paul II's thought, Williams pointed out that the pope studied and recited the works of Polish prophetic poets at the university and in the Rhapsodic Theater. Therefore, he must have absorbed the Polish Messianism which was so much a part of their writings. For the prophetic poets, the Polish nation imitated Christ. Just as Christ had suffered and died, so too the Polish nation had suffered and died through partition by Russia, Prussia, and Austria. Also like Christ, the Polish nation would rise again to save all nations. However, since resurrection could not be achieved without suffering, that suffering was not to be passively accepted, but rather embraced as a means of purification, eventually leading to a new age. According to Williams, there are traces of Polish messianic themes in John Paul II's writings and speeches, namely, his stress on the Christ visible in suffering and the hope for an advent of renewed humanity in the coming millennium.[38]

Events can be powerful image creators. On May 13, 1981, Pope John Paul II's body was pierced by an assassin's bullet. Instantly, the pope became the hero of a drama told around the world. Even John Paul II used the event as a modern morality play about the sacred. First, the pope was dramatically reduced to a mere human state. No longer within the majestic walls of the Vatican, and no longer robed in the dignified attire of the papal office, the pope was lying on a simple hospital bed, in an ordinary hospital gown, and hooked up to feeding tubes. What was even more shocking was that the world was permitted to see him in this state through photographs. But then, he began to talk of his brush with death, and how it was a sign from God that he was spared. The assassination attempt had been on the feast of Our Lady of Fatima, and having recovered, a year later, he went to Fatima to give thanks for being spared his life. According to apparitions of Fatima, conversion of Russia was possible if people would pray the rosary. Mary had protected John Paul II, just as she had promised at Fatima to save the world from being devoured by atheism. When he arrived at Fatima, he placed the bullet on the altar. Two years after the almost fateful event, John Paul II, saved from the assassin's bullet, walked into the cell of Mehmet Ali Agca, his Turkish assassin, to forgive him. The story is told over and over again, as photos and video capture the essential moments in the narrative. Even when Ronald Reagan came to the Vatican to call upon the pope, the media began linking the two because both had narrowly missed assassination.

Much has been written about the role of Pope John Paul II in bringing an end to communist domination of Eastern Europe. There is no question that John Paul II's position of using dialogue with firmness produced amazing results. Some believe that after the pope's first visit to Poland, the Solidarity movement was motivated to challenge the communist regime. Calling a strike, Solidarity workers demonstrated outside of the shipyards of Gdansk carrying photos of John Paul II. Negotiating his second trip to Poland, John Paul II insisted that he meet with Solidarity's leader, Lech Walesa. In many ways, the papal visits and the process of planning for these events provided a forum for the pope and church officials to deal with the Polish communist government. Eventually, the government accepted the reality that the church in Poland was enormously powerful in influencing public opinion. As a result, the church joined the government in working out a consultative mechanism through which Polish leaders, regardless of political persuasion, would advise on national policies. This dialogue between the church and communist government led ultimately to parliamentary elections.

The reshaping of Poland was a crucial first wedge in weakening the communist hold on Eastern Europe. The Polish case of the church pressuring the communist government for improved human rights and religious freedom served as a model in other Eastern European nations, and even in Mikhail Gorbachev's Soviet Union. John Paul II boldly talked of a unity of the entire European continent through its common Christian origins. With quiet revolutions, the walls between the East and West vanished during his papacy. His obvious success in steering the Vatican's policies regarding Eastern Europe and the Soviet Union, and his continued call for human dignity, rights, and freedom of religion in every corner of the world, lead critics to view John Paul II as "God's politician," whose travels are "part of his long-term political strategy."[39] Indeed, part of the rhetorical persona of John Paul II is his political acumen. The media, which is used to reporting on political leaders and events, is not often well prepared to critique the visits as religious, or even as deeply cultural events. In a sense, this "political" persona of the pope can help and hinder papal communication. His prestige as a successful advocate of human and political rights lends strong credibility to his words and actions. However, the same reputation sometimes clouds understanding of the ultimate religious and spiritual goals of his overseas visits.

Statements on Communication Policy

Five days after his election to the papacy, John Paul II was ushered into an audience room filled with journalists, and instead of proceeding to his chair to address the group, he passed between the rows of reporters, answering questions posed in various languages. "Will you go to Poland?" was one of the questions, and the pope answered without hesitation, "If they permit me." Valentina Alazraki, a Mexican journalist, claims that when John Paul II approached the press without any inhibition, journalists realized that the pope had launched a new era in the Vatican's relationship with the press.[40] This papal style of dealing with journalists plays an important role in the overseas visit and serves to foster communication with the local church and others in the world. Again, the personal experience and talents of John Paul II may be factors in the development of this style, but the institutional components should not be ignored. Modern communication means have been embraced by the Vatican with its newspaper, radio station, television capabilities, and now internet web site. Furthermore, the church had begun thinking and formulating normative policies on communications long before the election of John Paul II. The first encyclical on twentieth-century means of communication was *Vigilanti Cura*, written by Pope Pius XI in 1936 to support morally good films and counteract those considered morally unacceptable. His successor, Pope Pius XII, not only used electronic means of communications for his messages, but he spoke often about the subject of electronic communication. In many of his talks and writings, and particularly in his encyclical, *Miranda Prorsus*, Pius XII analyzed the purpose and effects of film, radio, and television, and drew certain conclusions regarding the problems and possibilities of using these means for pastoral teaching. In 1963, Vatican Council II instituted a new terminology, "social communications," to emphasize that communication, more than the technical means, is a human societal and cultural process. The Council decree established two features that guaranteed continued study and recognition for social communications: a world day of communications, whose celebration has produced a yearly pontifical message; and a proposed commission on social communications that published a pastoral instruction on the subject. The commission was quickly established by Pope Paul VI in 1964, and the instruction, entitled *Communio et Progressio*, was published in 1971 after an extensive consultative process involving bishops and communication representatives throughout the world. Although not a papal decree or encyclical, *Communio et Progressio* was approved by Pope Paul VI, and is considered to be a major statement on the theology of communication and how communication is a means to human progress.

At the time of Pope John Paul II's election to the papacy, there was already in place an established view on the indispensability of the means of communication in the church's task of evangelization. John Paul II continued the practice of issuing messages on World Communication Day, and included references to the role of modern communication in papal exhortations. His treatment of communication in his encyclical, *Redemptoris Missio*, demonstrated how important communication has become to the church's mission of preaching the gospel. He compared the church's strategy with that of St. Paul, who on arriving in Athens went to the Areopagus, or the cultural center of the people of Athens. He pointed out that today's cultural center at which people are taught, guided, and inspired is the world of communication. Young people are growing up in a new culture of mass media, and rather than neglecting this world, the church has to integrate the gospel with the new culture formed by modern communications.[41]

SUMMARY: BACKGROUND SETS STAGE FOR
OVERSEAS VISITS

The Vatican's system of communication combines age-old tradition and updated technical means. Whether it be the internal hierarchical organizational structure that is influenced by the traditional familial and court-like ties of loyalty, or the extension of the pilgrimage as a spiritual means of communicating with the sacred, Vatican ways of communicating are deeply connected to traditional roots. Written forms of communicating are still very strong factors in conserving church tradition, but modern technical systems and lifestyles have already had an impact on Vatican communications. Electronic means, modern audience hall facilities, a workday schedule that matches any chief executive officer of a large organization, and an updated outlook toward the theory of communication and the practice of press relations are all factors that have assisted in fashioning the rhetorical style of John Paul II and his new vocabulary for constructing sacred symbols.

In a sense, the visits of the pope to the local churches are within the same tradition of the pastoral visits of bishops to local parishes. The orientation is towards the congregation, whereby the bishop, or in this case, the pope, moves outward from the diocesan or papal center, in order to communicate directly with the people. These visits are special occasions when the local church congregation interrupts their regular schedule to reflect on their spiritual journey. Pope Paul VI startled the world by inaugurating the idea of a traveling pope. These visits served as important precedents for the massive travel schedule of John Paul II. Clearly, certain elements of Paul VI's nine overseas trips were incorporated into the standard organization of John Paul II's visits to local churches.

Within a few years after his election, John Paul II was "known" to people all over the world. The mythological development of his persona was rapid and dramatic, mainly because elements of his past and present fit so well into a heroic narrative. Much of his early background was so different from recent popes, many of whom entered the seminary early and spent most of their adult lives in Italy or in the service of the Vatican. In this sense, John Paul II was not one of them. He was an outsider, and therefore, unencumbered by the Vatican "insider" image. He had worked in a factory, acted in plays, written poetry, and stood up to communists. He was also young and vigorous, and his energy matched his hopeful message. His first visits, especially his emotional and courageous trip back to his Polish homeland, set the pace and style for his future trips. If there is one single event that people remember about this pope, it is his narrow escape from an assassin's bullet. The event was kept alive by both John Paul II and the media who followed his story. The pope stressed a sacred interpretation, suggesting that his life may have been spared by God so as to continue the work of evangelization. The media focused on the possibility that the assassin was part of an international communist-led plot. Both interpretations, the sacred and the secular, enhanced each other's narrative. In this sense, the historical rhetorical persona of John Paul II presented a consistent foundation for his rhetorical strategy.

NOTES

1. Robert A. White, "The New Communications Emerging in the Church," *The Way Supplement: Communication, Media, and Spirituality* 57 (Autumn 1986): 20.

2. Patrick Granfield, "The Theology of the Church and Communication," *The Church and Communication*, ed. Patrick Granfield (Kansas City, Missouri: Sheed & Ward, 1994), 1–18.

3. Pontifical Commission for the Means of Social Communication, *Communio et Progressio*, in *Church and Social Communication: Basic Documents*, ed. Franz-Joseph Eilers (Manila: Logos Publications, Inc., 1993), no. 11, 76.

4. Avery Dulles, "Vatican II and Communications," *Vatican II: Assessment and Perspectives*, vol. 3, ed. René Latourelle (New York: Paulist Press, 1989), 528–537.

5. Wilton Wynn, *Keepers of the Keys* (New York: Random House, 1988), 136.

6. Peter Hebblethwaite, *The Year of Three Popes* (London: William Collins, 1978), 10–15.

7. Peter Hebblethwaite, *Paul VI: The First Modern Pope* (New York: Paulist Press, 1993), 374.

8. Christine de Montclos, *Les Voyages de Jean-Paul II* (Paris: Centurion, 1990), 16; and Peter Hebblethwaite, *Paul VI: The First Modern Pope*, 564.

9. Peter Hebblethwaite, *In the Vatican* (Oxford: Oxford University Press, 1986), 184.

10. Jerrold M. Packard, *Peter's Kingdom: Inside the Papal City* (New York: Charles Scribner's, 1985), 105; and Peter Hebblethwaite, *In the Vatican*, 54–56.

11. Hebblethwaite, *In the Vatican*, 181.

12. Packard, *Peter's Kingdom*, 117–118.

13. Ibid., 115–116.

14. Nick Thimmesch, "On the Secular Press," in *The Pastoral Vision of John Paul II*, ed. Joan Bland (Chicago: Franciscan Herald Press, 1982),

170–171; also David Shaw, "Activist Pope Puts Catholics at Front of Media Attention," *Los Angeles Times,* 18 April 1995.

15. Valentina Alazraki, *Juan Pablo II: El Viajero de Dios* (Colonia del Valle, Mexico: Editorial Diana, 1990), 218.

16. Hugh Morley, *The Pope and the Press* (Indiana: University of Notre Dame, 1968), 67–69.

17. Wynn, *Keepers of the Keys,* 257–259.

18. David Shaw, "Coverage of UN Conference Shows Vatican Media Savvy," *Los Angeles Times,* 17 April 1995.

19. Don A. Schanche, "Pope John Paul II: CEO," *Los Angeles Times Magazine,* 13 September 1987.

20. Hebblethwaite, *In the Vatican,* 57.

21. Kathleen Jamieson, "A Rhetorical-Critical Analysis of the Conflict Over *Humanae Vitae*" (Ph.D. dissertation, University of Wisconsin, 1972), 38.

22. Archbishop Justin Rigali, interview by author, October 1992, Rome, Italy.

23. Boleslaw Taborski, Introduction to *The Collected Plays and Writings on Theater*, by Karol Wojtyla, ed. Boleslaw Taborski (Berkeley: University of California Press, 1987), 1–16.

24. After Wojtyla became pope, one of his plays, The Jeweler's Shop, became a radio play, and then a motion picture starring Burt Lancaster.

25. George Huntston Williams, *The Mind of John Paul II: Origins of His Thought and Action* (New York: Seabury Press, 1981), 72.

26. Tad Szulc, *John Paul II: The Biography* (New York: Scribner, 1995), 180–192.

27. Williams, *The Mind of John Paul II,* 147–151.

28. Kenneth L. Schmitz, "Modernity Meets Tradition: The Philosophical Originality of Karol Wojtyla," *Crisis* (April 1994): 30–36.

29. Williams, *The Mind of John Paul II,* 166.

30. Ibid., 186–194.

31. Szulc, *John Paul II: The Biography,* 242–244.

32. Ibid., 208.

33. Ibid., 251–252.

34. Hebblethwaite, *The Year of Three Popes,* 184–193.

35. Alazraki, *Juan Pablo II,* 150–151; Paul Johnson, *Pope John Paul II and the Catholic Restoration* (New York: St. Martin's Press, 1981), 93–96.

36. Szulc, *John Paul II: The Biography,* 297–310; Wynn, *Keepers of the Keys,* 206–207; Johnson, *Pope John Paul II and the Catholic Restoration,* 73.

37. Hebblethwaite, *The Year of Three Popes,* 183.

38. Williams, *The Mind of John Paul II,* 42–47, 311–317.

39. David Willey, *God's Politician* (London: Faber and Faber, 1992), xi–xii.

40. Alazraki, *Juan Pablo II,* 215–216.

41. John Paul II, *Redemptoris Missio,* in *Origins,* vol. 20, no. 34 (31 January 1991), no. 37c, 552–553.

CHAPTER 4

Sensing the Faithful

A papal visit can be viewed as a campaign, the purpose of which is to "build up" the church and therefore, although its external relationships are very important, the primary audience is the local church. Both the internal and external audiences are composed of numerous groupings or subpopulations. As George Cheney has observed, the Catholic Church can be studied as a complex organization, in which the corporate voice or rhetor involves the "management of multiple identities." Managing the diversity of roles, ethnic backgrounds, ages, interests, and cultural identities within the church requires a "process of message construction," in which the diverse and sometimes conflicting interests of these groups as well as groups outside the church feel that their interests are represented.[1] However, as noted earlier, the overriding concern of the church is to maintain its "plausibility." For a religious institution, this entails, above all, managing the delicate balance between its sacred and secular interests.

As persuasive campaigns, Pope John Paul II's visits to local churches are carefully planned. In observing the planning process, it is possible to learn if and how planners take into account the need to appeal to multiple audiences and their positions regarding the accommodating-resistance dialectic with relation to the sacred-secular realms. Planners are constantly dealing with the demands and implications of the "worldly" elements of the trip: crowd control, ticket distribution, and how to pay for it. In many ways, the planning process itself tends to gravitate toward the secular demands of the world. Making decisions on how to control the selling of souvenirs requires skills in "market-ing." Choices of physical background not only demand some knowl-edge of aesthetics, but also some familiarity with visual media effects. However, those within the church who resist employing these "canons of rhetoric and public relations" argue that the church is significantly different from other organizations.[2] Because of this difference, there is tension in the planning process between the sacred and the secular character of the trip.

A planning process must constantly be measured against purpose. When reflecting on papal visits, those involved in the planning process stress the pope's own characterization of his purpose: the pastoral na-ture of his visits. The Reverend Roberto Tucci, who has been in charge of the organization of the trips since 1982, used a quote from John Paul II in 1979 to illustrate the primarily spiritual dimension. Each visit is "an authentic pilgrimage to the living sanctuary of the People of God."[3] The pope's use of the concept of pilgrimage is an outgrowth of his experience as a bishop. During his Lenten reflection which he preached to Pope Paul VI in 1976, he used the same expression to illus-trate a bishop's visitation of parishes in the diocese. A "canonical" visit to a parish is part of a bishop's administrative duty. However, John Paul II, then bishop of Krakow, viewed the parish, not only as an administra-tive unit, but as a "sanctuary" where the "community of the People of God" possesses the "kingliness" or "dignity" of mankind that is shared in Christ. The bishop arrives at these communities or sanctuaries as a "pilgrim," knowing "how to detect and appreciate that 'kingliness,' that dignity." Cardinal Wojtyla saw these visits as "joyful and necessary events."[4] As Tucci notes, John Paul II's visits are pilgrimages with a global dimension since "the world has become his parish."[5]

In 1980, speaking before the college of cardinals and Roman Curia, John Paul II described the travels of a "Papa-pellegrino" as journeys of faith and prayer.[6] The primary, if not exclusive, reason for papal visits is the spiritual rather than temporal or administrative function. In a world that has become increasingly unaware of the spiritual or sacred dimen-sion of reality, planners constantly struggle with how to construct a visit in which the sacred will become meaningful. For a papal visit to be suc-cessful, it must accommodate to the secular world and all its modern means of communication. However, it must also possess a quality that distinguishes it from visits by other important personalities. In examin-ing how the visits are constructed, there is evidence that the planning process itself works to impose certain character and meaning on the symbolic production of the visit.

PREPLANNING: VATICAN AND LOCAL CHURCH INTERACTION

From the outset of the planning process, Vatican officials stress the local-universal church dialectic. Local bishops from churches all over the world must make an *ad limina Apostolorum* visit to Rome every five years. In this sense, the *ad limina* is a movement of local churches towards the universal symbol of the one Church. The pope's travels outward to the local churches has been called an "ad limina Ecclesiae" that represents "un movimento inverso e complementare" towards the local churches.[7] Vatican officials emphasize that the pope does not unilaterally determine his itinerary, but responds to invitations from local churches. Of course, a broad hint from John Paul II or Vatican officials can easily prompt these invitations.

On national or regional visits, the Vatican turns to episcopal conferences to help organize the invitations. The episcopal conference is a relatively new administrative unit in the church. To implement reforms, Vatican Council II asked bishops who headed dioceses in the same nation or region to form an association. Since then, national episcopal conferences have grown in experience and staff. In the 1987 trip to the United States when the pope wished to visit the southwestern and western areas of the country, the suggested itinerary was largely left to the National Conference of Catholic Bishops (NCCB). In practice, the Vatican, the national bishops' conference and the individual bishops interact in the symbolic production of a papal visit.

Early in the planning process, the approval of the government of the country to be visited must be obtained. If the pope were simply a religious leader, this approval process would have little impact on the rhetorical strategy of the visit. However, the pope is head of the government of the worldwide Catholic community which is recognized by most nations as an international sovereignty. The complex nature of the Holy See and its curious mixture of both religious and political functions makes meaning production even more difficult. Western journalists and political commentators often view the papal trips as part of the "political strategy" of the Holy See. Even when the religious dimension is obvious, they have a tendency to emphasize the social and political aspects. To counteract this tendency, Vatican planners work to control and manage the political appearances of the visits. First of all, they evaluate the "political" factors. For example, political events within the country may affect the trip's timing. Arriving during national election campaigning is generally avoided so as to prevent the possibility that political themes will undermine the "pastoral" nature of the trip.

For a trip to run smoothly, the host government should be willing to work cooperatively with Vatican officials on a variety of matters that can affect the pope's rhetorical strategies. An uncooperative government could be reason for delaying or canceling plans for the trip. For example, the government of Nicaragua gave its approval for the pope's trip in 1983, but its attitude was "ambivalent," and the pope was "badly treated."[8] When the pope's preaching was interrupted and severely limited by organized protest, John Paul II was visibly disturbed. This obscured his image as a self-confident leader, thereby affecting his ability to persuade his audience.

Mostly, governments are cooperative, but sometimes governmental leaders are too cooperative. During a papal visit, the Vatican attempts to contain meetings with government officials, usually allowing only a welcoming and departure ceremony. However, political leaders are constantly pressuring the Vatican for more opportunities with the pope. Occasionally, the Vatican bends its rules to accommodate them. The itinerary of the 1991 Brazilian trip conveniently included Alagoas in Macao, which happened to be the home base of Brazilian President Fernando Collor de Mello.[9] During the preparation for the pope's first trip to France, Jacques Chirac, mayor of Paris and a political rival of French president Valery Giscard d'Estaing, offered to host a ceremony for the pope at the city hall of Paris. The Vatican and local church officials resisted, contending that the pope makes official visits only to national leaders. When Chirac went to the Vatican and appealed directly to Pope John Paul II, the pope agreed.[10] On the first day of his visit to France, John Paul II met President d'Estaing in the center of Paris, and later the pope was officially welcomed to the city at city hall by Jacques Chirac.

In preparing the U.S. trip, the Reagan administration lobbied hard to include an event acknowledging Mrs. Reagan's efforts on drug prevention. Planners gave in, and scheduled a visit to a Catholic school with Mrs. Reagan present. During John Paul II's visit to the United States in 1995, leaders of the U.S. Senate and House of Representatives asked to meet with the pope. They were refused because "the pope generally meets with the head of state or a vice president, but not with opposition leaders when he visits democratic countries."[11] Keeping the governmental and political aspects of the papal visit within bounds is constantly on the minds of Vatican planners. Indeed, to counteract the tendency to misinterpret the papal mission, the Vatican insists on the local church invitation process.

Invitational Process: Vatican, Bishops' Conferences, Individual Bishops

According to the Reverend Roberto Tucci, John Paul II receives many invitations. Together with officials from the Vatican secretariat of state, Tucci reviews the invitations using criteria set by the pope and by the physical constraints of his calendar. Through experience, they have found that the pope can reasonably make four trips a year—one close to Rome, the other three farther away. Obviously, the Vatican planners attempt to space trips so that no one continent is favored over another. However, John Paul II feels that trips to Latin America and Africa should not be too far apart.[12] There seems to be a special concern on the part of the pope for these two continents where the church is viewed as potentially strong in numbers and vitality.

Because of the deep symbolic tradition of religious communication, Vatican planners look for a match between important themes on the pope's agenda and contextual elements of a trip that can serve as symbolic elements to help reinforce the theme. According to Tucci, a main reason for the pope's visit to Thailand was to address the world on the refugee situation and to do so from a refugee camp. On the island of Goree in Senegal, where there remain the ruins of a prison once used for holding Africans waiting to be sent as slaves to America, the pope could address the world on the horrors of slavery.[13] Vatican planners begin by reviewing invitations, but they clearly weigh the global implications of the visits, trying to balance needs, issues, and the symbolic contextual frameworks of the visits.

After the decision has been made to visit a country or group of countries in a continent, Tucci sends the local bishops a list of criteria to be used in their planning. These are mainly technical details such as time requirements for events. Usually a trip includes opportunities for the pope to meet with clergy, bishops, religious men and women, and laity. The Vatican requests that the sick and the poor be included in some event. Host governments are sometimes sensitive regarding papal visits to poor areas because they do not want to publicly acknowledge these problems. In some instances, governments agree to the papal itinerary, but the slums are cleaned up before the arrival of the pope. In Brazil, the pope insisted that the trip include a visit to a slum, but the government voiced legitimate concerns about security and access. Finally, to permit the pope to visit a poor area of Lixao, Vitoria, the Brazilian government built a heliport out of a basketball court and avoided bringing the pope in by road.[14]

Once the criteria from the Vatican is sent, responsibility for planning the proposed trip passes to the local bishops. Because the format of the trip depends largely on the local conditions of the church, Vatican planners rely on the local bishops to make decisions based on their specific needs. In Africa, lay catechists are an important constituency for the pope's visit because priests in this young church depend on them to help teach the large numbers who wish to enter the Catholic Church. In countries where the church is a minority, the papal visits include sufficient and meaningful meetings with the majority who may be Muslim, Hindu, or Lutheran.

In turning to the local church in the planning process, the papal visit is attempting to build a sacred cosmos that is plausible and relevant to the local culture. When speaking of plausibility, Berger emphasized the need for the church to appear massively real.[15] For the 1987 visit to the U.S., an ad hoc committee was formed within the National Conference of Catholic Bishops (NCCB) to decide on the visit itinerary. This committee's first criteria in choosing sites for the visit was "massivity." Certain sites were prime contenders for inclusion because they represented areas where the Catholic population was substantial and growing. The trip was to focus on the West and, therefore, certain sites were automatically considered: San Francisco and Los Angeles, where there are sizable Catholic populations; and New Orleans, a historic Catholic center. Although Florida's Miami posed some political issues, which will be discussed later in this chapter, its large Hispanic-American population would guarantee substantial, enthusiastic crowds at the beginning of the pope's trip.

Thomas Kelly, archbishop of Louisville, who had been the NCCB's general secretary during the time of the pope's last visit in 1978, was chosen to chair the ad hoc committee to plan the 1987 trip. Serving with him on the committee were four other bishops, none of whom headed a diocese that could be considered part of the current trip.[16] The goal was to create a committee of "neutral" people who would not have a vested interest in choosing one site over the other.[17] The NCCB's intent was to concentrate on the process by which objective, systematic, and fair standards could be applied to organizing the trip. As Reese has observed, the NCCB operates "within an American context." It has borrowed operational patterns from American political culture, namely a consultative process, parliamentary procedure, and an open government approach that tends to make their deliberations accountable to public opinion.[18]

By establishing the "rules" for planning the 1987 papal visit early in the process, the NCCB aimed to sustain the visit's "national" theme. In the previous visit of John Paul II, topics and themes were linked to geographic place and local audience.[19] Decisions on the composition of the audience and participants for the 1979 visit were largely influenced by the individual dioceses. For the 1987 visit, the NCCB played a greater role in managing the conversation between "universal" Rome and the "particular" local church. Some church members criticize this growing NCCB role because they are wary that the bishops' conference and its "consultative process" are controlled by an "elite" of a "new Catholic knowledge class" who have been heavily influenced by "post-Christian," "neopagan," "secular" sources.[20] They would have more confidence in certain individual bishops acting as spokesmen, rather than the NCCB.

For the most part, the planning process worked smoothly. Because the NCCB acted as the buffer between the Vatican and the local dioceses, it was easier for a diocese to offer legitimate excuses for not being included in the itinerary. For example, Denver was a logical choice for a western itinerary, but the city's Bishop Casey excused himself and his diocese, contending that he was too old to manage such an event and to raise the needed funds.[21] The process also allowed planners to eliminate and narrow the list either because of practical concerns or by reason of not fitting into the overall objectives of the "national" themes. In looking for a site where the Native American could be represented, the committee originally approached Tucson, but the diocese could not afford it financially. Santa Fe was also considered, but it had no suitable airport. The committee then settled on Phoenix as the southwestern component of the visit.

Not all decisions were made based on pragmatic concerns. The committee kept its focus on the symbolic themes and the audiences it had targeted. In Texas, the committee wanted to give the pope an opportunity to address the influence of Mexico on American culture. Houston was a strong possible choice, but the committee preferred San Antonio, because of the symbolism of its Spanish name. Also, Catholic Charities had already planned to hold its convention in San Antonio, and by moving the convention's schedule by a few days, it would be possible to include this "national" perspective of charitable service of the church in the San Antonio portion of the papal visit. Because Phoenix is well known for its medical complex and retirement community, the church's

long involvement in health care became an important reason for insert-
ing that city into the itinerary. New Orleans, with its Catholic heritage,
became an obvious choice for the southern portion of the pope's visit.
The committee also began to look upon the New Orleans site as an opportunity for the pope to address two important subjects: Catholic
education and African American Catholics. Xavier University, America's only predominantly black Catholic university, is located there.
Also, the Catholic educators had used the New Orleans Superdome for
its large conventions and were familiar with its facilities.

Because a papal visit to the United States has to take into account relations with other churches, interfaith meetings were an important part
of the planning. A proposal was made to hold the meeting with Protestant and Orthodox leaders in an area that was not predominantly or
heavily Catholic.[22] In other words, the pope would go to "Protestant
territory" as an invited guest. In that way, John Paul II was being sensitive to their legitimate existence in the United States. The committee
endorsed the proposal and began looking at sites in the "Bible Belt."
They settled on the University of South Carolina in Columbia, South
Carolina, where the papal meeting attracted more denominations than
at a similar gathering during the pope's first visit to the United States.
The NCCB's committee process by which it applied a fair, systematic
approach to balance the practical conditions with the symbolic demands of John Paul II's pastoral visit appeared to work smoothly. The
committee seemed to have been able to exert overall control over the
trip so that it retained a national and cohesive character.

Cheney noted that the U.S. bishops' management of multiple identities "necessarily involves the use of power" and consequently, "not all
identities are treated equally."[23] In the 1979 trip, the Polish American
community managed to bypass local control to be included in the itinerary.[24] As plans for the 1987 visit developed, Polish Americans who
were descendants of a farming community in Texas asked to be included in the schedule, but when Detroit, a diocese containing large
numbers of Polish immigrants, was added to the itinerary, the NCCB
eliminated the event in Texas. Nevertheless, a thousand Polish Americans were able to obtain access to the pope for a short meeting at the
end of his day in San Antonio.

In many of the pope's visits throughout the world, Polish communities are given recognition. As immigrants, their strong faith and loyalty
to the church deserve to be recognized. Furthermore, their inclusion as
an event in a papal visit offers opportunities for the pope to speak about
the importance of Christian heritage in one's cultural identity. The

meetings with Polish communities are occasions for joy and emotion where John Paul II can engage the audience with a naturalness that stems from his use of his native language. Symbolically, they remind the larger audience of his unique position of being a non-Italian pope. They also recall his unusual background which has enhanced his credibility with audiences around the world. At the same time, an overconcentration on the Polish background of John Paul II can prompt criticism. The pope is a symbol of universality and therefore must be available to all. Furthermore, critics of the current papacy have accused John Paul II of being too steeped in the conservative Polish tradition to understand and appreciate modern democratic culture. Some have even claimed that the Vatican bureaucracy, once heavily influenced by Italians, is now controlled by well-placed Poles. Even though these accusations and claims may not be totally accurate, the ability for Polish groups throughout the world to obtain an unusual amount of time with the pope can be misinterpreted. John Paul II is sensitive to this, and according to one report, he was not pleased with the inclusion of the Polish American meeting in San Antonio.[25]

That episode, however, was only a minor point that had loosened the systematic process of the NCCB's ad hoc committee. The larger issue was the inclusion of Detroit, which had not even been selected by the committee as a site for the pope's pastoral visit. The United States bishops had been informed of the pope's trip well in advance. In contrast to the ten-month hectic period of preparation for the 1979 trip, planners in the United States had two and a half years to prepare for the 1987 visit. Soon after the announcement of the visit, Edmund C. Szoka, then archbishop of Detroit, began lobbying both the NCCB and the Vatican to have Detroit on the itinerary. Even though the visit was intended to be directed toward the southern and western regions, Szoka argued that Detroit was an important archdiocese that had not been visited previously. He made his arguments to the NCCB, but was turned down. However, he refused to give up and continued lobbying for a whole year. When he met with the pope, the pope listened but gave no commitment.[26] In November 1986, Szoka was told that Detroit definitely would not be included, but in January 1987, the Vatican added a day to the length of the stay to include Detroit. Having to adjust to the Vatican's addition, the ad hoc committee moved the meeting with deacons from New Orleans to Detroit to give Detroit a "national" dimension. As a result, black Catholics gained more time in New Orleans.

The decision on Detroit illustrates two points: First, Vatican planners depend on local church input and indeed have relinquished a sizable amount of control to local planning committees. However, the Vatican is not hesitant to exert its ultimate control in making final decisions and, in this case, override local recommendations. Second, in making choices regarding his visits, John Paul II's sense of meaning construction does not fit the systematized, democratic process. There was no sense of "neutrality" in his approval of Detroit. Rather, it recognized the loyalty and affection between the local bishop and the pope. The final stop in the U.S. visit needed to be successful and the pope had personal confidence in Szoka's ability.[27]

Even though it operates within a rational, systematized process, the NCCB understands the importance of symbol in message construction. When a site was discussed for the 1993 youth conference, some Vatican officials logically argued for Minneapolis because it had a "better Catholic infrastructure" and a "more effective relationship with civil authorities." The NCCB proposed Denver because the spectacular "sky" country was an appropriate religious symbol. After all, the words sky and heaven are the same in Italian and Spanish. John Paul II agreed with the NCCB recommendation and chose Denver because of its communicative value.[28]

In preparing for the 1987 visit, the NCCB ad hoc committee not only wanted to operate the planning process according to the systematic procedures of American technical know-how, but it also wished to bring the character of the visit closer to the American cultural context. The committee was cognizant of NCCB discussions following John Paul II's first trip to the United States in 1979. In critiquing that visit, bishops felt that there had not been enough opportunities for dialogue with the pope. Some supported an amendment to a resolution on the papal visit that called for more dialogue. The amendment was never included in the formal public statement of the bishops' conference, but was sent to the ad hoc committee for future reference.[29] When an ad hoc committee was constituted for the 1987 visit, the bishop members intended to remedy the situation and proposed events that allowed the local U.S. church to speak to the pope. They proposed ten to twelve events during which the pope would listen to designated representatives and then respond to their remarks. To give these events a national character, they suggested that the audience be composed of people from all parts of the United States rather than from the host geographic site. They wanted each event to symbolize an aspect of the service of the church in the United States and proposed that the presentation to the pope be done by a representative of the national group representing the particular service being highlighted.

The NCCB wanted to stress the "pluralism" of the church experience and, at the same time, convey a unity. The theme of "Unity in the Work of Service" expressed the "unity in faith and charity" with the pope as "vicar of Christ." The composition of the visit also stressed a unity "with one another," that is, a unified church at the national level.[30] The theme of service allowed the visit to feature the different ways the church in America goes about its work. The addition of the "structured dialogues" permitted the expression of particular American problems and issues from an American point of view. In his discussion of the U.S. bishops' role in American public policy, Cheney concludes that, in order to be heard, constituencies must be "insiders" who share the organization's identity and interests.[31] Because the inclusion of dialogue into the papal visit represented a change in papal format, the proposal was likely to be heard at the Vatican if it were presented by loyal "insiders." In this case, the NCCB had remained loyal by not publicly criticizing the lack of dialogue during the pope's 1979 trip. Secondly, the NCCB presented the Vatican with a plan for "structured" dialogues wrapped within a strong unity theme.

The terms of the format whereby a representative would speak, and then the pope would deliver his message, was not entirely new. For the meetings with youth, members of the youth organizations often prepared questions to raise with the pope as part of the preparation for the visit.[32] However, the 1987 U.S. visit, as proposed, added a dimension that was unique. The representative was to be more than a greeter, or introducer of the pope; the speaker was expected to summarize for the pope, the group present, and the entire church, the most pressing current issues facing them. Because of the public character of the trip, there was always a risk that the pope would be "upstaged" by the presenter. Nevertheless, Vatican planners, and eventually the pope, approved the plan.

The Vatican relies on the national bishops' conferences and the individual bishops of the dioceses to plan events, suggest themes, provide current information, and in some cases, draft speeches. That the local churches have a considerable amount of input has both philosophical and practical considerations for the Vatican. John Paul II has described his role as twofold: to proclaim the evangelizing message and to energize the local churches themselves.[33] A papal visit encourages spiritual renewal, serving to "shake up" the local church.[34] It acts somewhat like an internal audit or review. The local committee examines the state of the church, assessing its strengths, weaknesses, and needs in order to choose the sites and themes which maximize the effects of the visit.

Much of this assessment occurs in the *ad limina* visits of the bishops to Rome, and therefore, there is a noticeable similarity of themes, as occurred in the trip to Brazil in 1991.[35] The bishops are the primary intermediaries between the local church and the Vatican. In this sense, the visits have become a constituent part of the collegial process. While the official *ad limina* visits of bishops to the Roman pontiff are the regularized and codified means of ensuring collegiality, the papal international visits and their process of preparation have provided another important forum for the local churches to communicate interactively with the pope.

Planning Participants and Decision Makers

Who is communicating and what is being communicated to the Vatican become crucial to the decision-making process. In effect, the Vatican draws its information from a variety of sources. In the 1987 visit, the NCCB committee played a key role, but so did the individual bishops. Archbishop Szoka had excellent contacts in the Vatican and was able to obtain a change in scheduling. Cardinal Mahoney of Los Angeles was instrumental in influencing the character of the California visit. The decision to use an "electronic" format of video conferencing for the youth meeting as well as the meeting with professional communicators, primarily for the movie industry, were his and his diocesan staff's ideas. The NCCB had originally planned for the pope to rest in Phoenix, but bishops in Texas contended that because of the "state's importance," they "deserved a little more than eight hours." The visit's planners relented and kept the pope overnight in San Antonio before going to Phoenix.[36] American bishops, either on their own or through the NCCB committee, made a number of visits to Rome during the preparation period for the 1987 visit. For those who understood the pope's managerial style, this was crucial to the decision-making process. When forming ideas for upcoming trips, John Paul II prefers to speak face-to-face with his bishop colleagues. Unlike his predecessor, Paul IV, who wanted everything in writing, John Paul II thrives on oral discussion.[37]

The consultative process through which the Vatican seeks input from the local church on the trips is enhanced by openness and long lead times. When Pope Paul IV ventured out for those first papal trips, the Vatican allowed no detailed publicity prior to ten days preceding the trip. The trip was announced in concept, but no dates were given, and all preparations for the visit were carried on in secrecy. With John Paul II, dates are announced early and details on sites, themes, and types of audiences are released as final decisions are made. The first trips made by John Paul II were hurriedly put together, but as the visit process became regularized, the pope's schedule was decided several years in advance so that local committees had ample time to participate in the planning.

The Vatican benefits from its reliance on the local bishops' committee to do most of the work in designing and carrying out the practical elements of the visit. By turning to the bishops' staffs in the local country, the Vatican can orchestrate these global tours using a minimum of their own staff. The overseas visits are under the direction of the "Sustituto" of the Vatican secretariat of state, a position that is equivalent to the second in command of the ministry of foreign affairs. The official texts of speeches of the pope are issued from the secretariat of state, but the drafting of speeches is often carried out in the local level. The logistical preparations for the trip are directed by the Reverend Roberto Tucci, S.J., president of the coordinating committee of Vatican Radio, who personally visits all of the sites of the papal itinerary in advance, making certain that all details, including the exact time requirements, are carefully thought out.

Besides acting as the funnel of all information, thereby systematizing the trip's preparation, the local committee is sometimes asked to make the difficult decisions. When the schedule becomes too loaded, Tucci asks the local committee to make the cuts, thereby protecting the pope from being blamed for any disappointments.[38] On good news decisions, the pope intervenes, such as happened with the inclusion of Detroit in the itinerary. On the bad news decisions, the local committee takes the blame. Vatican planners are constantly aware of their efforts in protecting and enhancing the reputation of the pope. In that regard, Vatican planners must sometimes work diplomatically to resolve issues that might escalate into larger problems. In preparing for the 1991 trip to Brazil, one of the Brazilian bishops, wary of Brazilian government intrusion, was reluctant to allow government security people into his residence where the pope planned to stay. Tucci resolved the problem by suggesting that the bishop regard only the second floor of the building as his residence. The security people would be confined to the first floor, and the bishop's and the church's privacy would be protected.[39]

In the preparation of the 1987 trip to the United States, most of the early consultative process involved bishops and their staffs of priests. As each diocese appointed a local committee to oversee the details of the visit, lay people were added. In many cases, the laity on these committees were chosen "to make an event happen" because of their technical and professional experience in media or public relations. For the most part, the laity had little input into the early decisions on content and context.[40] As the preparation proceeded, laity became more involved in the suggested content of certain meetings and in the drafts of the locally prepared papal speeches. The procedural organization of decision making in preparing for the papal visit followed largely traditional hierarchical lines.

THEMATIC DEVELOPMENT AND SPEECH DRAFTING

Each diocese to be visited set up a local site committee that gathered facts, background material, and drafted proposed papal speeches. As Briggs comments, "a ferocious paper chase had been set in motion."[41] The material was sent to the NCCB where staff members coordinated, edited, and redrafted parts of the package before it was sent on to the Vatican secretariat of state. At the NCCB, Russell Shaw was given the responsibility for "synthesizing" the draft speeches. According to Shaw, the local diocesan committees were given no guidelines other than the agreed upon themes and events. Material from the local committees was submitted in various forms: background notes, suggested points, outlines, and fully drafted texts. Shaw was also given some help in researching what the pope had said previously on various themes. The Reverend Alfred McBride, a religious education specialist, was tapped to write the pope's speech to educators in New Orleans. In the spring of 1987, Shaw took all the material home to work uninterrupted for ten days. Again, fairness in the consultative process was an important consideration. Shaw tried to use as much as he could of the suggested material, but there was far too much.[42]

For the structured dialogues involving the functional classifications within the church, the spokespersons for the group were, for the most part, selected by their peers. Speaking for the laity were Donna Hanson, a church worker from Spokane, Washington and the chairwoman of the bishops' lay advisory committee; and Patrick S. Hughes, director of pastoral ministry for the San Francisco Archdiocese. Samuel Taub, executive director of the U.S. bishops' Secretariat for the Permanent Diaconate, was chosen to speak for the deacons. Representing women and men religious, Sister Helen M. Garvey and Reverend Stephen Tutas were both presidents of their religious conferences. The four bishop spokesmen had actively served on NCCB committees. Reverend Frank McNulty, a pastor of a parish in New Jersey who had experience in leading retreats for priests, was chosen by the executive committee of the NCCB. All sought suggestions and comments from members of their group, but they were responsible for writing their own speeches which were then sent to the NCCB where Shaw wrote the draft of the pope's responses. McNulty's speech on behalf of the priests was the only one that was changed at the request of the Vatican.[43] However, McNulty claims that Vatican officials never asked him to tone down his remarks.[44] These dialogues were "structured," not only in actual presentational format, but by reason of the groups they represented and the relationship of the presenters to the institutional church. For example, all presenters were church workers, who received all or part of their livelihood from church funds. Being "professional" church members did not necessarily guarantee full agreement with Vatican policies and thinking. Indeed, church workers are sometimes criticized for being too progressive. Nevertheless, these presenters were fully engaged in the church's organizational structure and were committed "insiders."

By accepting the process of collaboration and the format of dialogue, Vatican planners had to deal with a new set of rhetorical circumstances. They had to have confidence that the presenters were sufficiently loyal as "insiders" to know how to craft their criticism and still remain faithful to the teaching authority of the church.[45] On the other hand, Vatican planners had to recognize that the presenters needed to demonstrate their allegiance to their constituents by expressing the shared views of their fellow group members. For the presenters to be heard, they had to manage the conflicting interests. This rule also applied to John Paul II. Vatican planners, in constructing the symbolic framework of the "structured" dialogue, had to balance the centrifugal and centripetal tendencies so as to permit only enough tension to sustain the idea of dialogue and at the same time preserve the unified church as symbolized by the Successor of Peter.

The Vatican seeks and depends on the material it receives from the local churches. The pope, with his writers and planners, reviews the local drafts and other material submitted. This locally prepared material is used as a "sounding board" during the many conferences between the pope and his Vatican advisors on the themes and textual material. Sometimes the drafts and concept are accepted, and at other times, the pope wishes to use his own insights to elaborate the theme of the talk. The way a talk unfolds is "unique for each situation."[46] In a sense, the Vatican is not hemmed in by hard and fast rules and systems in the method of speech preparation. This fluidity is also reflected in how the speech-writing tasks are assigned. Although the secretariat of state is always responsible for all final texts, the pope calls upon whomever he feels can get the job done. For the 1987 trip to the U.S., Archbishop Justin Rigali was responsible for the speech preparation. At the time, he was president of the Pontifical Ecclesiastical Academy which trains priests to become diplomats for the Vatican secretariat of state. Rigali had handled the speech material for the previous trip of John Paul II to the United States in 1979 and therefore, he was asked to assume this responsibility once again.

There may be a certain fluidity within the Vatican bureaucratic system, but there are certain patterns that have developed in this pontificate that are related to John Paul II's style. In preparing a visit, John Paul II tends to become personally involved in writing the sermons for the liturgies since he considers the sacramental events pivotal to the visit. Sometimes, he provides his staff with schema to be filled in as necessary. Very often, he writes full texts. The pope sometimes surprises his colleagues and advisors with his ability to construct a speech in short, concentrated periods of time. Less than a month before his first visit to France, John Paul II drafted one of his key homilies while traveling to Africa. In it, he treated elements of France's religious history and humanist philosophical tradition, topics that were "very natural" for him because of his knowledge of France and French thought.[47] Also, the Vatican had barely announced the pope's first trip to the U.S., when Pope John Paul II handed Rigali his handwritten draft for his speech to the United Nations.[48]

John Paul II writes both text and schema for his homilies in Polish which are then translated to the language to be used. Speeches that are drafted by others are written directly in the local language. The translated first drafts of the pope and those of the Vatican writers are worked on in the local language to make sure the speech is close to the cultural expression of the country to be visited.[49] The pope and his advisors meet frequently, sometimes at working lunches and dinners, to discuss the texts.

Vatican writers are concerned more with presenting the accurate thinking of John Paul II than with metaphoric style. They are constantly aware of the universal-particular church dialectic. Local and particular problems need to be addressed, but John Paul II's purpose is to "encourage local members to draw out of themselves and look at their problems with a new and different perspective."[50] This perspective is especially evident in the preparation of the textual responses to the presentations in the "structured dialogues" during the 1987 visit. The Vatican always maintained that the pope would listen, but he would not feel compelled to answer each and every point raised in the presentations.[51] Consequently, in many of his responses, the pope preferred to refer "obliquely" rather than directly to challenges that were raised.[52] Most of all, attention is focused on the speech's long-term value. Speeches are prepared so that they can be used for teaching.[53] Therefore, a speech's written, rather than oral, composition influences the character of the speech-writing activity.

For the more extensive trips, the secretariat of state reviews the events and their speeches as a unit to see if all important topics are covered. When the finalized versions of the speeches are ready, they are not sent back to the local bishops' conference for review. Sometimes, the Vatican calls upon a specific representative from the local church to go to Rome to review the texts for possible errors or omissions. Otherwise, the speeches are delivered to the local bishops' conference a few minutes after the pope arrives in the country.

The process of local consultation on the visits has developed with experience. Early in John Paul II's pontificate, there was little time and perhaps less confidence in both the Vatican and local churches regarding the drafting of texts at the local level. In preparing for the pope's first visit to France in 1980, the French church sent analyses of issues to the Vatican, but did not draft speeches. The U.S. bishops had much more time and experience to prepare more extensive and meaningful input to the Vatican for the 1987 trip. Like their U.S. colleagues, the Brazilian bishops' conference provided drafts of speeches for the pope's visit in 1991. Not only have the national bishop conferences improved their methods of preparation at the local level, but they have learned and borrowed from each other. Reporters have observed that, as staffs develop more experience, the format of the visits are "becoming a drill." They claim that the local churches are copying events so that the trips are taking on a "stock" appearance.[54]

Local Vatican Speech Drafts

A review of select draft material prepared for and by the NCCB and sent to the Vatican in preparation for the U.S. papal visit of 1987 demonstrates that local suggestions are indeed incorporated into the final versions of the pope's talks.[55] It also shows that the experience is mixed. A comparison of the draft and final speech reveals that one-quarter of the drafts have little if any similarity with the final version. Approximately one-third of the drafts show distinct similarity in sequence, themes, quoted material, and even some metaphors. Another third contain some references, themes, and basic outlines that were incorporated into the final version. One draft, which replaced an earlier version that was rejected at the NCCB level, was used with hardly any changes. The local planners had the most success in influencing the final speeches to particular groups in the church; they had the least success in the homilies and addresses to youth. This confirms the personal interest of Pope John Paul II in creating his own material for the Eucharistic celebrations. It also confirms the special place that youthful audiences have in the construction of the papal visit. For many of the youth events, the pope responds and reflects on the questions submitted by young participants in advance of the event.

In some of the drafts, local speech writers tried to have the pope defend American achievements and culture such as diversity, pluralism, and religious freedom. The final papal versions, while careful to include contextual acknowledgment of the audience, rarely gave the same praise suggested by U.S. drafts. Diversity and pluralism were not seen as ends in themselves, but rather as ways of working out unity and communion. Additionally, American drafts have included references to internal tensions and differences in the church, which Vatican final versions never admitted. For example, the draft speech to the laity mentioned problems in working out collaboration between men and women, clergy and lay, marketplace ministers and ecclesial ministers. The final version of the pope's talk treated this collaboration and consultation as "positive developments" that are "always rooted" in the "sound" church norms taught by Vatican Council II. In other words, there are no problems if the church employs sacred norms that preserve the differences between clergy and lay, and between women and men as complementary in their relationship to each other and to the whole church. Rhetorically, Vatican drafters emphasize sacred unifying movement of papal speech.

In several draft speeches, local writers tended to focus on motivating and fulfilling the needs of the audience as individuals or as members of groups such as families, parishes, and universities. In the final papal versions, the audience was motivated to think and act far beyond their localized spheres. For example, the draft on higher education treated the concerns that U.S. Catholic university administrators and faculty had with a Vatican draft document on higher education. The two main issues—the relationship of bishops to Catholic universities and the teaching of theology—concern two important tenets of the American cultural and legal frameworks for private universities: academic freedom and an independent governing board's responsibility to direct university policy. Instead of concentrating only on these specialized items that concerned the inner administrative workings of church and church-related institutions, the pope's speech in New Orleans reminded members of the audience of their role in the "pastoral care" of students and their ability to "enlarge their horizons" by drawing up "*blueprints*" that would influence the world on questions of peace and justice.[56] According to Vatican speech writers, the pope needs to show a certain amount of sympathy and understanding for the local problems and conditions, but his approach must also motivate his audience to rise above these problems and see them from a different, broader, and more universal perspective.[57]

Although the pope favors a universal perspective, he does not impose uniformity. In the draft of the pope's talk to deacons and their wives, local planners tried to convince the pope that the positive "lived experience" of this restoration of the diaconate in the United States "can and should be shared widely with the church in other lands." In the final version, the pope acknowledged that the diaconate in the United States is a "great and visible sign of the working of the Holy Spirit," but he refrained from applying the American experience universally to the church.[58] John Paul II maintained a balance between legitimating this evolving form of ministry and recognizing the contextual preferences of the local churches. Merely by his presence at the meeting with the deacons and their wives, the pope extended a strong worldwide endorsement of the permanent diaconate. However, sensitive to the preferences and authorities of the local churches, he refrained from telling others to follow the American lead. In Cheney's discussion of how the U.S. bishops had to be careful not to pursue their local interests to the point of violating the interests of the universal church, he mentions that organizations must avoid promoting competition between sub-units. This competition, which encourages the distinctiveness of the sub-units, can lead to a situation in which the interests of the whole organization become secondary to those of the subordinate groups.[59] Within Vatican circles, the U.S. church is sometimes suspect in this regard. Just as the United States is accused of exerting its powerful political and cultural influence over the entire world, the U.S. church, with its considerable financial resources, is watched carefully for any signs of unduly influencing the rest of the church. The Vatican's reticence to use the U.S. church's successful experience with the diaconate may be related to keeping competition between the local churches in check. They fear that the contextual experience of the American church may dominate and erase all others. For the universal symbol of church to exist, there must be a multitude of contextual experiences. Vatican Council II recognized this principle when it emphasized the need for "inculturation" of the church's symbolic system. In the draft speech to the deacons, local writers wanted to leap from the contextual U.S. experience to the universal; Vatican writers contained the U.S. experience as contextual.

Another difference between the local drafts and the final speeches is the tendency for the Vatican to include specific teachings and positions of the church on issues which might be difficult or controversial. In his speech to the laity, John Paul II followed drafters' suggestions to treat the church's outreach to the divorced and widowed; however, he also recalled for his audience the church rule that does not permit divorced persons who have remarried outside the church to be admitted to Eucharistic Communion. In the address to the deacons, the draft spoke vaguely of the bishops' direction and harmonious cooperation with the order of presbyters. In the final talk, John Paul II reminded the deacons that they are to be obedient to their bishops and respectful of priests; he reminded priests that they are to accept the deacons. Where the local drafts may have avoided talking about these potentially controversial issues, Vatican writers confronted them by reaffirming institutional norms. As a rhetorical strategy, this specificity adds external realism to the binding nature of church authority on individuals. Vatican writers are confident that listeners are ready to accept ecclesial authority, whereas local writers are still sensitive to the general distrust of institutional authority. Jablonski noted that bishops used "authoritative warrants" more often when they had confidence in their roles. During periods of change, they were more sensitive to potential sources of controversy and relied less on "tradition-bound appeals."[60] Following the arguments of Jablonski, Vatican writers, and the pope himself, have more confidence in the authoritative role of the pope and bishops than the bishops themselves.

When compared with the drafts, the final versions of papal speeches demonstrated a rhetorical preference for human interest symbolism. In the talk to deacons, the final version replaced the impersonal categories of work settings with a description of the people deacons serve. When the draft mentioned hospitals, nursing homes, and prisons, the final version talked of the homeless, refugees, street people, and the rural poor. People, not places or institutions, are the purpose of the deacon's mission. In the draft homily for the Eucharistic celebration at Dodger Stadium, diversity was measured in numbers of languages. The final version personified Christ as Anglo, Hispanic, and of other ethnic backgrounds. In the final version of the talk to leaders in Catholic higher education, the pope introduced the situation of the student through his own personal experience with university students, their questions, their personal backgrounds, and their need to be accepted and loved. Roderick Hart observed that presidents as persuasive speakers balance their ideological stands with attempts to "humanize" the shared understandings that they have with "their very heterogeneous listeners." Like other leaders in organizational settings, they "cannot tolerate for long a world of pure abstraction," and, therefore, are obligated to provide the "bridge" between theory and practical policy. The emphasis is on people, not things, since their mandate is constantly reaffirmed by the "will of the people incarnate."[61] Like presidents, John Paul II does not construct a church through abstract rules and norms alone. His communication binds the sacred to the people in very human ways.

As a process, the Vatican's solicitation of the local church for background and ideas has centrifugal overtones. Reaching out to local churches, Vatican planners and writers incorporate structural and textual material into the pope's visit that adapts to the contextuality of the local church. However, the process of adapting to local audiences also has binding effects. Being included in the early planning, members in the local church feel a special part of the papal visit. They have a stake in it, and are more committed to making it a success. Kenneth Briggs observes that after submitting their drafts, the various "interest groups" within the church waited to see "whether the points they had done the most to promote would make it into the final versions."[62] Although there were many differences, there were also many similarities between the drafts and the final versions. Local drafters of the talk on the laity wanted the pope to demonstrate some sympathetic attention to divorced and single-parent families. This recommendation was accepted. Drafters of the laity talk also wanted collaboration and consultation to be discussed. It was. Those who wrote the talk to the deacons wanted the pope to address the role of the deacon's wife. The pope acknowledged these women as "close collaborators" even in the spiritual formation of their husbands.[63] The drafters of the talk on higher education wanted the pope to demonstrate that there is no contradiction between faith and reason. This suggestion and others were incorporated into the final version as were a number of metaphoric expressions, such as "luminous presence," "lively sense of their Catholic identity" and "privileged settings for the encounter between faith and culture."[64]

At the same time, the local drafters tended to include expressions that they knew were favored by John Paul II and his Vatican collaborators. In other words, they demonstrated to the Vatican that they shared the same meaning construction. The draft on higher education talked of "authentic religious faith," "authentic presence," and "fundamental meaning." These preferences for the "authentic" and "fundamental" appeared in the final speech. Even though the final version of the homily given at the Los Angeles Dodger Stadium was quite different from the local draft, local writers made several suggestions that accurately anticipated or reflected the thinking of John Paul II. For example, knowing that a speech topic on the church necessarily would involve the relationship of pope to bishop and bishop to church, the local drafters suggested using the feast day of Saints Cornelius and Cyprian to symbolize the bonds of pope and bishop in church tradition. They also included the key phrase from a Vatican Council II document on the church that enunciates the unifying role of the pope and the bishops. Both of these recommendations were used.

External Influence on Papal Speech

During the preparation of a papal visit, external groups have the ability to influence the rhetorical strategy of John Paul II. The NCCB had included a meeting with American Jewish leaders in the papal itinerary for the 1987 visit to the United States. In June, three months before the visit, the Vatican announced that Austrian president Kurt Waldheim's request to meet with the pope had been granted. Jewish community leaders publicly called for Pope John Paul II to call off the meeting with Waldheim, who had been accused of knowingly aiding the shipment of Jews to Nazi death camps. When it appeared that the Vatican would not change its course, Jewish groups announced that they would boycott the upcoming meeting with the pope scheduled in Miami. The NCCB went to work to salvage the situation. Archbishop Keeler of Baltimore took the lead to negotiate a settlement.[65] During July, Vatican officials met quietly with American Jewish leaders both in the United States and in Rome. In August, John Paul II wrote a letter to Archbishop May, who was president of the NCCB, condemning anti-Semitism and the Holocaust. The pope also invited Jewish leaders to meet with him and Vatican officials in Rome. After an intense session with the pope during which Jewish leaders voiced their positions on a number of topics, many Jewish groups decided to drop their threats to boycott the September meeting in the U.S. However, because several Orthodox organizations decided to continue their boycott, Rabbi Gilbert Klaperman, who was scheduled to make the presentation to the pope, withdrew and Rabbi Mordecai Waxman took his place. Time was running out and Waxman's draft, which was finalized only three days before the meeting, was not ready for Vatican review. In the end, because of the intense two-month period of discussions with the Vatican, Jewish leaders had an extraordinary opportunity to influence the direction of the pope's message. The pope's remarks contained a strong statement on the Holocaust, acknowledging that Jews were the specific and primary victims. This was very important to the Jewish community, not only because of their belief that Catholics did not fully understand what the Holocaust meant to the Jews, but also their memories of centuries of misunderstanding and persecution of the Jews by Catholic populations. As Rabbi James Rudin recounted, Catholics charged the Jews with deicide, persecuted them during the Spanish Inquisition, and pillaged Jewish communities in the Crusades. Catholic attitudes and actions toward the Jewish community were so filled with suffering and persecution that "most Jews came to view the Roman Catholic Church as an eternal adversary, a powerful enemy."[66] In 1965, Vatican Council II issued a document, *Nostra Aetate*, to correct Catholic teaching by repudiating the false belief that Jews are collectively guilty for Christ's death. Since then, references in Good Friday liturgies have been changed, catechism and textbook materials have been updated, and scriptural scholarship has developed more accurate interpretations of the context and times of the life of Jesus.[67] Nevertheless, there are differences on theological, social, and political matters, and lingering attitudes on the part of many within both faiths. After John Paul II's meeting with the Jewish leadership during his 1987 visit to the United States, some Jewish critics were not certain that Jews had gained anything from their discussions with the pope.[68] On some points, such as the Waldheim visit and diplomatic relations with Israel, the pope's remarks indicated no change. Furthermore, the pope defended the actions of his papal predecessors during the Nazi period, thereby dismissing some historians' criticism that the church failed to openly and adequately act against the atrocities being committed against the Jews.

External relations with the host governments are factors in choosing to accept local church invitations. The Vatican works closely with the host government on the arrangements for the trip and also on the official portions of the visit with relation to the textual material used in the official statements. For the U.S. trip, these official meetings took place on the first and last days. Given the strong tradition of the separation of church and state in the United States, there is little, if any, input expected of government sources in the thematic or speech-writing aspects of the unofficial portion of the visit. However, one incident during the 1987 trip illustrated how governments, even those who presumably have a hands-off tradition with regard to religion, sometimes exert their influence. At the Eucharistic celebration at Westover Hills in San Antonio, the pope spoke of the "movement of people northward." He praised the "great courage and generosity" of those working "on behalf of suffering brothers and sisters arriving from the south" for showing "compassion in the face of complex human, social, and political realities."[69] Some who had been working in the sanctuary movement, a group helping illegal immigrants in the United States, interpreted these remarks as validation for their actions. They placed an ad in a Phoenix newspaper claiming the pope's support. As the pope and his party were traveling to Phoenix from Texas, Frank Shakespeare, U.S. ambassador to the Holy See, received a phone call from Attorney General Edwin Meese, who was in the office of the director of the Immigration and Naturalization Service. The attorney general told Shakespeare of the ad, and asked him to inform the Vatican officials of how this group was interpreting the pope's message. Meese was concerned that the pope's remarks were being used to support illegal activity. Shakespeare immediately spoke to Archbishop Rigali, who was in charge of the pope's speech writing.[70] As a result, the pope's press spokesperson, Navarro-Valls, issued a statement that stressed the pope's interest in undocumented immigrants on a "moral, not legal level." According to Navarro-Valls, the pope did not endorse a specific movement, nor encourage violation of any civil laws.[71] Later, at the Mass in Dodger Stadium in Los Angeles, John Paul II again commended the bishops for "helping several million undocumented immigrants to become legal residents." He defended their "pastoral care of the immigrant" as a "legitimate work of the Church."[72]

These two examples illustrate how groups external to the church have influenced the development and textual references of the papal speech. Vatican and local planners have accommodated the papal message in order to build shared meaning. At the same time, the rhetorical strategy of the pope is to retain a distinct identity. The pope did not change position on Waldheim, nor did he condemn the actions or lack of action of Pius XI and Pius XII regarding Nazi persecution of the Jews. However, he met Jewish expectations in regard to other issues. With regard to the immigration issue, Vatican officials took specific action to interpret the papal remarks to demonstrate respect for the legal requirements of the host government. Nevertheless, John Paul II continued to claim for the church a legitimate role in working to make immigrants legal. As Cheney contends, the church adapts when it speaks to outsiders, but it is careful to retain its identity in order to preserve its own authority with insiders.[73] To negatively judge the past actions of papal predecessors would jeopardize the authority of the current pope. To say that the work with undocumented immigrants is a mistake would seriously affect the church's reputation with a large and growing sector of the church. As John Paul II noted in his homily at Dodger Stadium in Los Angeles, the concern that the church shows to refugees, immigrants, and the poor is "closely aligned with the Church's evangelization."[74] In both examples, the church adapts to the external audience, but firmly holds to a "sacred" interpretation of its interests.

STRUCTURAL ARRANGING

In preparing for a papal visit, there is a constant interplay of setting, form, and meaning. To convey the purpose of the pastoral visit, planners are aware that decisions on location and format of events have symbolic potential in constructing meaning for the papal visit. They are bound to follow the pope's own enunciated purpose: to make an authentic pilgrimage to the sanctuary of the People of God. According to his interpretation, John Paul II is visiting a sanctuary or holy place of a community whose corporate identity is held together by a holiness that transcends the human experience. However, these visits are not divorced from the everyday activities of the members of the church; they are "to penetrate all areas of human life."[75] When making their decisions on setting and format, planners are responding to both sacred and secular demands. As discussed previously, the cumulative experience of papal visits has produced a set of generic rules which influence the range of choices available for both local and Vatican-based planners. Nevertheless, the visit remains a movement toward the local church, where local situations provoke decisions that produce variations in setting and format.

Setting and Form

The Vatican is especially sensitive to the need for the visit to be characterized as "pastoral" rather than "political." They have elaborated definitive protocols on the arrival ceremonies. Church dignitaries, rather than civil officials enter the plane on arrival. The pope descends and kisses the ground, an act that resonates John Paul II's own description of his mission: to visit the sanctuary of the local church. As a priest kisses the altar at the beginning of the Eucharistic celebration, the pope bends down to embrace the land, consecrating it as holy ground where Christ's gospel is being carried out. It is a symbol of the pope as universal church becoming intimately and permanently united with the local culture.[76] Only after this act of consecration does the pope greet civil authorities. The pope resides in a religious house, seminary, residence of the local bishop or nunciature.[77] When the pope travels by plane or helicopter within the country, religious rather than civil leaders accompany him. The boundaries that Vatican officials try to draw between the sacred and the secular are difficult because of the complex nature of the Holy See and its status as a temporal entity with recognized governmental powers. For example, papal trip planners take advantage of the privileges given to visiting heads of state, such as security, facilitated travel, and use of public facilities. They are also careful to meet any obligations, such as meetings with civil officials and special seating for officials at certain functions. The drawing of these boundaries varies with the cultural environment of the country. In the United States where church and state are separate, the lines between the civil and religious natures of papal trips are clear, especially with regard to financial obligations for the visit. However, in Brazil, the national government offered to pay for the airplane, communications, and some hotel accommodations for the papal entourage.

With the civil portion of the visit closely controlled by Vatican officials, local planners can concentrate on choosing settings and formats for the pope's visit to the local church. Above all, the settings chosen need to reflect the ritual character of the papal pilgrimage since the settings for these rituals are part of the creation of meaning. The pope as a religious symbol may be enclosed in a traditional religious place such as a church or shrine, or he may migrate outward to places where secular rituals are performed. The variation of settings in itself is a dialectic which reflects David Martin's description of the movement of sacred symbol from the constraining particulars to the breaking of partitions so that the sacred can be released in the search for a unified space.[78] In most papal visits, there is an obvious need for the pope to pay homage to the local church's physical symbols of its presence. However, the traditional religious structures pose physical limitations. They simply will not hold enough people, necessitating that planners turn to large enclosures, such as stadiums, or to open spaces. As a result, the schedule is constantly being balanced between religious and popular settings.

Christine de Montclos observed that papal visits often include a visit to the diocese's cathedral on the first day of the trip.[79] Following this same procedure for the 1987 U.S. trip, planners scheduled the pope to proceed immediately after the welcoming arrival in Miami to Saint Mary's Cathedral, the seat of the archbishop of Miami, the pope's first host on his itinerary. This prompt transition from official greeting to the sacred space of the cathedral where John Paul II was seen praying for the success of his trip reinforced the pastoral and religious nature of the visit.[80] It also confirmed the relationship of the bishop of Rome to the local bishop hosting the visit. Even though the NCCB wanted to give the visit a national character, it cannot change the fundamental apostolic organizational character of the church. The local church is united to Rome through the individual bishops, and not through a national structure. The first event was local in nature, where John Paul II prayed and addressed one thousand priests, religious, and laity from the archdiocese of Miami in the diocese's cathedral.

Although the prayer service at the cathedral was intended to focus on the sacred nature of the visit, its political ramifications were not ignored. The NCCB ad hoc committee discussed the subtle symbolism of the pope's first audience—Cubans who had fled the communist regime of Castro. The Vatican was keeping its doors open to Cuba and even discussing a possible papal visit there. Some in the church warned against a stop in Miami, fearing that an embrace of anti-Castro refugees could cause setbacks for the church's attempts in Cuba.[81] The NCCB committee believed strongly that the vibrant growth of the church in the Miami area needed recognition and the Cuban immigrants were very much a part of that growth. Furthermore, planners thought that the warmth and enthusiasm of Hispanic American Catholics would help the pope begin the trip in a positive framework. As with most speakers, the pope tends to become energized and relaxed when the audiences are visibly expressing their confidence in the church and its papal leader.

During the 1987 U.S. visit, patterns are evident in the choices of settings. At each site visited, the pope prayed within a church structure. Cathedrals were chosen for certain church group meetings, such as with priests, religious men and women, seminarians, and laity, during which the internal issues of the church predominated. The church walls contain its membership within a sacred space and hold its images apart from the world so that conversations focus on a sacred otherness. Participants, who have been socialized to behave within a church setting in certain deferential ways toward the sacred, have reverential expectations of the pope as a rhetor when he is inside these holy enclosures.

In California, planners took advantage of the existence of several mission churches associated with Spanish missionary work in the eighteenth century. Three churches were chosen, one at each of the sites on the pope's California schedule, to portray a visual image of the pope praying at shrines depicting the beginnings of Catholicism in America. However, what was to be portrayed as a tribute to the historical roots of

Catholicism in western states struck Native Americans as a reminder of a bitter past, some claiming that Spanish missionaries, such as Father Junipero Serra, participated in the genocide of Native American tribes because of their cooperation in the Spanish colonialization effort known for its cruelty and injustice. In response to the criticism, the Diocese of Monterey issued a "Serra Report," defending Serra, who had already been declared "venerable," a first step to recognition of sainthood. The Monterey diocese hoped that Serra's cause for sainthood would progress so that the pope could raise the priest to "blessed" during his visit to the Carmel Mission in Monterey where Serra is buried.[82] Thus, the Monterey site posed situational problems for rhetorical strategists. The setting chosen for its symbol of holiness was being challenged as unholy and insulting. Shortly before the pope's trip, Vatican officials announced that they were not ready to reach another stage in Serra's sainthood, and therefore, there would be no beatification. However, Vatican and local planners decided to defend the inclusion of the mission site. During the actual visit to the Carmel Mission's basilica, John Paul II used several occasions to portray Spanish missionaries as upholding the rights of Native Americans and spoke of their "holiness of life that can truly be called heroic."[83] Using the mission setting, John Paul II emphasized that "more than words and deeds" the lives of people like Serra "speak to us still" of their personal commitment and loving service as a type of holy image that "draws people to Christ."[84]

Not all meetings with church groups were held in church settings. Meetings with Black Catholic leaders, as well as Catholic educators, were held in areas of the New Orleans Superdome, where the pope attended a youth rally immediately following these meetings. Utilitarian factors, such as time constraints and efficiency of movement, dominated over sacred symbol in choosing these settings. However, there were some symbolic advantages in that participants had the chance to fashion their own contextualized settings. For example, the Black Catholic group hung banners bearing the drawings of the Acacia, a tree cited in the Old Testament and found in parts of Africa. The deacons met in Detroit's Ford Auditorium, useful for showing the pope a videotaped presentation of their ministry.

Catholic churches, as well as other churches, synagogues, and temples were avoided for the interfaith meetings so they could be conducted on "neutral" grounds. More than the physical facilities, geography played a significant role in the choice of setting. The pope met with Jewish leaders in Miami where there is a sizable Jewish population. The interreligious faith meeting with non-Christian religious leaders was scheduled in Los Angeles because of the city's racial and ethnic diversity. A specific location in the Bible Belt was sought for the meeting with Christian church leaders. Since there was no other reason for the pope to journey to South Carolina, this portion of the trip took on special meaning. The pope was indeed going "out of his way" to meet with Protestants, whereas the meetings with the Jewish and interfaith groups were conveniently scheduled in areas where the pope visited with specific Catholic populations.

Each day of the visit, the pope celebrates the Eucharist, a central sacramental rite of the Catholic faith. Since these celebrations are the events to which large crowds are invited, their settings are determined by pragmatic concerns of allowing access to and controlling large numbers of people. In most cases, these events are held in facilities associated with secular activities: sports stadiums, parks, and convention halls. As Goethals noted, these are the sites of the secular rituals of contemporary Western culture. Just as the sacred enclosures of churches provide a place where the extraordinary world of the sacred can be created apart from ordinary reality, superdomes and stadiums are places where people "escape humdrum routines of daily life."[85] These secular rituals of football games and rock concerts are popular weekend pastimes, often competing with the ritual offerings in the church's sacred places. The use of secular ritual spaces for the central events of the papal visit presents a unique set of challenges to papal visit planners as they bring together two sets of symbolic environments.

An important challenge involves the transformation of the secular space into sacred space. The efforts in Phoenix were exceedingly effective. In Arizona State University's stadium, the symbolic depiction of the sun devil mascot was covered up and a seventy-foot cross of copper and steel was erected. Behind the altar, lighting on the vividly colored backdrop of a phoenix rising from the mountains of Arizona had a startling effect against the clear night sky. The symbolic setting was so effective that the phoenix as a symbol of Christ's resurrection became an important textual theme in the pope's homily.

In other sites, symbolic transformation was not as complete and stadiums presented a meeting place for both sacred and secular symbols. Scoreboards used to flash greetings to the pope stood next to advertising signs for soft drinks and beer. Exuberant participants waved flags, sang hymns, displayed banners, chanted prayers, and wore tee shirts emblazoned with papal memorabilia. It was hard to separate cultural expressions of sacred ritual from the secular. Often the meeting of the two realms increased the emotional feelings of participants who were trying to cope with this extraordinary juxtaposition of the two seemingly divided symbolic worlds. A college student who attended the New Orleans youth rally told about how she started crying as the pope entered the Superdome, "I was just overwhelmed. Maybe it was seeing a symbol of so much holiness. The pope looked so angelic."[86]

The voyaging of John Paul II is movement toward the local churches and one of the visit's purposes is, in the pope's words, to "penetrate" all aspects of the life of the local People of God.[87] The NCCB ad hoc committee wanted John Paul II to come in contact with the many aspects of America's diverse culture in order to better understand the church's work and service. For the youth rally in the New Orleans Superdome, the committee scheduled a Mardi Gras parade, including colorful costumes, masks, and floats. In Phoenix, the Veterans Memorial Coliseum was transformed into a Native American territory. Feathers were hung overhead, and a place was made for a charcoal fire which would be used in a ceremonial blessing of an eagle feather. In Detroit, the pope was lifted by a glass-enclosed elevator to a platform overlooking Hart Plaza, a public square in the midst of the downtown area. The setting, among modern office buildings, was designed to emphasize the everyday life of office workers in the capital of U.S. auto manufacturing.

At nearly every site, there was a planned motorcade, in which the pope used the "popemobile" to greet and bless the crowds. The purpose was to allow as many people as possible to see and be blessed by the pope. Passing through the cheering and adoring crowds, these motorcades symbolically enhance the celebrity status of the traveling pope. However, encased in the specially made secure device, he is both accessible and separate. Also, during the 1987 trip to the U.S., the motorcade drew lower numbers of people than estimated. Some felt that secret service security had been too tight, causing areas to be sealed off and making access to parking very difficult.[88] Others reasoned that pretrip publicity warning of crowds and traffic jams had "scared people off."[89]

Apportionment and Sequencing

The NCCB committee approached the scheduling with balance and fairness. First, the pope spent an equal amount of time at most of the sites. Los Angeles was the exception, hosting the pope for just short of two days, including two large Eucharistic celebrations. With three and a half million Catholics, the Los Angeles diocese was by far the largest on the pope's itinerary, and since its physical facilities could accommodate large gatherings, that city became the focal point for the pope to address the U.S. church in its national perspective. Los Angeles was where the pope met with the bishops, and at the mass that followed at Dodger Stadium, the pope gave a comprehensive address on the state of the church. Second, at every site except Monterey, the NCCB scheduled an event with a national perspective, drawing representatives from all over the United States to these events. Third, the structured dialogues were interspersed throughout the trip. Again, one was held at each site, except Monterey. By scheduling them as a daily event throughout the trip, the national and dialogic character became symbolically a substantive part of the entire visit. Also, in terms of news coverage, the press had a national and newsworthy event to write about each day.

Besides sustaining themes and maintaining balance, the NCCB had a few problems to address regarding the sequence of the trip. For example, NCCB planners anticipated that the meeting with the priests would present some challenging issues, such as celibacy. Opinion polling of Catholic priests indicated that about half believed that celibacy should be optional, and many who left the priesthood claimed that celibacy was the primary reason. However, some Vatican officials did not accept these claims and cited evidence of other reasons why priests had asked to be released from their vows.[90] When the pope upheld the celibacy requirement, some priests viewed his firmness as a sign that he was unsympathetic to priests with problems. Another issue involved a theologian at the Catholic University of America. In 1986, the Congregation for the Doctrine of the Faith found the Reverend Charles Curran unsuitable to teach moral theology because his support for flexibility of moral decisions on sexual norms dissented from the teaching of the magisterium of the church. Some priests supported Curran's stand on these issues, others feared that cracking down on dissent would silence discussion on other theological matters. Given the tense atmosphere, the NCCB decided to place the meeting with priests early in the schedule because they reasoned that, if done well, the meeting would dispel the reticence and discomfort that priests seemed to be feeling about their relationship with John Paul II. The committee took a risk. They had to achieve both objectives or they would fail: do it early and do it right. Obviously the local planners had confidence in both the pope's ability and the ability of their chosen "structured dialogue" format to be successful. In shaping the relationship between audience and rhetor, the NCCB committee emphasized to the priests the unprecedented dialogical nature of the meeting. At the same time, the bishops advised John Paul II to demonstrate compassion by simply telling the priests that he loves them.[91]

The other consideration involved demonstrations. Knowing that there would be planned protests, the NCCB wanted to take whatever steps necessary to prevent the pope from being drawn into the demonstrators' confrontational tactics. The church in the United States had been grappling with how to minister to the needs of AIDS victims without relenting on the church's stand regarding homosexual activity. In October 1986, an instruction from the Vatican's Congregation of the Doctrine of Faith confirmed the church's condemnation of homosexual acts as immoral and urged bishops to establish pastoral programs for AIDS victims who were in full accord with the church's position on homosexuality. The statement sparked reaction from gay activist groups who advocate acceptance of homosexual behavior in stable relationships. Because of its large homosexual population, San Francisco had been hard hit by AIDS cases. John Quinn, archbishop of San Francisco, was especially sensitive to the issue and had established a number of ministries for AIDS victims. Several months prior to the papal visit, he wrote an article to explain more fully the Vatican's recent instruction to bishops on homosexuality.[92] Archbishop Quinn and NCCB planners for the papal visit anticipated that there would be demonstrations by gay activists in San Francisco, and that the issue would draw media coverage. Planners recommended that the church highlight its role as compassionate caregiver rather than moral legalist. At the pope's first scheduled event in San Francisco, one hundred AIDS victims and their families were invited to be among the thousand participants, mainly sick and elderly. AIDS victims, including a priest who had contracted the disease, were invited to be close to the pope who, by touching them, could confirm his words, "God loves you all, without distinction, without limit."[93] The image of John Paul II hugging AIDS victims provided a powerful antidote to attempts on the part of gay activists to portray a discriminatory church.

In addition to placing the AIDS victims at the start of Pope John Paul II's entrance into San Francisco, planners also recommended that the pope begin talking about the AIDS issue before his arrival in California. It made sense to include it in the pope's address to Catholic health care representatives in Phoenix where the issue could be approached in a nonconfrontational atmosphere. Mentioning AIDS as one of the "new challenges" of health care professionals, John Paul II identified it as a "crisis of immense proportions."[94] This was the first time that the term AIDS had been mentioned in a papal speech.[95] Textually, the themes of love and solidarity were woven through the speeches of John Paul II at both the San Francisco and Phoenix occasions when AIDS was mentioned. The sequencing of the AIDS issue during the trip and the textual and nontextual symbols of compassion were designed to rhetorically tone down any attempt on the part of gay activists to heighten controversy.

Characterization and Control of Audience

Since the Eucharistic celebrations are the most important daily events of the visit, organizers must concentrate on making them successful. First of all, planners must consider how large numbers of people can be attracted to participate in these events. Then, since the Eucharist is the central ritual of the Catholic Church, the audience should be composed largely of church members who can participate fully in the ritual. Therefore, planners must strike a balance between presenting an open event to which all are invited, and controlling an event so that most in attendance are Catholics, and hopefully, enthusiastic and loyal. For the large-scale events in the U.S. trip, crowds were both encouraged and controlled by tickets. Unlike American secular events, where ticket distribution is usually done at a central location on a first-come, first-serve basis, tickets for Eucharistic celebrations were distributed through the local church structure, primarily at the parish level. Each parish was given a certain number of tickets and the parish decided how to distribute them. The Vatican insists on separating the decisions on ticket distribution from monetary contributions. Tickets cannot be sold, nor can tickets appear to be sold by offering them only to financial contributors. Proposals by certain U.S. diocesan planners to link tickets to contributions in order to pay for the trip's expenses were quickly stifled by planners at the national and Vatican levels.

The system of ticket distribution uses a contractual approach to access to the papal events. Although the method of distribution at the parish level attempts to include wide-scale geographic, cultural, and economic participation, ticket holders are mainly Catholics known to their parish priest as active participants in the life of the parish. In some cases, parishes employed a lottery system to choose among the many parishioners requesting tickets. Local planners also relied on the same techniques employed by event managers of rock concerts. Printed tickets, with sophisticated counterfeit-proofing safeguards, were not distributed until shortly before the event.

This reliance on modern worldly means of ticket distribution is a product of John Paul II's preference for large-sale events. If meetings were small, these elaborate measures would be unnecessary. However, smaller meetings encourage exclusivity. For John Paul II's trip to Switzerland, a small group of clergy were chosen to meet with the pope. When another group of clergy petitioned the Vatican to be permitted into the meeting, John Paul II insisted that they be invited.[96] For his first visit to France, the pope wanted his meetings with workers and laity to be open and inclusive. The French bishops committee agreed that the meeting for workers should be geared to large numbers, but they recommended a closed and limited meeting of only representatives of lay organizations that maintained official relationships with the French church.[97] The contrast between the compositions of the papal events for French workers and lay organizations reflects the classic differences between popular and intellectual appeals. As Italian journalist Luigi Accattoli observes, the masses are sympathetic to John Paul II, whereas the Western European intellectuals are skeptical of the crowd mentality of this papacy.[98] The intellectuals prefer small meetings of elites to reflect deeply on issues, but the pope wants to touch and inspire as many people as possible. Accattoli attributes this quest for numbers to John Paul II's missionary and messianic compulsion to preach the gospel to the whole world. If the church ceases to expand, it will risk losing its nature.[99] The interaction of the pope with large numbers becomes a crucial element in sustaining the plausibility of the church.

The pope prefers crowds and inclusiveness. However, even this policy preference presents problems in actual program. Crowds must be controlled by heavy security measures. After the U.S. visit in 1987, church officials complained that security measures were sometimes too strict, cutting down on the numbers expected at motorcades and other public events. Security also threatened to direct the rhetorical strategy of the U.S. papal visit with regard to anticipated demonstrations. In California, state law allows people to demonstrate within the line of sight. Nevertheless, the secret service sometimes imposes restrictions that push these demonstrators further away from the actual event. The NCCB pressured the secret service to permit various groups of protesters to demonstrate. They worried more about the church being criticized for stifling protester action than about the consequences of the demonstrations. To visit planners, it was important that the church allow discussion. Although the pope would not engage the demonstrators in debating the issues, a free and open public posture would better serve their theme of dialogue. Local planners admitted that they had "good intelligence" on the size of groups protesting, and since these groups did not appear to pose any significant threat to the papal visit's goals, they were comfortable with their policy of noninterference.[100] In effect, the demonstrators remained apart from the insider crowd of ticket holders for the major events. This was not the case in Nicaragua where, according to some observers, the government allowed and encouraged demonstrations inside the event to disrupt the pope's homily.[101]

Media Variables

There is a definite relationship between the visit's emphasis on crowded events and the media. Large-scale events generate interest on the part of the media, but small, elite meetings are closed to the public and the media. As Accattoli noted, small, exclusive meetings, which were tried on several papal visits, worked well for those who attended because the meeting style encouraged frank exchange and reflection, but they ended there. Accattoli concluded that, in John Paul II's strategy, action prevails over reflection and message prevails over probing.[102] The mass media thrives on action and does not handle well the reflective and investigative mode. The numbers of people attending the large-scale events add to the dramatic action of the visit, thus guaranteeing media attention.

The mass media attention in the planning stage is also an important factor in guaranteeing crowds. As previously noted, unlike Paul VI, John Paul II publicizes his trips well in advance. During the planning for the 1987 papal visit to the U.S., individual dioceses turned to lay experts in event management and media to help promote and plan their portions of the trip. Part of that promotion was to emphasize the size of crowds expected and the logistics for handling these crowds. Reporting on a briefing of media coordinators, *The Los Angeles Times* wrote that an estimate of "10 million people are expected to personally see the pontiff."[103] The media coordinator from Miami was quoted, "to make everyone happy, we need a front row that can seat a quarter-million people."[104] This emphasis on numbers had its drawbacks. At events where crowds were less than expected, media commentators noted a marked difference between the estimates and actual numbers. Some church officials blamed media reporting of expected crowds. They reasoned that people, fearing that the crowds would be too great, chose to stay home and watch the events on television.

The papal visit is filled with sacred and secular rituals that offer occasions for large numbers of people to break from their ordinary lives to participate in an extraordinary event. In ritual, individuals come together to celebrate symbols of common beliefs and value that give meaning to their lives. Gregor Goethals contends that the mass media, television in particular, has taken over some of the ritual functions once provided by religion. An array of media images and carefully constructed narrative of news coverage "present accounts of 'reality'" that "explain what is happening in the world" thus enabling us "to understand ourselves in this complex society."[105] The televised coverage of important events provide the means for people from all geographic areas, ethnic backgrounds, and religious persuasion to come together to form a community of viewers. They follow the "pilgrimage" of John Paul II and become involved in the enthusiastic and emotional responses of crowds portrayed on their television screens. This mass media production of the visit demands that the church employ people who are well versed in the technologies of the media.[106] Conflicts arise between these technocrats and those who wish to protect the purity of the religious symbol. A frequent criticism is cost. When queried about the costs of arranging for these large-scale events, Monsignor Robert Lynch, overall U.S. coordinator for the pope's visit, remarked, "you couldn't buy the attention, the coverage, the significance that his presence brings, even with what we end up paying for it."[107] One of the projects produced by these "technocrats" was a television documentary used in dioceses to promote participation in the visit's events. Another project, pooling television coverage, provided continuous and complete coverage to local television stations and cable systems throughout the United States.[108]

Halford Ryan noted that President Franklin Roosevelt understood how to obtain the most coverage from his speeches by giving hints as to what he would say at an upcoming event. He was thus able to direct three persuasive messages to the American people: anticipation of the address, the actual address, and the subsequent reporting on the address. Papal visit planners utilize the same principle. The Vatican controls the final drafts of the speeches, imposing secrecy on all those who work on them. They are not released until just prior to the speech. However, Vatican officials cooperate to a certain extent with media in pre-event publicity. Prior to the U.S. visit, *The Los Angeles Times* met with a number of Vatican officials who gave the reporters background on the pope's views regarding the need for affluent nations such as the United States to act responsibly to the world. Knowing that these reporters needed something more specific, Joaquin Navarro-Valls, the Vatican press spokesman, hinted that the pope would praise the American Constitution: "He has great esteem for the Constitution, and I wouldn't be surprised if he mentions that at the outset on his arrival in Miami." The Navarro-Valls hint became the lead to their story, casting a positive contrast to predictions of speeches that "will make some uncomfortable."[109]

Although the "structured dialogue" concept was designed to meet the needs of the local U.S. church, planners were also aware of its value in capturing journalists' attention on religious matters. Admitting that "there is no real spontaneity," Russell Shaw, communications director for the U.S. bishops, pointed out that "it's a real presentation of two points of view from two parties expressed over a period of time."[110] Those two points of view became newsworthy elements of conflict or tension. In general, journalists reporting on the upcoming papal trip to the U.S. tended to make the following distinctions: American Catholics "most ardently agree" with John Paul II's stands on political matters such as his "anticommunism" or his support and "admiration for the Constitution," but religiously and socially, American Catholics saw John Paul II "at odds with American values and the spirit of democracy."[111] Reflecting their culture, American journalists create distinctions between what is religious and what is political. The social teachings of the church are considered political because Americans have been able to find some common agreement on principles that are no longer seen as connected to a religious culture. Religion, having been removed from public discussion of these matters, comprises only the inner spiritual life and personal moral decisions based on individual conscience. Therefore, journalists interpret the pope as being open to the modern world when he speaks of social issues, because, in their view, he is not talking about religion. When he speaks about personal morality, he is discussing religious or spiritual issues, and in this domain, he is closed to the world because he insists on publicly drawing standards. To reorder this cultural discussion of religion is John Paul II's major challenge.

Part of the problem in approaching papal visit planning, especially the media component, is that the American media has become expert in covering the sociodrama of political figures and campaigns. As Gronbeck pointed out, expectations generated by the media play as much a role as the actual event in helping to form public opinion about a candidate.[112] Not having much experience with religion and religious ritual, the media approaches the papal visit as if it were a political campaign. Taking this into account, planners tend to build excitement about the visit, emphasizing its spectacular nature, and the enthusiastic throngs of people to be accommodated in massive settings. Planners for the 1987 trip fulfilled most of these expectations by providing impressive physical settings with huge altars and striking backdrops. They also enlisted top musical performers and choreographed picture-perfect liturgies for the electronic media. Most of all, the large-scale events, attended by enthusiastic participants, provided cheering, praying, and crying faces for the television crews. "The thunderous acclaim," "high-spirited reverence," and "adoring crowds" that "endured hot weather and long hours" for the pope act as a counterpoint in the sociodrama that the media interprets.[113] The *Washington Post* could not quite grasp the "odd mixture of moralism, pageantry, cultural expression, emotion, debate, and music," but in trying to judge it a success or failure, the *Post* writers admitted that "it is hard to speak too critically of something wrapped in such overwhelming beauty."[114] From the point of view of media relations, the large-scale events and their numbers demonstrate for political-minded journalists that the pope is a "winner" regardless of the opinion polls on certain moral issues. The crowds, as visible symbols of a plausible church, act to marginalize activist criticism.[115]

SUMMARY: SHARED MEANING CONSTRUCTION

Viewed from the Vatican, where decisions on international papal visits emanate, the initial period of planning directs meaning construction toward the sacred by defining the visit's purpose, restricting the political or diplomatic portion of the visit, and placing the sacramental ritual at the center of each day's schedule. As the planning process for each visit unfolds, local church planners assume primary responsibility for choosing themes, sites, and audiences, and although the sacred purpose remains a powerful centripetal referent, these local planners most often assume the role of opening the universal church to the issues and problems of the particular culture and the times. Soon after John Paul II's second trip to the U.S. was announced, local planners began imposing a consultative character on the visit that reflected the rational and systematized organizational approach of Western democratic culture.

Not only by physically leaving the Vatican walls does the papacy as universal symbol of the Catholic church open itself to particular church needs and demands. John Paul II increases the possibility of tension between the sacred center and the secularizing trends of the local culture because, as in the case of the 1987 visit to the U.S., the process through which the local church designs and carries out the visit often energizes and enhances the national church structure. In a sense, this tension accentuates borders between the sacred and secular, but it also presents opportunities to resolve the conflicts between the church and the world. As illustrated in my discussion of the comparison between local drafts and papal speech texts, John Paul II's personal writing and direction to his staff challenge local church audiences to engage themselves in a broader and deeper discussion of their problems. Often cued by local church suggestions, the pope's textual response invariably aims to draw the audience out of their limiting individual subjectivity to a larger communal framework defined by sacred norms.

Knowing that the textual planning effort will only have a limited effect on meaning construction, planners schedule opportunities for John Paul II to employ powerful visual symbols of identification, such as his touching of AIDS victims, his participation in a Native American blessing, his embrace of dialogue participants after their hints of dissent. Rather than attempt to resolve differences on issues through rational discussion or textual battles, planners build into the visit's schedule these moments that stimulate movement of the heart.

From time to time, the planning process is called upon to manage conflict involving outside groups, such as occurred with the Jewish leaders and the Native American community. Again, the planners use consultative tactics of systematic dialogue, and tensions are contained to some extent through human tactics of compromise. Knowing how the sacred symbol resists resolution with the secular, Vatican writers and planners act to preserve some differences, seeking in their texts to identify with audiences through appeal to sacred meaning rather than human means.

With experience, planners on both the Vatican and local levels appear to be drawn more and more into the mechanics of the visit, often to serve the visit's popular and mythic narrative requirements. Planners "engineer" events with pretrip publicity, media pools, "structured dialogues," national audiences, and stadium spectacles. In other words, these secular means aim to create a mythic narrative of sacred meaning.

Through the planning process for these international papal visits, the church has become more comfortable with the worldly tactics of creating meaning, but the process also encourages a closing of ranks to protect this sacred meaning. Hierarchical distinctions are preserved in both the planning function and in the visit itself. Furthermore, the process encourages participants to become stronger insiders, thereby increasing local church identification with its universal symbol.

From the moment that the local church invitation is accepted, the papacy, once enclosed within Vatican walls to protect sacred symbol, begins to relinquish control over meaning construction to local churches. In the case of the 1987 U.S. visit, local church planners were prone to emphasize the secular sources for meaning construction such as diversity, operational technique, and consultative dialogue. At the same time, local church planners were very much aware of the need for sacred symbol to present majestic contrast to the daily humdrum of everyday lives.

NOTES

1. George Cheney, *Rhetoric in an Organizational Society: Managing Multiple Identities* (Columbia, South Carolina: University of South Carolina Press, 1991), 164–167.

2. Paul A. Soukup, "The Church as Moral Communicator," in *Mass Media and the Moral Imagination*, eds. Philip J. Rossi and Paul A. Soukup (Kansas City, Missouri: Sheed and Ward, 1994), 199.

3. Roberto Tucci, "Come gli Apostoli Pietro e Paolo, pellegrino verso i santuari viventi del Popolo di Dio," *L'Osservatore Romano*, 16 October 1985.

4. Karol Wojtyla, *Sign of Contradiction* (New York: Seabury Press, 1979), 144–145.

5. Tucci, "Come gli Apostoli Pietro e Paolo."

6. John Paul II, "Discourse to College of Cardinals," 28 June 1980 in *Insegnamenti di Giovanni Paolo II*, vol. III, part 1, (Vatican City: Vatican Polygot Press, 1980), 1886.

7. Pasquale Borgomeo, "In visita 'ad limina Ecclesiae,'" *L'Osservatore Romano*, 18 October 1988. See also Gianpaolo Salvini, "I viaggi di Giovanni Paolo II, annunzio itinerante del vangelo e 'segno' per il nostro tempo," *Civiltà Cattolica* IV (1985): 550.

8. Reverend Roberto Tucci, S.J., president of the coordinating committee of Vatican Radio, interview by author, 13 February 1992, Rome, Italy.

9. Gilberto C. Paranhos Velloso, ambassador of Brazil to the Holy See, interview by author, 5 November 1992, Rome, Italy.

10. Gérard Defois, archbishop of Sens, France, interview by author, 24 March 1993, Sens, France.

11. *Washington Post*, 8 October 1995.

12. Tucci, interview by author.

13. Ibid.

14. Velloso, interview by author.

15. Peter Berger, *The Sacred Canopy: Elements of a Sociological Theory of Religion* (Garden City, New York: Doubleday, 1969), 150.

16. The four members were: William A. Hughes, bishop of Covington, Kentucky; John F. Kinney, bishop of Bismarck, North Dakota; John R. McGann, bishop of Rockville Center, New York; and Arthur N. Tafoya, bishop of Pueblo, Colorado.

17. Robert N. Lynch, general secretary of the National Conference of Catholic Bishops, interview by author, 28 August 1992, Washington, D.C.

18. Thomas J. Reese, *A Flock of Shepherds*, (Kansas City, Missouri: Sheed and Ward, 1992), 302–306.

19. Lynch, interview by author.

20. Joseph A. Varacelli, *The Catholic and Politics in Post-World War II America: A Sociological Analysis* (St. Louis, Missouri: Society of Catholic Social Scientists, 1995), 25–31.

21. Ibid.

22. Ibid.

23. George Cheney, *Rhetoric in an Organizational Society: Managing Multiple Identities* (Columbia, South Carolina: University of South Carolina, 1991), 179.

24. The Polish community in France also bypassed the local committee and worked directly with the Vatican to obtain a meeting with John Paul II on his first trip to France in 1979. Defois, interview by author.

25. Lynch, interview by author.

26. Cardinal Edmund Szoka, president of the Prefecture of Economic Affairs, interview by author, 8 November 1992, Rome, Italy.

27. Less than a year after the 1987 visit, Edmund Szoka was made a cardinal, and later, John Paul II brought him to Rome to take control of the Vatican's financial affairs.

28. Cardinal Pio Laghi, prefect of the Congregation for Catholic Education, interview by author, 21 September 1992, Rome, Italy.

29. Reese, *A Flock of Shepherds*, 160.

30. Most Reverend John L. May, preface to *Unity in the Work of Service*, by John Paul II (Washington, D.C.: National Conference of Catholic Bishops, 1987).

31. George Cheney, *Rhetoric in an Organizational Society*, 168.

32. During his first trip to France in 1980, John Paul II changed his prepared speech to a rally of fifty thousand young people in order to respond to twenty-one questions he had received from the youth. See Jean Paul II, *France, que fais-tu de ton baptême?* (Paris: Le Centurion, 1980), 165–179.

33. *L'Osservatore Romano*, 12 May 1985.

34. Tucci, "Come gli Apostoli Pietro e Paolo."

35. Velloso, interview by author.

36. Russell Chandler, "Pope's Visit a Tug of War," *Los Angeles Times*, 22 February 1987.

37. Tucci, interview by author.

38. Ibid.

39. Velloso, interview by author.

40. Lynch, interview by author.

41. Kenneth A. Briggs, *Holy Siege: The Year That Shook Catholic America* (San Francisco: HarperCollins, 1992), 336.

42. Russell Shaw, vice president, Public Affairs, Knights of Columbus, interview by author, 8 August 1992, Washington, D.C.

43. Lynch, interview by author.

44. Cathleen Decker, "The Papal Visit: Speech to Pope Puts Priest in Spotlight, Creates Ripple," *Los Angeles Times*, 12 September 1987.

45. See George Cheney, *Rhetoric in an Organizational Society*, 168–169.

46. Monsignor James M. Harvey, interview by author, 21 November 1992, Vatican City.

47. Defois, interview by author.

48. Archbishop Justin Rigali, interview by author, October 1992, Vatican City.

49. Harvey, interview by author.

50. Ibid.

51. Rigali, interview by author.

52. John Travis, Catholic News Service, interview by author, 28 October 1992, Rome, Italy.

53. Harvey, interview by author.

54. Thavis, interview by author.

55. I reviewed drafts of eleven papal speeches prepared for and by the NCCB for the U.S. papal visit of 1987. Drafts of seven speeches are from the personal collection of Russell Shaw, vice president of the Knights of Columbus, who served as press secretary to the NCCB 1969–1987, and was responsible for preparing the final drafts that were sent to the Vatican. Drafts of four other speeches are from the files of the general secretary of the NCCB.

56. John Paul II, "Meeting with Leadership in Catholic Higher Education," no. 8, in *The Pope Speaks to the American Church* (New York: HarperCollins, 1992), 198.

57. Harvey, interview by author.

58. John Paul II, "Meeting with Deacons and Their Wives," no. 1, in *The Pope Speaks*, 338.

59. George Cheney, *Rhetoric in an Organizational Society*, 169.

60. Carol Jean Jablonski, "Institutional Rhetoric and Radical Change: The Case of the Contemporary Roman Catholic Church in America, 1947–1977" (Ph.D. Dissertation, Purdue University, 1979).

61. Roderick P. Hart, *Verbal Style and the Presidency: A Computer-Based Analysis* (Orlando, Florida: Academic Press, 1984), 44–45.

62. Briggs, *Holy Siege*, 336.

63. John Paul II, "Meeting with Deacons and Their Wives," no. 6, in *The Pope Speaks*, 342.

64. John Paul II, "Meeting with Leadership of Catholic Higher Education," nos. 2, 6, 9, in *The Pope Speaks*, 194, 197, 199.

65. Reese, *A Flock of Shepherds*, 65–66. See also Briggs, *Holy Siege*, 393–394, 424–425.

66. James A. Rudin, "The Dramatic Impact of *Nostra Aetate*," in *Twenty Years of Jewish Catholic Relations*, ed. Eugene Fisher (New York: Paulist Press, 1986), 9–18.

67. Rudin, 9–18; also Michael J. Cook, "The Bible and Catholic-Jewish Relations," in *Twenty Years of Jewish Catholic Relations*; and Eugene J.

Fisher, "Reflections on the Thirtieth Anniversary of *Nostra Aetate*," *Pace* 25 (January 1996): 9–25.

68. Richard Cohen, "They Should Have Criticized the Pope," *Washington Post*, 15 September 1987.

69. John Paul II, "Homily at Westover Hills," no. 8, in *The Pope Speaks*, 204–205.

70. Ambassador Frank Shakespeare, interview by author, 16 May 1995, Washington, D.C.

71. Briggs, *Holy Siege*, 529.

72. John Paul II, "Homily at Dodger Stadium," no. 8, in *The Pope Speaks*, 293.

73. Cheney, *Rhetoric in an Organizational Society*, 170.

74. John Paul II, "Homily at Dodger Stadium," no. 8, in *The Pope Speaks*, 293.

75. John Paul II, remarks made to author, 13 February 1993, Vatican City.

76. John Paul II consecrates the ground through a kiss only on his first visit to the country.

77. A nunciature is the Holy See's diplomatic mission or embassy, which is headed by a nuncio or ambassador.

78. David Martin, *The Breaking of the Image: A Sociology of Christian Theory and Practice* (Oxford: Basil Blackwell, 1980), 39.

79. Christine de Montclos, *Les Voyages de Jean-Paul II: Dimensions Sociales et Politiques* (Paris: Editions de Centurion, 1990), 63.

80. On his first trip to the United States in 1979, Pope John Paul II was greeted by President Jimmy Carter's wife, Rosalynn. In 1987, the pope was greeted by President Ronald Reagan. Neither President Reagan nor Mrs. Carter attended the cathedral ceremony after the official greeting. In 1995, President Clinton broke this custom. He greeted Pope John Paul II at Newark Airport and met officially with the pope at the archbishop's residence. After the official meeting, President Clinton went to the cathedral in Newark, New Jersey.

81. Lynch, interview by author.

82. There are three steps to sainthood: venerable, blessed, and saint.

83. John Paul II, "Visit to the Carmel Mission Basilica," no. 2, in *The Pope Speaks*, 302.

84. John Paul II, "Visit to the Carmel Mission Basilica," no. 3, in *The Pope Speaks*, 303–304.

85. Gregor Goethals, "Symbolic Forms of Communication," in *The Church and Communication*, ed. Patrick Granfield (Kansas City, Missouri: Sheed and Ward, 1994), 65.

86. John Paul II, *"Building Up the Body of Christ": Pastoral Visit to the United States*, ed. National Catholic News Service (Washington, D.C.: National Catholic News Service, 1987), 33.

87. John Paul II, remarks made to author, 13 February 1993, Vatican City.

88. Szoka, interview by author.

89. John Paul II, *"Building Up the Body of Christ,"* 107.

90. See National Opinion Research Center, *The Catholic Priest in the United States* (Washington, D.C., 1972); *National Catholic Reporter,* 8 May 1987; Giuseppe Versaldi, "Priestly Celibacy from the Canonical and Psychological Points of View," in *Vatican II: Assessments and Perspectives,* ed. René Latourelle, vol. 3 (New York: Paulist Press, 1989), 131–157.

91. Lynch, interview by author.

92. John R. Quinn, "Toward an Understanding of the Letter on the Pastoral Care of Homosexual Persons," *America,* 7 February 1987, 92–93.

93. John Paul II, "Visit to Mission Dolores Basilica," no. 5, in *The Pope Speaks,* 306; Valentina Alazraki, *Juan Pablo II: El Viajero de Dios* (Colonia del Valle, Mexico: Editorial Diana, 1990), 115.

94. John Paul II, "Meeting with Catholic Health Care Representatives," no. 7, in *The Pope Speaks,* 235.

95. Briggs, *Holy Siege,* 526.

96. Rigali, interview by author.

97. Defois, interview by author.

98. Luigi Accattoli, "Un pontificato missionario," in *Wojtyla: Il nuovo Mosè,* by Domenico Del Rio and Luigi Accattoli (Milan: Arnoldo Mondadori Editore, 1988), 90–95.

99. Accattoli, "Un pontificato missionario," 111.

100. Lynch, interview by author.

101. Alazraki, *Juan Pablo II,* 130.

102. Accottoli, "Un pontificato missionario," 115–116.

103. Russell Chandler, "Pope's Visit: A Tug of War: Church Leaders Vie for Extra Time, Attention," *Los Angeles Times,* 22 February 1987.

104. Ibid.

105. Gregor Goethals, "The Expressive Face of Culture: Mass Media and the Shape of the Human Moral Environment-1," *Mass Media and the Moral Imagination,* eds. Philip J. Rossi and Paul A. Soukup (Kansas City, Missouri: Sheed and Ward, 1994), 14–19.

106. Raymond Lemieux, "Charisme, mass-media et religion populaire: Le voyage du Pape au Canada," *Social Compass* XXXIV, 1 (1987): 18–19.

107. Russell Chandler, "Pope's Visit: A Tug of War."

108. Reese, *A Flock of Shepherds,* 228.

109. Don A. Schanche and Russell Chandler, "The Papal Visit; Speeches May Discomfort Some Americans; Pope's Call to U.S.—Behave Responsibly," *Los Angeles Times,* 6 September 1987.

110. Russell Chandler, "The Papal Visit: Exchange of Ideas with John Paul Are Staged with Care," *Los Angeles Times,* 15 September 1987.

111. Raymond Coffee, "Among Americans, It Seems, the Pope Is Losing the Game," *Chicago Tribune,* 20 September 1987; Don A. Schanche and

Russell Chandler, "The Papal Visit: Speeches May Discomfort Some Americans," *Los Angeles Times*, 6 September 1987.

112. Bruce E. Gronbeck, "Electric Rhetoric: The Changing Forms of American Political Discourse," paper based on lectures at Hayward Conference on Rhetorical Criticism, California State University-Hayward, 1989.

113. Cathleen Decker, "The Papal Visit: Dodger Stadium Mass Gives Immigrants a Night of Joy," *Los Angeles Times*, 17 September 1987; and Ari L. Goldman, "Ideas and Trends: Can a Patriarchal Aura Close the Gap Between a Pope and His Flock?" *New York Times*, 13 September 1987.

114. David Maraniss and Laura Sessions Stepp, "Pope Leaves Amid Contradiction, Affection," *Washington Post*, 20 September 1987.

115. Lemieux noted that during the pope's Canadian visit in 1984 criticism was "submerged by the force of the event." Raymond Lemieux, "Charisme, mass-media et religion populaire," 14.

CHAPTER 5

Textual Address: Audience Identification and Characterization

In all rhetorical situations, the relationship between speaker and audience is key. To induce cooperation and eventual identification, a speaker must know how to arouse the desires of the audience. This entails an understanding of the internal voice of the audience, that is, the symbolic meanings that have been constructed and internalized by audiences in their sociocultural settings. Edwin Black pointed out how the rhetorical critic can examine a text for "a hypothetical construct that is the implied auditor." Because actual auditors look for cues in the discourse, the critic can find in the speech text an image of how the rhetor views the audience and a "model of what the rhetor would have his real auditor become."[1]

This critical approach to the text searches for patterned forms of address that bind the speaker and audience into types of associations with each other and into varying relationships with others.[2] In the view of Duncan, strategic choice of a form of address can shape the content of the intended models because this form "determines *how* we address each other and thus how we affect each other."[3] Inasmuch as the forms of address the rhetor uses are "a way of experiencing reality,"[4] they can provide concrete clues as to how John Paul II would have his audience act as models in constructing a new vocabulary of the sacred. These forms of address can shape the content of the vocabulary by closing down on the sacred or moving out toward the secular world.

GREETING THE FAMILY AS TEACHER

Most traditional religious leaders approach their audiences as those who know more than their audience and are charged with guiding them. Roman Catholic tradition and teachings describe the pope as the church's supreme ruler and teacher. [5] With the end of the church's temporal power, usage of the ruling titles that emphasized authority diminished and pastoral descriptions of the papacy became more prevalent. This symbol of pastor most often contained the idea of a dedicated and kindly teacher who leads, disciplines, and dispenses knowledge. However, with the expressive revolution, teaching as a controlling and legitimating function began to recede in favor of a more egalitarian concept which encouraged self-learning. Nevertheless, as Bernice Martin observed, when the pendulum began to swing too far in the direction of the liberal egalitarian ideology, educators began to reintroduce some of the classic modes of control. Form and structure, as well as authority based on objective knowledge returned, but the open style of pedagogy that tends to blur the lines between teacher and student is still favored.[6] Because John Paul II characterizes his trips as pastoral, the way he approaches the audience reveals whether his pastoral style favors a dominating presence or an egalitarian posture.

In every speech, including homilies, Pope John Paul II employs an initial salutation to identify the audience in some specific way.[7] The salutation is a form of greeting, and people tend to greet each other in ways that conform to the cultural codes of their particular societies. These codes of greeting very often indicate rank or status, or relative position within the society. In some cultures, greetings are intricate, formal, and extremely deferential to those of higher rank. In other cultures, especially those influenced by egalitarian and utilitarian concepts, greetings tend to be informal, inclusive, and short. In fact, in informal situations, speakers feel quite comfortable eliminating the salutation altogether.

The majority of John Paul II's speeches begin with a salutation of "Dear Brothers and Sisters," or "Dear Brothers and Sisters in Christ" or some variation of this phrase, reflecting the format of early church letters or Epistles.[8] These forms of salutation act to structure the church as a family. In his 1987 visit to the United States, John Paul II also used this same form of salutation when addressing Christian, Jewish, and other religious leaders, indicating that there is a familial bond between all who are engaged in constructing and maintaining religious meaning. "Brothers and Sisters" are distinguished from "Friends," a salutation John Paul II reserves for diverse audiences who come together based on secular interests and specialization. Because family blood is what binds the sacred community together with one another, the relationship is much more permanent than the intimacy of friendship.

The use of brotherhood and sisterhood in the formal salutation is historically significant. Encyclicals, and even speeches of previous popes, included a parental relationship, addressing the faithful as "Sons," as well as "Brothers."[9] John Paul II has dropped the parental salutation in favor of the more equalizing tone of brethren prevalent in the Epistles of the apostle Paul. As teacher to family members, even as an elder sibling rather than a parent, John Paul II can demand loyal reflection, whereas advice from a friend can be accepted or rejected. With the youth, John Paul II becomes more teacher than family member. He puts aside family symbolism, addressing these audiences as "Dear Youth," or "Dear Young People," thereby creating a unique and special position for these youthful audiences.

In his formulas of salutation, John Paul II upholds the traditional hierarchical order of the church. Brother bishops are addressed before other brothers and sisters, brothers almost always before sisters. Only once during a joint meeting of religious women and men did John Paul II change the order to place sisters before brothers. Most of John Paul II's salutations assume an audience whose identification with the church is constructed through the mystification of hierarchy, that is, through the maintenance of hierarchical distinctions in rank, even between men and women.

As Pearson noted, both in the salutation and within the body of the speech, John Paul II often conveys messenger status on his audience.[10] As a rhetorical strategy, this tactic opens the speech to a much larger audience. As discussed in the chapter on planning, the strategy of representation was part of the 1987 trip's national character that highlighted the diverse missions of the church in the United States. Representatives of these various church activities and services throughout the country gathered at designated locations to hear an address by the pope on the issues related to those services. In New Orleans, the pope sent greetings to "all the members of the black community throughout the United States" by addressing his audience of those "who make up the black Catholic leadership in the United States."[11] Similarly, the pope addressed representatives of Catholic education, Catholic charitable works, and Catholic health care services. The tightly drawn and systematic audiences representing the diverse services in the church are indicative of twentieth-century American society in which life, as observed by

Bellah et al., is compartmentalized "into a number of separate functional sectors."[12] By acknowledging and enhancing the representative status, the pope's rhetorical strategy builds participation within the sector. However, following Bellah's reasoning, there is a risk that individual participants view the church only from a limited perspective. Their interrelationships with other functions and sectors largely become abstractions and therefore less meaningful. Accommodating to secular trends, this rhetorical strategy encourages members to construct a sacred cosmos that is very much defined and limited by the service and function which they and their peers are performing.

DIALOGUE WITH CONTEXTUALIZED MODELS

Duncan observes that when we speak to the audience using the second person, "you," we consider an audience of "others significant to us as friends and confidants with whom we talk intimately." In addressing the "you," the rhetor is naming the other, forming a relationship between the self and the other, the other and the self. The naming conveys individuality and selfhood, for in address of an "I" to a "you," the "you" takes on an existence and is then able to respond. Rhetors in dialogue with the audience make choices regarding the character of the "you" they are designating as truly participating and acting in dialogue.[13]

Naming

In most of his homilies, John Paul II refers to a "you" that is marked by cultural diversity and contextuality. He names the specific ethnic groups of America's "multicultural society," the "Cubans, Haitians, Nicaraguans" and "the cultures of France and other European nations, of black people, Hispanics, and more recently, Vietnamese." Celebrating this multicultural diversity, John Paul II uses civic experience to inform the audience of its sacred identity. The composition of the church in America is the same as that of the nation. Because America's diverse population has learned to live as one nation, the church can experience "*this mystery of unity in diversity* in a very real sense."[14]

Additionally, the pope draws from the American contextual life experiences of the audience to identify those qualities of the "you" audience that have positive value and can lead to sacred meaning. The pope constructs his audience in the midst of the "dynamism and expansion" of contemporary society and its various industries such as communication, tourism, and space exploration. It is an audience that is seeking "to build a better life" and "an even better life for your children." The American dream of being able to improve one's lot in life is accepted as part of the church member's identity. John Paul II also connects the audience with their physical setting, leading them "to look about you to see the many *wonderful gifts* conferred by the mighty Mississippi . . . and by the riches of the sea," "snowcapped mountains and deep lakes . . . mighty redwoods, a land among the richest and most fruitful of the earth."[15]

In using these contextual experiences to identify his audience, John Paul II depicts his audience as inseparable from their American culture. Even though the church and the civic community are distinct entities, he underscores how they live the same history, often affected by each other's development. For example, in Florida, the dynamism and expansion of secular life is matched by the *"rapid growth in building up the body of Christ."*[16] In San Francisco, John Paul II mixes the sacred and secular hopes of those who came to the city: those propelled by wealth and those looking for souls. Together, all faced setbacks such as the earthquake and fire of 1906 which "took effort and determination for the city and the Church to recover."[17]

This movement outward to recognize the "historical destiny" of American Catholics is counterbalanced, as John Paul II draws his audience inward toward a recognition of their sacred identity. Warning his audience that "your abundance" may cause the audience to "forget the Lord," John Paul II implores his audiences of friends and confidants to "hold fast to your Christian faith."[18] Sacred meaning has to be continually constructed and reconstructed through a dual relationship with the American culture. In many instances, John Paul II asks the "you" to defend the church and themselves against this culture, to be unpopular and countercultural. At the same time, the pope urges the friends and confidants to "continue to work in harmony for the good of the society you belong to."[19] Whether it is a pull toward or a tug away from the culture, religious theologies become meaningful when they are put to the tests in public life. Wuthnow has observed that there is a bifurcation of religion, not in terms of denominations, but within the three main religious groups of Protestants, Catholics, and Jews.[20] This tug of war between conservatives and liberals is taking place in the public forum with relation to the culture. Through his juxtaposition of incultural and countercultural messages, John Paul II is encouraging the ferment at both ends of the accommodating-resistance spectrum, giving new meaning to religious revival.

Models of Sacred-Secular Tensions

The "you" address in two specific homilies illustrates the interplay of rhetorical strategies that advocate an opening and closing. At Dodger

Stadium in Los Angeles, John Paul addresses the entire American church or "*all the faithful* of this land." The Dodger Stadium event was designed as the central celebration of the visit to address the church as a national unit. Taking place shortly after the pope's meeting with the bishops, the event was attended by most of the U.S. members of the hierarchy. The array of cardinals, archbishops, bishops, monsignors, and priests visibly demonstrated the hierarchically delineated leadership of the church. John Paul II's homily, especially his prayer for the American church and all Americans that he added at the end of his homily, underscored the hierarchically arranged roles and functions of church members. The pope begins by praying for bishops, and then proceeds to priests, deacons, religious, and laity. After establishing the traditional roles within the church, John Paul II then turns to special categories which also follow an order: families, women, young, elderly, and finally the single people. In the second section of this prayer, the audience is characterized by their engagement with the "great Christian struggle of life." First, this struggle involves centripetal movement to understand and live according to God's norms. Then, the struggle moves outward to cope with human everyday concerns of the poor and needy. The third part of the prayer looks beyond church bounds to baptized Christians and citizens. The primary focus is clearly to strengthen the American Catholic Church community "living corporately" according to the sacred norms with distinct roles and traditional lifestyles. Once the church is firmly established, it moves outward to deal with everyday needs, and embraces all—even non-Christians.[21]

The second example of the interplay of rhetorical strategies of opening and closing is found in the homily to people associated with farm work and food distribution at Monterey, California. In contrast to the hierarchical classifications used at Dodger Stadium, the pope uses identifiers that acknowledge the systematized "highly complex" life of modern society. He calls his audience growers, workers, processors, packers, distributors, retailers, and consumers. Although they work at different jobs, no one person is greater than the other in the eyes of God. There is no hierarchy, but instead equality. Even the relationships within the church, between bishops and the faithful members who are farmers are characterized by moments of intimacy. "Your bishops and the whole church . . . are listening to the voices of so many farmers and farm workers." The voices of the "you" addressed as well as "the voice of the poor" are being listened to and heard, indicating a relationship of dialogue between the bishops, including the pope who is a bishop, and the audience.[22]

Throughout his talks, John Paul II consistently addresses certain models in the audience who underscore the themes of struggle and suffering. A favorite papal model is the immigrant. Leaving one's native land is one of the "saddest phenomena in our century" and through this suffering, an immigrant nation has fashioned "a community of compassion."[23] In other words, the struggle is ennobling and necessary for a Christian because it brings rewards and bestows heroic glories. Americans understand this theme when it is illustrated with the familiar story of immigrants. It becomes less comprehensible when John Paul II speaks about the "special mission" of the sick and the elderly. The modern culture looks for cures and a pain-free death, whereas John Paul II advocates that the sick and dying are to bear their sufferings with "courage" and "embrace" the cross.[24]

Inasmuch as suffering is a mark of strength, John Paul II urges his audience, regardless of role or function, not to simply submit to suffering but to relish it. The pope tells priests to "recognize" and "not resent" their personal suffering because the duties and lives of priests will "definitely entail hardship." He sees the laity as they "toil and work" and "bear" these sufferings. Even to the youth, John Paul II describes a future in which there may be "suffering and pain."[25]

Critics of Pope John Paul II complain that he "condemns" the world.[26] They consider his message too negative and fatalistic. Some claim that his emphasis on the positive aspects of bearing pain acts to condone and accept the inhuman and unjust suffering of the poor and the oppressed. John Paul II anticipates his critics by employing the technique of symbol inversion. Christian interpretation of suffering is not "fatalism or passivity," but the *"negation of passivity."* He turns to models in his audience to show that there is no "abstract" answer to the "why?" of suffering. Immigrants, the sick, priests, lay people provide a practical means of making sense out of sickness and pain.[27]

In one sense, John Paul II addresses his audience as a realist, tapping into the anxieties and hurt experienced in their everyday lives. On a personal level, sin remains a problem; on a societal level, a utopian earthly world is impossible. When rational attempts to cure ills, prolong life, and fashion peace give way to new afflictions and renewed conflicts, the audience is not asked to deny the inconsistencies, but rather to capitalize upon them. In a Burkeian dramatistic view, themes of struggle provide the division lines of separation that invite resolution and identification. What does not make sense can be the key to understanding. For John Paul II, suffering, is an "opportunity," and a *"call, a vocation"* to resolve sin and injustice. The sacred image inverts. Suffering is no longer suffering, but "spiritual joy"; pain is no longer pain, but "inner peace."[28]

Dialogue as Conversation

According to Duncan, the "you" address is indicative of a conversation or dialogue with a significant other. The distinguishing feature of the 1987 papal trip to the United States was its attempt to introduce conversation and dialogue. At thirteen events,[29] representatives addressed the pope, to which the pope then responded in his own speech. One sees similarities and distinctions between the audience as constructed by representative speakers and the audience implied in the pope's speech.

In meetings with church groups, representatives in the "structured dialogues" often sought to test the position of the pope on a number of issues that aimed to move the borders of the church's cosmos to embrace new and expanded meanings. A few were echoed by the pope, most were modified or redirected in emphasis, and some were totally ignored. The dialogue with the priests in Miami in 1987 serves as an example of this rhetorical strategy. Many U.S. priests considered John Paul II's position on celibacy and theological dissent as indication that he neither understood nor sympathized with the plight of priests working in Western secular culture. Priests, in general, were demoralized by the thinning of their ranks that occurred during the sixties and seventies when so many priests left the priesthood. With the importance of religion threatened by secularization, priestly roles began to be devalued. Priests were often isolated, sometimes overworked and frustrated by falling church numbers. On an organizational level, priests had recently gained acceptance of diocesan priest councils composed of those elected from their ranks. Instead of individual priests working through their pastors or other superiors, priest councils could discuss problems and concerns directly with their bishops. The audience of priests for the 1987 visit of John Paul II was composed of the elected heads of priest councils throughout the United States, and therefore, this audience included those actively engaged in pressuring for consideration and solutions to the concerns of priests.

Reverend Frank J. McNulty, chosen to present the views of priests from dioceses throughout the country, constructed a moving and eloquent speech on priestly life and work in the United States. An analysis of the speech demonstrates that his remarks are structured within an emotive rather than rational framework. Presumably he realized that there would be no meeting of the minds on several issues. Therefore, to bridge these differences, he poses an image of priests and pope committed to communion by warmth, affection, and intimacy. He speaks for an audience who "open up their hearts" to a poet-pope, and poets "know the human heart."[30] Likewise, John Paul II reciprocates by declaring his desire to "open my heart to you."[31]

The speeches of John Paul II and Reverend Frank J. McNulty raise many of the same issues, namely: the joys and problems of the special mission of priests; the problems of morale and increased pressures of their work; the need for compassion; the shortage of priests; the value of collaboration; and the balancing of freedom of inquiry and fidelity to the truth. The treatment of these same issues encourages an awareness among the audience that a real conversation is unfolding. Only one of the issues raised by the priest representative is totally ignored by the pope, that of the service of women in the church. Despite the similarity in issues, there are differences in perspective and therefore in meaning construction. McNulty's audience is actively engaged in "knowing the Shepherd" through "walking" with him in their priestly ministry. These priestly activities which "enflesh" the Vatican documents and share so completely their community's "journey" often leave little time for priests to develop an "inner life" of prayer.[32] In contrast, the identity of the audience as constructed by the pope is formed by an objective sacred being, "*that Shepherd whom we all know*," rather than the audience's act of knowing the Shepherd.[33] It is striking that the talk of John Paul II is replete with references to the sacred, whereas comparatively speaking, McNulty refers to the sacred sparingly.[34] As described by McNulty, an outer directed ministry is the center of the audience's lives. Although the priesthood entails service and care for the People of God, John Paul II states that "the Good Shepherd—is *the very center of your life, the very meaning of your priesthood.*" Therefore, prayer is not an "option" but an "*essential.*" The rhetorical direction of papal speech points less toward an audience defined by active engagement with their people and their people's needs, and more to an audience that is "invited," "entrusted," and "called" by the sacred.[35] John Paul II's implied audience has an ontological connectedness to the sacred; the audience's existence and being takes precedence over activity.

McNulty's audience is very sensitive to the declining image of the church. The priestly audience is concerned with a communal church that sounds "harsh" and "is not as credible" as they would like it to be. Priests blame the "technical approach of some of our ecclesial documents." John Paul II agrees that priests should be concerned about what people expect of the church, but he focuses on how people look to priests as models. John Paul claims that "the example of priests" through the sacraments, especially in their repeated conversion through the Sacrament of Penance, is what is "noticed" by the community. In McNulty's speech, image depends on how an administrative church writes its documents. In John Paul II's speech, image is constructed through visual and sacramental signs.[36]

On the lack of vocations, John Paul II agrees with what McNulty has said regarding prayer, role models, and the need for priests to "personally invite" young men to the priesthood. However, the pope does not answer McNulty's suggestion that celibacy still presents a problem for those considering the priesthood. Instead, the pope reminds the audience that Christ is the attraction and priests have to proclaim this fact. The pope reorients his audience toward a powerful and awesome being who can "overcome" the problems of the world. However, John Paul II does not abandon the human factor. For John Paul II, if priests continually talk about the obstacles, there will be no hope. If priests present the positive attraction of the priesthood, then "we have a right to expect" that God will answer our prayers.[37] The sacred is a factor in our construction of meaning, but the implied audience plays an important role by building a more positive image of Christ and the future of his church.

Identification occurs when there is difference. The essence of persuasion is to promote social cohesion, bringing together the divided and contending voices. Burke reminded us that the images of division and conflict "can figure as a terminology of reidentification" as in transformation or rebirth.[38] Differences are often used by John Paul II to explain the need for "renewal." As Duncan explained, leaders of a social institution understand that social order cannot depend on perfect obedience. Therefore, leaders must explain how disobedience can occur and how the individual can be reeducated. Rulers arouse in us a guilt and then articulate ways in which we can expiate that guilt. Authorities "mystify us through appeals to some great transcendent principle of social order. They teach us that disobedience threatens . . . the whole principle on which social order rests."[39] In his argument regarding the need or lack of vocations, Pope John Paul II does not discuss ways to change the rules to make it easier to become a priest. Instead, he suggests that priests have not attracted young men to follow them because priests themselves have not had sufficient faith and trust in the Lord. He arouses guilt in his audience, and shows them ways to deal with this guilt.

If John Paul II's rhetorical strategy with the priests is an attempt to move his audience from their secular surroundings to a sacred center, his strategy with Native Americans employs an opposite tactic. The Native American complaints are two-fold: the association and possible collaboration of Spanish missionaries with the cruel treatment of Native Americans by the Spanish colonial forces during their expansion into the southwestern part of the United States; and the contribution of missionaries to the disintegration of Native American culture by forcing them to abandon or hide their traditional religious beliefs and practices. Social anthropologist E. H. Spicer studied the results of Catholic missionary activity among the Native American populations in the southwest and concluded that many consider themselves Catholic, but in practice, their religion is a syncretic fusion of both religious traditions. In some cases, the religious practices of the past traditions are simply added to Catholic ritual ceremony and liturgical celebrations. However, Spicer observed that many Native American Catholics do not accept many Christian concepts, such as heaven and hell.[40] The U.S. Catholic Church still supports many Indian missions, particularly in southwestern reservations, and the Bureau of Catholic Indian Missions has been a strong advocate for Native American causes.

Knowing the past and current context of the plight of Native American peoples, John Paul II's rhetorical posture of address is to move the audience toward their individual and secular responsibilities. The pope listens to Native American spokesperson Mrs. Alfretta M. Antone characterize the audience as proud of their heritage, but sadly abused and in need of help. She asks the pope "to do all in your prayer, power, and influence to help us secure" twelve wishes and demands. The pope acknowledges history's "harsh and painful reality," but claims Native Americans have benefited from positive encounters with European culture. Ignoring their pleas for help, John Paul II tries to convince Native Americans that they are worthy and capable of helping themselves, the church, and others. He acknowledges that there are biases to be changed, but "the greatest challenge is to you yourselves."[41] The pope's speech recognizes that the audience's Native American heritage is deeply spiritual and cognizant of a dependence on a sacred being. What he finds lacking are human initiative and self-determination. Rhetorical movement in this case is not toward the sacred; it is toward worldly accomplishment.

In analyzing the process of dialogue, it is not enough to examine if and how John Paul II addresses the issues set forth by the representative speaker. Indeed, the pope agreed with many points, and maintained his differences with others. However, if the analysis considers the sacred-secular dialectic, the pope's intent is to supply the missing ingredient, whichever aspect of the symbol system is missing, the sacred or the secular. This strategy not only is applied to Catholic audiences, but also to those groups external to the church. For example, during the meeting with Jewish leaders, Rabbi Mordecai Waxman called for a "common agenda" of specific secular requests. Among these requests was Vatican diplomatic recognition of Israel.[42] John Paul II's response was markedly different, relying often on biblical references to characterize a "common heritage" and a "spiritual fraternity." In referring to the Holocaust, John Paul II spoke about the "meaning" of "this mystery of suffering."[43] From John Paul II's point of view, the discussions in July and August with Jewish leaders at the Vatican had relieved the tension concerning the Vatican's decision to receive Kurt Waldheim, allowing the pope to move beyond these temporal events to discussions on the sacred realm of "spiritual fraternity" established by God's "covenant of eternal love."[44] Reflecting afterward about the meeting with the pope in Miami, Rabbi Leon Klenicki of the Anti-Defamation League believed that in contrast to the speech given by John Paul II, the Jewish presentation had "projected secular feelings and concepts." He explained that the theological sections in the speech draft had been vetoed by other Jewish colleagues. According to Klenicki, the historical experience of persecution makes Jews fearful of theological conversations outside of the Jewish community.[45] For the Jewish audience, meaning construction remains almost entirely on the level of common service in the secular world. For John Paul II, meaning construction includes a sacred-secular continuum.

Frequency of Dialogic "You" Address

In Duncan's view, the "you" address invites dialogue and discussion between friends. Dialogue takes place because there is a distinct identity placed on the audience, separating that audience from the speaker and thereby setting the stage for identification and resolution. In his Eucharistic homilies, John Paul II uses only a small portion of his speech to signify audience action that is distinct. The "you" address gives contextual features to the audience, but it is usually placed within a speech that is overwhelmingly characterized by the "we" of agreement. However, when the pope addresses specific groups within the church, there are observable differences in the mode of address. In comparing the speeches to the laity and the priests, there is an inverse relationship of the forms of address "we" and "you." The overwhelming perspective of address to the priests is the "we" of community guardians, whereas there is little use of "we" address to the laity. The opposite occurs in the "you" address. There are only three instances where the priests are addressed solely as "you." In the speech to the laity, the pope specifies a "you" audience thirty-one times.

The predominant use of "you" in address to the laity is employed less as a cultural or contextual marker, and more as a device to separate the identity of the lay person from that of the priestly speaker. John Paul II makes clear that lay people take different paths than priests. In fact, he ignores a lay presentation that calls for the pope and lay people to walk in each other's shoes. Vatican Council II was considered to be a turning point for laity within the church. Catholic lay people, once largely uneducated in contrast with the priestly class, were not only achieving new heights in secular fields, but they were also being permitted to study and teach theology. On the parish level, the church began instituting reforms, including the creation of parish councils in which the laity eagerly took part, assuming that they would be equal partners in the decision making of all except the sacramental aspects of the parish. This tide of change was not without friction. Some priests resisted lay intrusion into parish affairs, especially finances. When diocesan bishops asked prominent businessmen and women to head fund-raising efforts, some of them accepted on condition that they be involved in deciding how to spend the money. At the time of John Paul II's visit in 1987, a National Advisory Committee (NAC) was already in place, composed of bishops, diocesan priests, religious, and laity that advise the U.S. bishops on upcoming agenda items for bishops' meetings. The chair of NAC, Donna Hanson, was chosen as the representative speaker for the meeting with the laity during the pope's 1987 visit to the U.S. Being aware of the potential of close collaboration with the bishops through this committee, Hanson sought an even stronger role for laity to "truly share responsibility."[46] Her speech attempts to portray the pope and the laity walking together as a "we."

John Paul II's response distances itself from this solid collaborative approach. Instead, he tells the "you" of the laity that they must walk in the "everyday world" and engage themselves in "secular professions and occupations." The pope acknowledges the laity's increased "collaboration and consultation" in ecclesial life since Vatican Council II, then switches to the "we" form to claim agreement between the audience and himself on the need to hold back the church from pursuing unconditional equality. John Paul II warns that if lay service is not "rooted in *the sound Catholic ecclesiology*" of Vatican Council II, "we run the risk of 'clericalizing' the laity or 'laicizing' the clergy." Confusing the identities results in "robbing" priests and laity of "their specific meaning and their complementarity."[47] John Paul II argues that the meaning system of the church depends on differences. According to Kenneth Burke, these subtle differences provide the mystery of strangeness that intensifies social bonds.[48]

John Paul II closes down movement to a more equal and indistinct church membership by turning to Vatican Council II documents to enhance agreement on the issue.[49] The Council attempted to give a positive description of the lay person by emphasizing a more mystical rather than juridical definition of the church. Previously, laity meant all others who were not priests or religious. In stressing unity and communion, the Council spoke of all Christians sharing in one mission. In fact, the Council avoided terms that emphasized categories or status, and instead employed terms such as charisma and gifts to indicate differentiation. John Paul II continues this tradition by focusing on identity and meaning rather than hierarchical rank, status, or even sociological role. At the same time, he constructs an oppositional relationship between lay and clergy, not only by arguing for complementarity, but also by separating himself from his lay audience through the consistent use of the "you" form of address.

ADDRESS OF BELONGING: THE "WE" AND THE "THEY"

If the goal is a shared social identity, the rhetor will look for plausible ways to use "we."[50] The rhetor takes on risks when using the "we," because this assumes agreement of the audience. Prior to Vatican Council II, a hierarchical or institutional model dominated the church's form of communicating. Teaching about the faith involved a top-down movement. With scriptures and tradition originating from God, communicating about the faith passed through papal and episcopal authority to the clergy and finally to the faithful whose response was one of acceptance and adherence. Most papal communication was in the form of written decrees.[51] This tradition of declaration affected the way popes spoke, causing them to use very formal techniques, including a corporate "we." Because there was no "I" form, all first-person statements contained "we." The pope assumed that he was not addressing others in order to court their agreement, but he was speaking for them, expressing their automatic assent to whatever was being declared as official doctrine. This formal mode of speaking continued through the papacy of Pope Paul VI.

Because of the contrast with the personal pronoun form in the speech of John Paul II, it is possible to view his use of "we" within a communication model that allows for a free response from the audience. In his writings, John Paul II has been a strong advocate of freedom, insisting that "man cannot be forced to accept the truth."[52] The pope's challenge is to hold together a diverse and tension-filled church by persuading, not forcing, his audience to identify with a communal "we" that they can recognize as making sense to them. The pope as a leader of the Catholic Church must be constantly concerned with shoring up the meaning systems by which Catholics define reality. He needs to convince his audience that the "we" of the Catholic community is still defined through its sacred dimension. During John Paul II's 1987 visit to the U.S., he addressed audiences who viewed themselves as part of the church, but lived in a culture permeated by secular values and behavior. Like most Americans, they have difficulty envisioning communal agreement unless it allows for compromise and individual choice. They understand how to come together based on pragmatic grounds, often to satisfy personal needs and interests. As Bellah noted, Americans are not totally cut off from society; they have a "penchant for 'getting involved.' "[53] Therefore, any reappropriation of tradition would appropriately build upon the American need for active involvement.

Communal Pull of the Sacred

At first, it would seem that John Paul II's rhetorical strategy ignores this need for active involvement because he portrays the members of the church in a dependent relationship with this sacred Other. We pray, ask, and "plead like the servant" to this Other being because "we belong to God." The truth is synonymous with God's word that "comes to us from the Apostles" and is "stored in the depths of the Church's memory and in Sacred Scripture." In other words, John Paul II asks Catholics to listen and recall a well-defined tradition that has been written and codified by an institutional church. All norms originate from the sacred above and pass through the pope and bishops to the faithful members. This vertical dimension tends to restrict meaning and act centripetally to reinforce an institutional church of which John Paul II is the head.[54]

On the other hand, John Paul II draws his audience as active participants in communal acts of remembering. The pope persuades people to stick together, because only as a communal act can the "we" of the church pose unifying symbols of transcendence. Usually at the beginning of his sermons, John Paul II includes his audience in the act of constructing the nomos by recalling that "we" hear, read, and know the Word of the Lord during the Eucharistic ritual. Because large numbers of people gather from various parts of the region or country to take part in the sacramental ritual, these liturgical celebrations heighten the audience's awareness of a collective "we" who are involved in recalling, remembering, fixing "our gaze" on the sacred nomos.[55]

John Paul II does not neglect the personal and individual relationship with one's God. His audiences have been conditioned to be in touch with their interior, subjective selves. Their sense of communal identity has faded, leaving them to face life alone, filled with anxieties about themselves and their future. To these troubled individuals, John Paul II promises a relationship of intimacy with a sacred Other. God touches our lives, gives gifts to us, and calls us in special ways. The Other is posed as someone "to whom our hearts speak."[56]

Marsha Witten's interpretation of Protestant preaching points out how the insecure, privatized self receives solace from an intimate God, not from the human community.[57] John Paul II's preaching on an intimate God may also console individuals, but the community is essential to the consoling, intimate relationship with the sacred. In the pope's speech, the audience cannot have a relationship with God unless they are "reconciled among ourselves." They will never find the answers to ultimate questions about life if they are alienated "from God and our fellow human beings."[58] The church members do not just stand next to each other in a crowd, but they have deep interpersonal relationships that require forgiveness and compassion. As Avery Dulles noted, communion-type ecclesiologies have great appeal because they are viewed in contrast to the "oppressive and depersonalizing" institutions of modern life.[59] Participants interviewed at large-scale Eucharistic celebrations often cite their consciousness of being unified with all who attend these gatherings.[60] This consciousness is enhanced by the audience's situation. At Westover Hills, Texas, the audience included a large number of Hispanic Americans, who would tend to interpret the call to reconciliation according to their own experiences with racial oppression. In Los Angeles, the pope's call to compassion stands in contrast to life in this sprawling urban setting where the affluent and the needy hardly ever cross paths.

The Force of Opposition

Communicating an understanding of the communal "we" requires the audience to "*confront* the implications of division." The "we" of the church are in dialogue with other voices and respond to the appeals of antagonist and protagonist in order to make sense out of these conflicting loyalties.[61] John Paul II's rhetorical strategy leads the audience to confront division as a contemporary reality.[62] He often constructs an oppositional "they" in order to solidify the group in its stand against the opposition, although this presents several problems. If John Paul II articulates impenetrable borders between the "we" of the church and the "they" of the secular opposition, belonging to the "we" becomes a requirement for survival. Individuals may only congregate because they seek a safety zone as a refuge for maintaining their personal interests. Janice Peck claimed that televangelists need the antagonist "they" in order to produce cohesiveness and belonging.[63] Even though the "they" performs an important function in that it maintains an oppositional tension, rhetorically the church's meaning has to be sustained by a sacred Other and not simply by a negation of an evil world.

Another reason why care must be taken with regard to the use of an antagonist "they" is that the church's communal myth is universal and all-inclusive. To reach perfection "we must all come *to maturity 'together' in the community of the Church.*"[64] The "they" can be a source of potential members. Luigi Accattoli contended that the missionary theme, represented in and by John Paul II's worldwide travels, has become the dominant idea giving shape to the pontificate of John Paul II. He compares the thinking of Protestant theologian Karl Barth with that of John Paul II. Both see a missionary church destined to spread itself to the whole world, otherwise it will lose its nature, surrendering to the world, risking its disappearance.[65] If papal rhetoric draws such impenetrable borders between the "we" and "they," the church will have to give up its claim to new possibilities.

In six of his homilies, John Paul II employs an opposing "they" in contrast to the "we" of the committed church members. In the first two homilies of the 1987 trip, the borders are rigidly drawn to separate the faithful of the church who know and recall the sacred from "modern man," who "easily *forgets that he has received a great gift.*" The pope delineates how the *nomos* of the faithful community guardians is "challenged and even directly opposed by ideologies and lifestyles."[66] When John Paul II lists the challenges to Christian values, they make sense to a wide variety of people: crime, violence, terrorism for those living in the urban areas of Miami; dishonesty and injustice "in business and public life" for those concerned about white-collar crime; spending on armaments at the expense of poor for those active in social justice causes; alcohol, drug abuse, and the exploitation of sex, especially for those working with youth; and adultery, divorce, fornication, contraception, abortion, and euthanasia for those distressed about eroding family values.

At times, John Paul II describes the antagonist in terms very familiar to the church community he is addressing. He uses the third person to distinguish the discordant from the harmonious "we," but it is clear that the American audience can recognize its own cultural traits. "A part of the human family—the most economically and technically developed part—is being specially tempted . . . to forget God."[67] Using a rhetoric of jeremiad, John Paul II warns of the possibility of an impending danger to all the world's civilization, and "we," the church in America, can save the world from this disaster. The jeremiad, a recurrent rhetorical pattern in religious sermons and American political discourse, is very familiar to audiences in the United States.[68]

At first, the pope's contrasts between the sacred and the secular appear to be consistent with a fundamentalist condemnation of the modern and material world. Indeed, there are significant numbers of Catholics who are drawn to both Catholic and Protestant fundamentalist movements because of their zealous world-denouncing rhetoric. Catholic theology has always embraced a world that has the potential for being good, but it has also recognized that the potentiality for evil is always present. In some respects, Vatican Council II and the enthusiasm it generated for reaching out to the world led to a mentality that played down the existence of evil and sin. Sermons on the four last things, death, judgment, heaven, and hell, were considered too negative, and therefore, were discarded as part of the past. Instead, the church looked upon the tangible and finite world as potential carriers of the divine presence.[69] Now, a number of church members question whether this view was too optimistic. Others fear that by reintroducing the negative, the church will undo what it attempted to correct. John Paul II includes references to hell and Satan in his sermons. He preaches often about the need for individual use of the Sacrament of Penance and presents these "objective truths of faith" as "firm and unchanged." On the other hand, to appeal to an audience of radically interior and individualized selves who may not want to recognize evil as an objective reality, John Paul II adds arguments drawn from modern psychology. Even though he stresses the sacramental nature of confession, the pope admits that the effects of confession may be measured and valued as psychologically liberating to the human self.[70] If the audience does not accept sin as an objective reality, perhaps they will see the value of confession for therapeutic purposes.

Softening the Opposition

John Paul II's symbolic posing of an oppositional "they" centers on the "spirit" and "ideologies" of the modern world. He does not separate Christians from the "things" of this world, but from the way we see and measure experience. For example, the pope contends that new technological improvements and progress in research and technology should not be labeled good or evil, for this progress simply "increases what we can do" and therefore increases the possibilities among which we "must choose between good and evil."[71] The American audience is relieved that the pope supports their insatiable need for technological improvement, but they also understand this plenitude of choice. They may not be able to identify right from wrong, but they rebel when their freedom is curtailed.

Chastising people directly for their sins can have demeaning effects on the audience. John Paul II usually casts the blame on the "they," carefully placing them at a distance from the "we" of his audience. For example, in Monterey, only "a part of the human family" are the culprits. In his homily at Westover, Texas, John Paul cites those "in different parts of the world" who neglect the Sacrament of Penance because they are unwilling to "accept maturely and responsibly the consequences of the objective truths of faith." The implication is that the "we" who are mature and responsible members of the church accept objective norms, whereas those who neglect to follow the church's instructions are immature and irresponsible because they practice their religion according to their own subjective feelings. John Paul II sometimes softens the rhetorical division between the sacred and secular by offering reasons or excuses for the immature and irresponsible neglect of the norms. He cites "inadequate instruction," improperly formed conscience, or lack of serious understanding, even "hesitation" or "unwillingness."[72] Consequently, there is provision for the private realm of the individual conscience, but always in relationship to the objective norms defined by the church.

Another rhetorical device that John Paul II uses to protect the "we" from his condemnation of the world is the externalization of secular evils. The "we" of the church face "a growing *secularism* . . . insidious *relativism* . . . materialistic *consumerism* . . . alluring *hedonism*."[73] All these "isms" are societal attitudes that deny the absoluteness of God's truth and thus influence the normative functioning of our lives. Rhetorically, even though John Paul II personifies the "ism" or ideology as "growing," these "isms" of secularism, relativism, consumerism, and hedonism are terms that "oversocialize" the human subject, emphasizing an impersonal social environment over which the human person has little control.[74] This externalization of impersonal social science constructs produces a dramatic contrast with the "we" of the People of God who need "inner" fulfillment and satisfaction for the "human heart."[75] However, as a rhetorical strategy, the impersonal ideologies may be so abstract that the audience fails to see them as threatening or relevant to their lives.

For Burke, communion or consubstantiality involves paradox because it brings together the divided, and at the same time does not destroy individual identity. After drawing clear borders between the threatening world and the remembrance of the sacred, John Paul II attempts to reconcile "these two realities," that is, our "duties before God and before society." "As Christians *we live and work in this world,* but at the same time, we are *called to work in the vineyard of the Lord.*"[76]

The two worlds of sacred and secular are different, but each world is defined by the other. John Paul II's clearest statements of resolution of the two worlds of sacred and secular through love take place in speeches to audiences whose composition is characterized by the large numbers of laborers: Monterey with immigrant farm workers; Detroit with office and factory workers. [77] John Paul II seems more confident that the audiences who are less affluent and therefore struggling on a daily basis with primary needs may be more receptive to his message of love as a mystical force that brings the community together in its diversity and divisions.

Adjustments to Audience

In examining the use of the "we" address in John Paul II's speeches to specific groups within the church, there are several observations to be made. By far, the pope uses the "we" address abundantly in his speeches to priests. He constructs the priestly "we" more actively than passively: knowing, loving, growing, ministering, working, serving, praying. However, because John Paul II poses no threatening external world to the priest audience, he portrays the priestly identity as distinct and disassociated from the world. Meaning for priests is derived totally from their sacred function. The overabundance of "we" form of address and the absence of the secular world focuses the rhetorical action inwardly, binding priests and pope together. It is a concerted effort on the part of the pope to desire "all distances to be bridged."[78] Planners for the trip knew that the pope's meeting with the priests would be difficult. Among America's priests, who are declining in numbers, there is reduced morale and outright opposition to the pope's preaching. The priestly function is of prime importance to John Paul II's quest for unity, and therefore he works hard to encourage identification with the papacy. If it were not for the pope's touching self-references, his speech at the meeting with priests would be overbearing in its formal appeal for association. By contrast, in the pope's speech to the youth in Los Angeles, there is hardly any "we" address. When speaking to the young people, the pope uses a much more intimate conversational style. He is both teacher and friend. Unlike his task with the priestly audience, he does not have to work as hard to win the rhetorical agreement of the youth. He knows that there are no barriers between them and the "we" of identification is assumed.

At meetings between the pope and representatives of other religions, the pope concentrates on points of agreement, drawing the audience into an all-inclusive "we" of Catholics with followers of other religions. There is no distinction between the Catholic Church and other Christian churches. The implied audience is united not only in service, study, and meeting, but also by "our Christian identity" that "intimately unites us among ourselves." If there are barriers, they are caused by human tactics that entail "measured calculation . . . efficiency . . . advantage and influence." The rational, scientific approach fails, but a "conversion of heart" can lead to complete unity. However, in the same address to the ecumenical leadership, John Paul II supports those human tactics of systematic committee work and evaluation that are so much a part of the modern rational approach to common meaning construction.[79]

With the Christian community, barriers are formed by human tactics and are capable of being broken. With the Jewish audience, common agreement in some areas cannot wipe away "our distinctive identities." For example, the pope switches his use of "we" as an identifier of the common Catholic and Jewish leaders who are present to an identifier of the Catholic Church which the pope represents. "We [the Catholic Church] proclaim" about Jesus Christ and "we [the Catholic Church] recognize and appreciate" the religious belief of the Jewish people.[80] This change in implied audience for the "we" address tends to amplify the distinctions between the "we"—Catholics and Jews, and the "we"—Catholics, not Jews. The distinctions that John Paul II draws are to indicate that Catholics do not expect union with the Jews as they do with other Christians and recognize Jews as respectfully continuing their belief in the special covenant of God with the Jewish people.

PERSONA: THE PROCESS OF SELF-DISCLOSURE

Examining the personal references of John Paul II in his public discourse gives us some cues as to the rhetorical persona that seeks identification with the audience. These choices of symbols reveal the motives and interests of the audience as understood by the rhetor. By placing the rhetorical persona on the sacred-secular continuum, we can determine whether John Paul II's investment of self in his speeches is evidence of a unifying, tradition-bound motive, emphasizing unchanging role and function; or an indication of accommodation to the more dispersed, interior, individualized perception of identity.

It is important to view John Paul II's rhetoric within a papal rhetorical tradition to understand fully the implications of self-revelation in public. Those Catholics who remember the pronouncements of Pope Pius XII recall a highly impersonal mode of speaking. The calling to the papacy was a renunciation of selfhood, and thereafter the pope spoke as a corporate head, never as an individual. The form "we" was the preferred mode to demonstrate that popes did not make individual decisions, but spoke as successors of Peter, inspired by the sacred, conveying the authority of a position directly traceable through nearly two thousand years. Furthermore, the papal forms of rhetoric were perfected when the cultural norms of the day were dependent on a regal, monarchical authority. Rulers were clearly distinguished from all others and the borders were not crossed by personal revelation: the Crown wished, His Majesty proclaimed, and the Successor to Peter did the same.

Gradually, republican traditions began eating away at these borders, and the leveling influences of equal citizenship made it incumbent on most leaders of newly democratic societies to reveal to their constituents more and more about their individual selves. So, too, modern popes. Pope Paul VI simplified many aspects of papal dress and ceremony, and became the first pope to travel by air to far-off corners of the world. However, he continued the formal speaking style of popes using the papal "we." Even during occasions when Paul VI gave glimpses of his personal background to his audiences, he could not abandon the formal "we." For example, in attempting to relate more closely to an audience of journalists, Paul VI spoke about his own family, "Our father, Giorgio Montini, to whom We owe Our natural life and so very much of Our spiritual life, was, among other things, a journalist."[81] Personal revelation made papal speech very cumbersome until John Paul I, during his short pontificate, inserted the use of "I" in his speeches. This change in style was indicative of deep changes in the culture.

Returning to the theoretical framework of Peter Berger, the Catholic Church, along with other established churches, was losing its massivity and hence the appearance of durability.[82] Adjusting to a pluralistic world, Catholic teachings were no longer self-evident and the "we" of the corporate church no longer had the same strength or meaning. To be connected and relevant to human present activity and understanding, the "we" needed to relate to the age of individual self-fulfillment.

According to Burke, the connection between the "I" and the "we" is produced and reproduced at least through words. It is the dramatic tension of separation and joining, or courtship, that intensifies social bonds.[83] The absence of an "I" continually denied that tension. By revealing his individual self, John Paul II provides the missing ingredient in the dialectic process of identification.

In every speech during his 1987 trip, Pope John Paul II addressed the audience using "I." The noting of these self-references interspersed throughout the body of the speech text, their frequency, and their relation to the audience and persuasive message is a way of interpreting "distinctions and connections, contrasts and parallels" in the symbolic structure of the discourse.[84] To facilitate the classification of verbal motives and actions in relation to the implied audiences, these "I" statements of John Paul II can be grouped into five categories: personalized greetings, persuasive courtship, narrative intimacy, managerial role-bound self, and sacred invocation.

Personalized Greetings

In most of John Paul II's speeches, "I" statements are used regularly in the introduction to express greetings and appreciation, a practice that conforms with the patterns of Western rhetorical tradition. These personal greetings recognize the process of invitation, a process that is often emphasized in the structuring of the papal visit. Pope John Paul II himself makes the final decisions on where he will travel, but his choices are limited by the invitations. The Vatican and the pope are in a responding posture, rather than in an initiating one.

Therefore, the rhetorical formulas of hospitality in the papal speech are humbling symbolic acts. A pope only goes where he is invited. He is thankful for being invited and thankful that people have come to listen to him. The contrast is evident. In this divinely established office of the papacy, the pope exercises full supreme and universal power in the church. At first, it would seem that since the papacy has succumbed to a "fair" process of invitation by consensus, the pope is no longer endowed with full and complete authority, a condition of its divine origin and sacredness. A pope no longer speaks in majestic terms employing corporate formulas of "we," but instead greets the audience with personal expressions of familiarity and emotion—joy, warmth, pleasure, embrace, happiness—telling the audience how thankful he is that he was invited, and that so many have come to hear him speak.

Duncan wrote that the structure of the relationship between speaker and audience determines "*how* we address each other and thus how we affect each other." Rhetors "petition superiors in reverence and awe," or "cajole, coach, exhort, or instruct inferiors." However, with equals there is discussion, argument, agreement, and play. Audiences and rhetors play roles, but these roles are not permanent; they change. An effective speaker plays different roles, and shapes these changing roles and relationships during a speech. Duncan reminded us that "we are not *either* superior and inferior or equal, but both superior, inferior *and* equal."[85]

Most of the papal greetings, such as "I am grateful," are not particularly unique. They are expressions of modesty conforming to rules of taste in society's social play.[86] Greeting each other, the rhetor and audience anticipate the experience of coming together in joyful social play, during which all, as equals, are submitting themselves to agreed-upon rules of invitation and hospitality. Some of the greetings of Pope John Paul II move him beyond the role of invited guest to express his natural affection. For example, in his meeting with priests representing the clergy throughout the United States, the pope opens his remarks with "Coming here today, I wish to open my heart to you."[87] It is no accident that this greeting is special. When discussing the preparation for this meeting with the priests, U.S. advisors, knowing that the priests would be one of the most critical audiences of the papal visit, urged Pope John Paul II to simply say that he loves them.[88]

Persuasive Courtship

The pope's self-references signal persuasive action and, in this regard, these "I" statements mark the purpose of the pope's speech-making. Predominant use of expressions, such as "I ask you," "I urge you," "I make this appeal," "I invite you," please an audience that is steeped in a pluralistic situation where allegiance is voluntary. Believers cannot be coerced, but need to be courted.[89] Because even a pope can only ask, not command, John Paul II employs an intimate style to help him persuade his audiences. When calling for action, the self-references of John Paul II are sometimes unusually polite and often loaded with verbose phrases that tend to distance the one who asks from the asking. Despite the introduction of self-references, formality and indirectness of language persist in papal speech-writing.

In certain speeches during the 1987 visit to the United States, the use of "I" abounds, whereas in other speeches it is controlled or limited to almost formula-type situations. Because conversational style contains free use of self-references, a group of people who are familiar with the speaker, and indeed are used to one-on-one working relationships that are more informal and conversational would expect a consistency of style from that speaker. Such is the case in the pope's discourse to the U.S. bishops, in which there are many instances of self-reference. Bishops are appointed by the pope, and in the United States at the time of his visit, many of the American bishops had been appointed by Pope John Paul II. Every bishop is obliged to make a special *ad limina* visit to Rome every five years. Some bishops are more familiar with Rome than others, either because of their prior schooling or current work on special projects and commissions. For many U.S. bishops, the meeting during the 1987 visit to the U.S. was not the first exchange with John Paul II.

Furthermore, the relationship between bishops and pope is more complex than a reporting line of an organization. This relationship, known as collegiality, is not a juridical, but a theological concept, and was one of the more far-reaching doctrines defined by Vatican Council II.[90] The pope is both a member of the College of Bishops and head of that college. The body of bishops, together with and never without its head, the Roman pontiff, has supreme and full power over the church.[91] Because the future of the church depends on the unity and solidarity of its bishops together with the pope, there is a need for a familiar mode of address between the pope and bishops. The progression of self-references used by John Paul II in his speech to the U.S. bishops reflects a familiar tone, as well as the complex issue of collegiality. In his opening remarks, he uses self-references to personally thank the bishops for all the efforts they made in preparing for the visit, but, more importantly, for being with him as partners "in the Gospel." In this case, the pope's act of thanking moves beyond friendship to an acknowledgment of a shared responsibility. Then, this "I-you" relationship becomes symbolically a "we," in which the bishops together with the pope discuss "our collegial ministry." After his discussion of collegiality, John Paul II again uses "I" statements to attest to "my role as Successor of Peter in a spirit of fraternal solidarity with you." The "I" testifies to his personal dedication to collegiality and his wish "only to be of service," but John Paul II also reminds the bishops of "my specific responsibility," one which no other bishop has, that of confirming all bishops in "their own collegial ministry."[92] The pope reveals a self that is role-bound by the formal teachings of the church, reaching out in solidarity to bind the bishops to himself, and at the same time, preserving a lead role for the papacy.

Kathleen Jamieson contends that self-disclosure which accelerates the audience's sense of intimacy can insulate the rhetor from the "sting of unpopular policies."[93] It is perhaps because, as equals, the audience and the rhetor expect conflict. However, unlike superior-inferior relationships, they create social forms so their differences can be resolved. They expect a successful outcome and therefore anticipate being convinced.[94] Using the personal "I" form, the pope creates familiarity and equality of partnership with his audience. For example, the papal persona refrains from giving outright orders to his bishops. Instead the bishops hear him saying, "I encourage you," "I ask you," "I urge you." At times, those urgings are for pointed and strong policies: making sure that those who dissent from the church's teachings understand that this dissent can be an obstacle to receiving the sacraments; safeguarding the Catholic character of Catholic colleges and universities; seeing that seminarians study and accept the dogmatic and moral teaching of the church.[95] The pope makes these demands very clear, but his tone is always one of persuasion and not command.

Even with the increased use of self-references to persuade friends and family, there is still a sense of formality and indirectness in the pope's style. For example, the pope often uses the conditional form of the verb and other devices of politeness. This is much more evident in the discourse to the U.S. bishops in Los Angeles than in his homilies at the Eucharistic celebrations and even in his discourse to the priests. For example, these expressions, "I wish to support you," "I feel a particular desire to support you," "I would ask you,"[96] clearly build a formal veil between the speaker and the audience, emphasizing the official nature of the talk. Again, the pope is speaking with "collaborators" and there are no direct orders given, but instead strong wishes and desires.

Narrative Intimacy

Another type of "I" statement that is considered to be profoundly revealing is the self-reference interwoven into the text as a personal narrative, examples of which can be found in the pope's speeches to priests and young people. In his address to the priests of the United States in Miami, John Paul II talks about "my love for the priesthood" which he celebrates and praises.[97] In telling his audience about his own feelings for the priesthood, he establishes a common ground between himself as a priest and the priests present. He also endows the common identity of priesthood with status and prestige. This enhances his own credibility, for in praising the unit he praises himself as member.[98]

Self-revelation normally increases the audience's expectation of intimacy, but the tone established by these statements can indicate an opening toward, or a closing down of meaning. In making statements such as, "I know from listening to many priests," and "I learned as a Bishop to understand firsthand the ministry of priests," John Paul II demonstrates that his knowledge is from his own experience and first-hand information.[99] As Wuthnow noted, frequent "I" statements that tend to make the narrator more intrusive in his own narratives convey an unchallenged authority. The speaker has already found the answers through his own experience and when he observes others problems and confusion he can readily supply them with the answers.[100]

In personal narrative, one unmasks the self before an audience. This unmasking becomes more dramatic when the layers of the mask are thick and weighty. Such is the case for a pope whose role has been formed in a two thousand-year tradition. It is striking when John Paul II occasionally sprinkles his speech with narrative about his life and experiences before his elevation to the papacy. In his speech to the youth in Los Angeles, he refers to early days when he was a young priest. He tells them, "I have spent many hours talking with students on university campuses or while hiking along lakes or in the mountains and hills. I have spent many evenings singing with young men and women like yourselves." This persona of a priest seems very different from the one revealed in his discourse to priests. It is an idyllic scene of relaxation and pleasure, one that is in close harmony with young people and the natural surroundings. In this same speech to the youth, John Paul II continues the narrative, revealing his personal habits as a pontiff by saying, "Even now as Pope, during the summer months, various groups of young people come to Castelgandolfo for an evening and we sing and talk together." John Paul II admits in his address that he seeks out meetings with youth when he travels around the world because he sees hope for the future "in your eyes."[101]

By revealing himself more intimately and more often to young people, Pope John Paul II shows the youth that he respects them and has confidence in them. Young people respond very positively to this special treatment. When parents are too busy and grandparents show disapproval for their lifestyles, the pope as an attentive listener and optimistic supporter strikes a responsive chord. Unlike other members of his generation, John Paul II seems less concerned about instructing young people in the rules and regulations of life. Instead, he exhibits a profound sense of trust in their ability to form the future for the church. He rarely uses a "we" form of address with the youth because he does not seek their agreement on matters of today's church, nor does he use metaphors to help them understand the current church community. Since young people will reconstruct and renew the church, there will be new metaphors and new issues. Identification between the pope and young people is built upon intimacy and love. In his own writings, Pope John Paul II observes that young people often lack direct contact with the heroic traditions that influenced his own generation to struggle for freedom and equality. For that reason, the pope seems to want to supply those romantic traditions that are lacking in the culture surrounding young people. In his opinion, young people *"need guides*, and they want them close at hand. If they turn to authority figures, they do so because they see in them a wealth of human warmth and a willingness to walk with them along the paths they are following."[102]

In revealing himself to his young audiences, John Paul II becomes more of an equal with his audience. Duncan contended that "even the most authoritative social order must have moments of equality," for equality acts "as a counterweight against the power of authority." The singing, the conversational talking, and the hiking with young people are forms of "social play" in which the other becomes an equal as "social distance narrows." These moments of "sociation" are so important to human relationships because in such joy and gaiety "new energy" is given to "our social bonds."[103] When John Paul II talks about his great joy in being a priest, he contends that "Nothing has ever changed it, not even becoming a Pope."[104] Rhetorically, his dismissal of his pontiffness breaks down barriers that may exist because of his high office. He sheds that high office, confiding to his audience his most intimate thoughts. At the same time, he remains a priest. The image he constructs of a priest is not one who is removed from the audience by hierarchical rank within a highly systematized church, but it is an image of a friend, a confidant, a companion with whom the audience can sing, talk, and take hikes.

Managerial Role-Bound Self

Another category of John Paul II's "I" statements addresses implied audiences who need to be assured of a competency in the church. That competency is personified in a leader who is so self-confident that he says how much he knows, and writes, and says. In contrast to the humbling act of expressing thankfulness and the equalizing moments of self-revelation, this set of self-references is designed to appeal to the audience's need for hierarchical distance. First, they convey cognitive affirmation, such as "I know," "I am aware," "I affirm." Employing no expressions of doubt or uncertainty, the rhetor appears sharply differentiated from many in modern society who are unclear and anxious about their lives. He stands above the unsure, closely aligned to an all-knowing sacred cosmos.

In John Paul II's speech to the U.S. bishops, there is frequent use of the "I" to refer to what he has written and said previously in letters, official remarks made at *ad limina* visits, and encyclicals. The talk's dependence on current church documents reveals the institutional resources and processes of governance, and portrays an institution that is severely restricted by written documents and official pronouncements. In a businesslike fashion, the pope uses his managerial persona to report to his bishops what he has said, what he requests them to do, and how he wants them to follow up on points. Unlike the more familiar and affective tone of previous self-references, these tend to signal reliance on rational systems of messages, reports on actions, and outcomes.

With external groups, such as ecumenical meetings, John Paul II is less revealing. Mostly, his use of self-references reminds these religious leaders about his key actions or writings as milestones in their relationship. The use of "I" is not intended to reveal, but to establish credibility for the church and its leadership. At the meeting with world religious leaders in Los Angeles, John Paul II established what his leadership meant to the dialogue by using expressions such as, "throughout my pontificate," and "on my personal visits around the world." At the meeting with ecumenical leadership in Columbia, South Carolina, John Paul II's rhetorical persona is engaged in "this process," "pontificate," "consultation," and "meetings." Despite the pope's contention that collaboration "is not a matter of measured calculation," the "I" statements reveal a systematic approach to managing the contacts with other religions.[105] In these cases, self-revelation does not seem to have the same effect of making the conversation more intimate. The pope is speaking of his personal approval and personal efforts to steer the church's governing systems and mechanisms. The relationships of rhetor to audience become systematized by "meetings" and "collaboration" in which the various parties "struggle and compete with each other under rules."[106] These rules or vocabularies of bureaucratic and organizational structure are "suspect" because they are the language of the highly specialized and fragmented culture of modern society.[107]

After twenty years of a pontificate in which the personal pronoun has appeared regularly in papal speech, the deliberate return to a formalized style of papal "we" serves as a reminder of the pope's rights and privileges as pastor for the universal church. Only in one homily did John Paul II use the papal "we" almost exclusively. This occurred at Dodger Stadium in Los Angeles where almost all of the American bishops, together with hundreds of priests and thousands of Catholic laity, gathered to hear the pope. The speech themes are corporate, not personal, and John Paul II used his formal corporate titles to tell the audience that the church in the United States "is visited today by the Bishop of Rome, the Successor of Peter."[108] Supported by references to church documents, the pope attempts to explain the mysterious universality and unity of the church. Only once during this homily does Pope John Paul II use the personal "I" when he specifically commends the bishops and "those working closely with you" for helping undocumented immigrants to become legal residents. The immigrant issue is extremely immediate and contextual in relation to other points of the homily. Through the use of "I," John Paul II peels off the layers of pontiffness to personally identify with those working on an issue which was not fully supported from within and without the church's ranks. The switching from impersonal, formal style to one that employs self-reference acts to reinforce meaning, sending a signal that the line between the sacred and secular is shifting, and tension develops between the universal and the contextual.

Sacred Invocation

In addressing the sacred other, humans act out their role as inferiors, humbling themselves as they ask for favors. In praying, the pope also takes on the role of an inferior in relation to the Other, but in relation to the audience the personal references of prayer act inversely. The audience is the witness and sometimes the subject of his approach to the sacred. It is not the corporate "we" of the church, that is, pope and people, praying together as inferiors. The prayer, addressed in these personal "I" terms, is a conversation between the sacred and the pope who, as head of the church, makes pleas on behalf of those present. During this personal act of prayer between the sacred and one person, the audience stands outside this conversation, listening to the exchange. Thus, the use of self-references to describe and act out a personal conversation with the sacred increases the distance between rhetor and audience and enhances the mystery of the occasion.[109]

Immediately after the homily in Dodger Stadium, Pope John Paul II uses the "I" form to pray to Mary, the Mother of Jesus. Instead of a corporate "we," so prevalent in the homily, the pontiff vocalized his direct and singular prayer before thousands present and millions viewing. Roderick Hart suggested that increased self-references in presidential speeches may be related to the tendency of American voters to hold their presidents more personally accountable for the government and the nation.[110] Using the same reasoning with regard to John Paul II's use of self-referencing in his prayer for the U.S. Catholic Church, the pope is obligated to show what he personally can and is doing for the U.S. church. He speaks to Mary, the Mother of God, giving her the status of confidant and friend.[111] The audience watches this "courtship," but also senses that the subject of this courtship and dialogue is the audience itself.

As Duncan observed, invocations to the gods are a form of public self-address, in which the speaker pleads a cause with those selected to overhear the dramatic soliloquy. They are statements about "the principle of order which the speaker holds sacred." They can also be evidence that the speaker is struggling "to act under conditions where discrepancies exist between principles and practice in social order."[112] The prayer in this homily at Dodger Stadium is an approach to the holy and the sacred, but it is also a set of objectives or wish list for the U.S. Catholic Church. This repetitive use of "I" closes down meaning, making these petitions the goals of this particular pontiff, John Paul II. His prayer arranges bishops, priests, religious, and laity in their hierarchical order. It speaks of obeying the Commandments and responding to the needs of the poor. It asks that women discover the secret of their femininity and that children be preserved in their innocence. As each group of persons within the church is named in this litany-like prayer, it is the use of "I" as a form of self-reference that conveys specificity, not only to the selection of issues, but also to the audiences named. John Paul II is willing to invest his own person in praying for specific groups and goals within the church.[113] He lets the audience overhear this dialogue with the sacred so that all will recognize themselves in this vision of "the whole church in America."[114]

SUMMARY: FORM SHAPES VOCABULARY

The form of John Paul II's address to his audience shapes the content of his new vocabulary of the sacred. First, compared to other popes, John Paul II structures a more egalitarian relationship between the implied audience and himself. As teacher, he maintains an authoritative posture, and at the same time introduces elements of style that tend to blur the lines between the papacy and the people he addresses. His modes of address demonstrate that he is very cognizant of his audience's need to remain whole, appealing to their contextualized culture and secular civic experience to inform a sacred identity. On the other hand, he often approaches his audience from sacred otherness, asserting defined norms, hierarchically arranged roles, traditional lifestyles, and mystical interpretations of suffering to offer a way for his audience to order their secular lives and give them meaning.

The rhetorical strategy of John Paul II is not static; he adapts his modes of address to his audience according to where he locates them on the sacred-secular continuum. Sometimes his appeals are audience-driven, naming those forms of identity or opposing challenges that conform to his audience's tendencies to favor a more open or closed church. At other times, he examines his audience for deficiencies, calling Native Americans to be more responsible to self, priests to withdraw from secular forms of self-identity, and Jewish leaders to seek dialogue on spiritual as well as temporal issues.

An examination of the differences in John Paul II's choice and frequency of mode of address indicates how these differences create boundary lines between his audiences. The most striking example is the difference between priest and lay audiences. Priests have an ontological connection with the sacred. Their human identity is constructed by and through the sacred, and is not informed by any reference to outer secular challenges. On the other hand, the lay members are immersed in secular activity and bombarded by oppositional forces in order for them to construct sacred meaning.

John Paul II's predominant mode of address involves the construction of a plausible "we" of the church. He follows the traditional papal path by articulating a well-defined authoritative dependence on the sacred norms. On the other hand, he adds to his vocabulary of the sacred a forceful call to inner feelings and emotion. Notwithstanding his respect for individual conscience and freedom, John Paul II entices his audience to move beyond their privatized understanding of intimacy towards a new language of close collective involvement. For larger, mixed audiences at the Eucharistic celebrations, his stirring of a universal intimacy matches the audience's emotional experience as they stand together before him. For those audiences who are tightly drawn as representatives of specific services in the church, John Paul II's terminology of the sacred collectivity tends to support the compartmentalized life of modern society.

In most of his homilies, John Paul II employs strategies of address that help define the collective community in opposition to external forces. This tactic of withdrawing from the world for the sake of saving it is familiar to Americans in both religious fundamentalist preaching and political discourse. Calling on his audiences to be countercultural, he draws borders by naming and denouncing certain worldly ideologies and practices. However, when John Paul II uses terms of social science to describe these threatening human conditions, he distances his audience from these conditions because the impersonal terminologies seem so irrelevant to everyday experience. As a result, the intended boundary lines between what is to be opposed and what is to be embraced are weakened, and therefore, less meaningful.

John Paul II appeals to a wide range of audiences, allowing for broad interpretations, but he also singles out certain audiences for deeper understanding of how the sacred and secular can best be reconciled. Clearly, in his 1987 visit, he favors audiences who are laborers. Because his reconciliation of the sacred-secular tendencies involves continued tension, inversion, and mystical possibilities of communion, he assumes that audiences of popular masses rather than specialized intellectual groups are more likely to accept these interpretations.

John Paul II's forms of address continue the tension between the sacred and the secular. On one hand, the pope addresses his audience by applying normative tradition, striking a familial posture, and drawing a distinctive identity—all indicators of sacred movement. On the other hand, his address is attentive to the self-indicators and contextuality of his secular audiences. He launches in one direction, then turns in the opposite direction. For example, he employs forms of communal intimacy, then characterizes his relationship with his audience in business-like rational terms of an organizational manager. This juxtaposition of symbols and messages encourages ferment at both ends of the accommodation-resistance spectrum. In this sense he attempts to fashion a vocabulary for a new form of religious revival.

There is no question that John Paul II's use of self-references tends to pull aside the curtains that distanced the papacy from the world. These self-references appear in all his speeches, but they are far from overwhelming. During the U.S. visit in 1987, the personal pronoun was used most frequently in his address to priests. However, when compared with U.S. presidential discourse, the ratio of "I" statements to the rest of the speech is very low.[115] Nevertheless, John Paul II's use of self-reference represents a change in papal speech style even though it is rare. Because it is rare, it takes on additional meaning. According to Bellah, audiences are bereft of objective criteria to order their lives. Therefore, they look to the self and its feelings for moral guidance. The papal self-references allow audiences to peek under the protective coverings of the papal office for cues about the self.

NOTES

1. Edwin Black, "The Second Persona," *Quarterly Journal of Speech* (April 1970): 112–113.

2. Gronbeck (1986) uses a similar approach to his close textual analysis of President Reagan's Inaugural Address, in which he examines the first, second, and third-person voices with relationship to the organizational segments of the speech and the subject matter: Bruce E. Gronbeck, "Ronald Reagan's Enactment of the Presidency in His 1981 Inaugural Address," in *Form, Genre, and the Study of Political Discourse*, eds. Herbert W. Simons and Aram A. Aghazarian (Columbia, South Carolina: South Carolina Press, 1986), 232–236.

3. Hugh Dalziel Duncan, *Communication and Social Order* (New York: Bedminster Press, 1962), 290.

4. Kenneth Burke, *Counter-Statement* (Berkeley: University of California Press, 1968), 143.

5. Vatican Council II affirmed the previous Vatican Council I's teaching on the primacy of the pope. However, it also viewed the pope as head of a college of bishops who together lead the church.

6. Bernice Martin, *A Sociology of Contemporary Cultural Change* (New York: St. Martin's Press, 1981), 199–200.

7. Michael Vincent Pearson uses the opening salutation as one of six criteria to classify papal speeches by intended audience: Michael Vincent Pearson, "Audience Adaptation and Argument in John Paul II's American Speeches—October 1979: A Textual Analysis" (Ph.D. dissertation, Temple University, 1987).

8. Similar comparisons are made between encyclicals and the New Testament Epistles in Kathleen Jamieson, "A Rhetorical-Critical Analysis of the Conflict over *Humanae Vitae*" (Ph.D. dissertation, University of Wisconsin, 1972), 50–51.

9. Pope Paul VI's address to the church members at Yankee Stadium in New York referred to "brothers and sons" in Bill Adler, *Pope Paul in the United States* (New York: Hawthorn Books, 1965), 93. This same phrasing is discussed in relation to Paul VI's encyclical writing. See Jamieson, "A Rhetorical-Critical Analysis," 54.

10. Pearson, "Audience Adaptation," 49.

11. John Paul II, "Meeting with Black Catholic Leadership," no. 1, in *The Pope Speaks to the American Church: John Paul II's Homilies, Speeches, and Letters to Catholics in the United States* (New York: HarperCollins, 1992), 171. Material quoted from John Paul II's speeches is referenced by the numerical sections of the speeches. Hereafter, speeches from the 1987 visit to the U.S. will be noted by the title of the speech and numerical section.

12. Robert N. Bellah, Richard Madsen, William M. Sullivan, Ann Swidler, and Steven M. Tipton, *Habits of the Heart* (Berkeley: University of

California, 1985; reprint New York: Perennial Library, Harper and Row, 1986), 43–44.

13. Duncan, *Communication and Social Order*, 292, 298–299.

14. John Paul II, "Homily at Westover Hills," no. 1; "Homily at Tamiami Park," no. 2, 6; "Homily at New Orleans Mass," no. 5; in *The Pope Speaks*, 150, 153, 192, 200.

15. John Paul II, "Homily at Tamiami Park," no. 2; "Homily at New Orleans," no. 5; "Homily in the Silverdome," no. 1; "Meeting with Members of the Laity," no. 2; "Homily at New Orleans Mass," no. 5; "Homily at Laguna Seca," no. 1; in *The Pope Speaks*, 150, 192, 296, 316, 354.

16. John Paul II, "Homily at Tamiami Park," no. 2, in *The Pope Speaks*, 151.

17. John Paul II, "Homily at Candlestick Park," no. 5, in *The Pope Speaks*, 323.

18. John Paul II, "Homily at Laguna Seca," no. 9; "Homily at Westover Hills," no. 8; in *The Pope Speaks*, 205, 301.

19. John Paul II, "Homily at New Orleans," no. 5, in *The Pope Speaks*, 192.

20. Robert Wuthnow, *The Struggle for America's Soul* (Grand Rapids, Michigan: William B. Eerdmans, 1989), 31–36.

21. John Paul II, "Act of Entrusting to the Blessed Virgin Mary," nos. 1–3, in *The Pope Speaks*, 294–296.

22. John Paul II, "Homily at Laguna Seca," nos. 5–7, in *The Pope Speaks*, 299–301.

23. John Paul II, "Homily at Tamiami Park," no. 6, in *The Pope Speaks*, 153.

24. John Paul II, "Homily at Arizona State University," no. 8, in *The Pope Speaks*, 247.

25. John Paul II, "Meeting with Priests," nos. 1–2; "Meeting with Members of Laity," nos. 2, 7; "Address at Youth Teleconference," no. 3, in *The Pope Speaks*, 135–136, 253, 316, 319.

26. Richard P. McBrien, "The Hard-Line Pontiff," *Notre Dame Magazine* (Spring 1987): 27–29.

27. John Paul II, "Homily in Los Angeles Coliseum," nos. 4–5, in *The Pope Speaks*, 262–263.

28. Ibid., no. 5, 263.

29. The thirteen events include meetings with: priests, Jewish leadership, ecumenical leaders, Catholic educators, leaders of Catholic higher education, Black Catholics, young people, Native Americans, the bishops, non-Christian religious leaders, men and women religious, laity, and permanent deacons and their wives. In addition, following diplomatic tradition, President Ronald Reagan, as head of state, delivered a speech of welcome to John Paul II, as visiting head of state, to which the pope responded.

30. Frank J. McNulty, "Presentation by Reverend Frank J. McNulty," in John Paul II, *Unity in the Work of Service* (Washington, D.C.: U.S. Catholic Conference, 1987), 7.

31. John Paul II, "Meeting with Priests," no. 1, in *The Pope Speaks*, 135.

32. Frank J. McNulty, "Presentation by McNulty," in John Paul II, *Unity*, 7–8.

33. John Paul II, "Meeting with Priests," no. 1, in *The Pope Speaks*, 135.

34. The pope's speech contains sixty-three references to a sacred other, whereas McNulty's speech only refers to the sacred sixteen times.

35. John Paul II, "Meeting with Priests," nos. 1, 6, in *The Pope Speaks*, 135, 140.

36. McNulty, "Presentation by McNulty," in John Paul II, *Unity*, 9; John Paul II, "Meeting with Priests," no. 5, in *The Pope Speaks*, 139.

37. John Paul II, "Meeting with Priests," no. 4, in *The Pope Speaks*, 138.

38. Kenneth Burke, *A Rhetoric of Motives* (New York: Prentice-Hall, 1950), 45.

39. Duncan, *Communication and Social Order*, 285.

40. Duane Champagne, ed., *The Native North American Almanac* (Washington, D.C.: Gale Research, 1994), 680; Edward H. Spicer, *The Cycles of Conquest* (Tucson: University of Arizona Press, 1962), 504–516.

41. Alfretta M. Antone, "Presentation by Antone," in John Paul II, *Unity*, 107; John Paul II, "Meeting with Native Americans," nos. 2, 6, in *The Pope Speaks*, 239, 242.

42. Mordecai Waxman, "Presentation by Waxman," in John Paul II, *Unity*, 22–25.

43. John Paul II, "Meeting with Jewish Leadership," nos. 1, 4, 5, in *The Pope Speaks*, 145, 147.

44. John Paul II, "Meeting with Jewish Leadership," no. 1, in *The Pope Speaks*, 145.

45. Leon Klenicki and Richard John Neuhaus, *Believing Today: Jew and Christian in Conversation* (Grand Rapids, Michigan: William B. Eerdmans Publishing Company, 1989), 38–39.

46. Donna Hanson, "Presentation by Hanson," in John Paul II, *Unity*, 201.

47. John Paul II, "Meeting with Members of the Laity," nos. 2, 5, in *The Pope Speaks*, 316, 318.

48. Burke, *A Rhetoric of Motives*, 115; Duncan, *Communication and Social Order*, 117.

49. Vatican Council II documents are now accepted as established church tradition. This was not the case in the United States immediately after the Council. It required a combination of rhetorical strategies by the U.S. bishops. See Carol J. Jablonski, "Promoting Radical Change in the Roman Catholic Church: Rhetorical Requirements, Problems, and Strategies of the American Bishops," *Central States Speech Journal* 31 (1980): 282–289.

50. For other studies of the rhetorical use of the corporate "we," see George Cheney, "The Rhetoric of Identification and the Study of Organizational Communication," *Quarterly Journal of Speech* 69 (1983): 143–158; and W.J.M. MacKenzie, *Political Identity* (New York: St. Martin's Press, 1978).

51. Avery Dulles, *The Reshaping of Catholicism: Current Challenges in the Theology of Church* (San Francisco: Harper and Row, 1988), 112–116.

52. John Paul II, *Crossing the Threshold of Hope* (New York: Alfred A. Knopf, 1994), 190.

53. Bellah et al., *Habits of the Heart*, 167.

54. John Paul II, "Homily at New Orleans," no. 1; "Homily at Westover Hills," no. 4; "Homily at Candlestick Park," no. 6; in *The Pope Speaks*, 189, 201, 324.

55. John Paul II, "Homily at Los Angeles Coliseum," no. 7, in *The Pope Speaks*, 264.

56. John Paul II, "Homily at Tamiami Park," no. 8, in *The Pope Speaks*, 154.

57. Marsha G. Witten, *All Is Forgiven: The Secular Message in American Protestantism* (Princeton, New Jersey: Princeton University Press, 1993), 37.

58. John Paul II, "Homily at Westover Hills," nos. 7, 9; "Homily at Los Angeles Coliseum," no. 5; in *The Pope Speaks*, 204, 205, 263.

59. Avery Dulles, *Models of the Church* (New York: Doubleday, 1987), 59.

60. Fox Television news coverage, Eucharistic celebration at Meadowlands, New Jersey, 5 October 1995.

61. Duncan, *Communication and Social Order*, 159, 295–296.

62. A "we" or a "they" is a "given terminology" which is a "reflection of reality" and "by its very nature . . . it must be a selection of reality; and to this extent it must function also as a deflection of reality." Kenneth Burke, "Language as Action: Terministic Screens," in Kenneth Burke, *On Symbols and Society*, ed. Joseph R. Gusfield (Chicago: University of Chicago Press, 1989), 115.

63. Janice Peck, *The Gods of Televangelism* (Cresskill, New Jersey: Hampton Press, 1993), 185.

64. John Paul II, "Homily at Tamiami Park," no. 5, in *The Pope Speaks*, 152.

65. Luigi Accattoli, "Un pontificato missionario," in *Wojtyla: Il nuovo Mosè* by Domenico Del Rio and Luigi Accattoli (Milan: Arnoldo Mondadori Editore, 1988), 111–112.

66. John Paul II, "Homily at New Orleans," no. 5; "Homily at Tamiami Park," no. 7; in *The Pope Speaks*, 193, 154.

67. John Paul II, "Homily at Laguna Seca," no. 2, in *The Pope Speaks*, 297.

68. See Kurt Ritter and David Henry, *Ronald Reagan: The Great Communicator* (Westport, Connecticut: Greenwood Press, 1992); and Kurt Ritter, "American Political Rhetoric and the Jeremiad Tradition: Presidential Nomination Acceptance Addresses, 1960–1976," *Central States Speech Journal* 31 (1980): 155–171.

69. Richard P. McBrien, *Catholicism*, vol. 1 (Minneapolis: Winston Press, 1980), 220–228.

70. John Paul II, "Homily at Westover Hills," no. 6, in *The Pope Speaks*, 202–203.

71. John Paul II, "Homily in Los Angeles Coliseum," no. 4, in *The Pope Speaks*, 262.

72. John Paul II, "Homily at Laguna Seca," no. 2; "Homily at Westover Hills," no. 6, in *The Pope Speaks*, 202, 297.

73. John Paul II, "Meeting with Members of the Laity," no. 7, in *The Pope Speaks*, 319.

74. Joseph R. Gusfield, "Bridge Over Separated Lands: Kenneth Burke's Significance for the Study of Social Action," in *The Legacy of Kenneth Burke*, eds. Herbert W. Simons and Trevor Melia (Madison, Wisconsin: University of Wisconsin Press, 1989), 38.

75. John Paul II, "Meeting with Members of the Laity," no. 7, in *The Pope Speaks*, 319.

76. John Paul II, "Homily in the Silverdome," no. 7; "Homily at Laguna Seca," no. 7; in *The Pope Speaks*, 300, 357–358.

77. John Paul II, "Homily at Laguna Seca," no. 7; "Homily in the Silverdome," no. 6; in *The Pope Speaks*, 301, 357.

78. John Paul II, "Meeting with Priests," no. 1, in *The Pope Speaks*, 135.

79. John Paul II, "Meeting with Ecumenical Leadership," nos. 2–5, in *The Pope Speaks*, 159–162.

80. John Paul II, "Meeting with Jewish Leadership," no. 3, in *The Pope Speaks*, 146.

81. Hugh Morley, *The Pope and the Press* (Notre Dame, Indiana: University of Notre Dame Press, 1968), 29.

82. Peter Berger, *The Sacred Canopy: Elements of a Sociological Theory of Religion* (Garden City, New York: Doubleday, 1969), 150.

83. Kenneth Burke, *A Rhetoric of Motives*, 115.

84. Robert Wuthnow, *Rediscovering the Sacred* (Grand Rapids, Michigan: William B. Eerdmans, 1992), 80–81.

85. Duncan, *Communication and Social Order*, 289–290, 326–331, 345.

86. Ibid., 328–329.

87. John Paul II, "Meeting with Priests," no. 1, in *The Pope Speaks*, 135.

88. Monsignor Robert N. Lynch, general secretary of NCCB (now bishop of St. Petersburg, Florida), interview with author, 28 August 1992, Washington, D.C.

89. Burke, *A Rhetoric of Motives*, 208.

90. Patrick Granfield, *Limits of the Papacy* (New York: Crossroad, 1987), 77–106.

91. Vatican Council II, *Lumen Gentium*, in *Vatican Council II: The Conciliar and Post Conciliar Documents*, ed. Austin Flannery (Wilmington, Delaware: Scholarly Resources, 1975), no. 22.

92. John Paul II, "Meeting with the American Bishops," nos. 1, 4, in *The Pope Speaks*, 266, 269.

93. Kathleen Jamieson, *Eloquence in an Electronic Age* (New York: Oxford University Press, 1988), 182.

94. Duncan, *Communication and Social Order*, 340.

95. John Paul II, "Meeting with the American Bishops," nos. 5, 7, 15, in *The Pope Speaks*, 270, 272, 280.

96. Ibid., nos. 6, 11, 17; in *The Pope Speaks*, 271, 274, 281.

97. John Paul II, "Meeting with Priests," no. 1, in *The Pope Speaks*, 135.

98. George Cheney, "The Rhetoric of Identification and the Study of Organizational Communication," *Quarterly Journal of Speech* (May 1983): 146.

99. John Paul II, "Meeting with Priests," no. 3, in *The Pope Speaks*, 137.

100. Wuthnow, *Rediscovering the Sacred*, 77.

101. John Paul II, "Address During a Youth Teleconference," no. 1, in *The Pope Speaks*, 251–252.

102. John Paul II, *Crossing the Threshold of Hope*, 121.

103. Duncan, *Communication and Social Order*, 337–338.

104. John Paul II, "Address During a Youth Teleconference," no. 4, in *The Pope Speaks*, 253.

105. John Paul II, "Meeting with Interreligious Leaders," no. 2; "Meeting with Jewish Leadership," nos. 3–4; "Meeting with Ecumenical Leadership," no. 5; in *The Pope Speaks*, 146–147, 162, 285.

106. Duncan, *Communication and Social Order*, 343.

107. Bernice Martin, *A Sociology of Contemporary Cultural Change*, 17.

108. John Paul II, "Homily at Dodger Stadium," no. 2, in *The Pope Speaks*, 288.

109. Burke, *A Rhetoric of Motives*, 115.

110. Roderick P. Hart, *Verbal Style and the Presidency* (Orlando, Florida: Academic Press, 1984), 48.

111. Duncan, *Communication and Social Order*, 292.

112. Ibid.

113. Hart, *Verbal Style*, 16.

114. John Paul II, "Act of Entrusting to the Blessed Virgin Mary," no. 3, in *The Pope Speaks*, 296.

115. Comparing the pope's discourses to the three hierarchical groupings in the church's membership—bishops, priests, laity—the pope uses "I" expressions more frequently in his speech to the priests. However, in his speech to the priests, John Paul II's "I" statements are five times less frequent than

those in U.S. presidential discourses. In shorter speeches, such as his speech to the ecumenical leadership, "I" statements are between two and three times less frequent than U.S. presidents. The only occasions where "I" statement frequency approached that of U.S. presidents are in the arrival and departure ceremonies. These speeches are heavily influenced by diplomatic protocol and the role of the pontiff as head of state. See Roderick P. Hart, *Modern Rhetorical Criticism* (Glenview, Illinois: Scott Foresman, 1990), 300.

CHAPTER 6

Textual Analysis: Symbol Choice

METAPHORIC CLUSTERS

Roderick Hart characterizes rhetorical imagery by movement. Persuasion aims to move auditors to agreement. Imagery, particularly metaphoric imagery, moves meaning from the literal to a range of relational possibilities.[1] Rhetorical critics have discovered how metaphorical concepts which relate one kind of thing in terms of another in an audience's experience can form a coherent system, structuring meaning toward that one relational concept.[2] The predominant metaphor can narrow vision and reduce options.[3] At the same time, metaphoric concepts are never totally structured, only partially structured, because one concept can never be the other, only understood in terms of the other.

Metaphors have a special function in religious meaning. The sacred other can never be completely and literally described by terms of actual human experience. Nevertheless, humans construct images of God by describing the sacred in terms of another human experience. Metaphorical language attempts to make the complex and indiscernible more simple, more concrete, channeling the meaning in a certain direction. However, the channeling can never be complete because the term used to describe the other is never literally equal to the other. Humanly constructed images of the divine are also incomplete or "broken" because there will always remain a blockage between the sacred and human conceptions of it. Moreover, the infinite cannot be limited to one particular form.[4] A religious metaphor attempts to describe the sacred from one human framework, but it is not enough. Hence, other metaphors are constructed to describe meaning, and even the original metaphor itself is reinterpreted.

Because Christian theology has used and reused certain metaphors, there is a rich tradition of their interpretation. To favor one model over another can relate to its applicability at the time. When images are imprinted and held behind church boundaries, they become reified over time and need to be changed.[5] Because Christian metaphoric language carries with it an extensive historical tradition, the change or reinterpretation is prevented from straying too far from the relational concept. On the other hand, examining a specific metaphorical concept's use is a study of "gloss upon gloss, use and reuse of the figures which comprise an interweaving of meanings so complex that the possible readings are never exhausted."[6] The study of religious metaphoric language has also revealed both closed and open tendencies. Wuthnow discussed Frye's assertion that metaphor opens up multiple layers of meaning, thereby generating a centrifugal force that exposes the sacred text to larger interpretations. Often these interpretations are initiated by a desire to relate them to current worldly experience. Metaphor can also be restricted to more literal and narrow interpretation that refrains from questioning the words and meaning.[7]

The rhetorical critic searches for clusters of metaphors that are predominate in discourse, thereby revealing more precisely the rhetor's choice of motives that are considered by the speaker to be "salient in society at a given time."[8] As demonstrated in rhetorical studies, the predominance of certain metaphors and images and the recurrent patterns of adaptations over time can indicate the changing relationships between rhetor and audience.[9]

Frye makes the point that the Bible is written in "the literary language of myth and metaphor" and religious " 'truth' can be reached only by passing through myth and metaphor."[10] Because so much of Christian preaching is based on the scriptural texts, certain images and metaphors become part of sermonic tradition. This is not to say that Christian preaching is necessarily rich in metaphoric language. Especially during the modernist period in Protestantism, preaching tended to stray from the scriptures and focus on current problems. A topical approach to preaching was popular even in Catholic circles. The reforms of Vatican Council II returned the Catholic Church to the more expository style of preaching, prescribing that sermons during Eucharistic celebrations should be based on the scriptural readings of the day.

Imagery and metaphoric style can vary, even when dealing with the metaphoric imagery of the Bible. Religious discourse, in its attempt to make sense out of the metaphoric language of scriptures, can aim to demystify, using factual and nonambiguous language of rational science. Religious preaching can also aim to intensify mystery through rich imagery that evokes the sensual and emotional motives of the audience. The degree to which Christian preaching is "hot" or "cold" (emotional or rational) can indicate where the preacher intends to position the audience with relation to the self and the world.[11]

Metaphors for the Church

Time, nearly two thousand years of Christianity, has layered scriptural metaphors with meaning. Audience familiarity with images and metaphors of the Bible are part of the meaning structures of the differing forms of Christian belief. For Catholics, metaphoric symbols have been a part of their understanding of the church itself and its relationship to the world. Avery Dulles pointed out that throughout centuries of Catholic tradition, theologians and scholars have studied and meditated on the numerous biblical images used to describe the church. These images are such an integral part of the Catholic tradition that "it is difficult to draw the line between proper and metaphorical usage."[12] The metaphors become something more than metaphors. This point can be seen in the use of two current and widely accepted images of the church: the Body of Christ and the People of God. The Body of Christ became a dominant metaphoric image in the early twentieth century. Pope Pius XII defined the church as the "Mystical Body of Christ." By the time Pope John XXIII called for a Vatican Council II, the "mystical" modifier had been dropped in favor of a simpler and more concrete image of the church as a body. Even though both the People of God and Body of Christ are strong models of community, the Body of Christ metaphor bases communion on an organic structure that has both visible and invisible elements that bind it together. It has also been used to describe the "institutional" church as a living body of members, with its head that forms one unified church. Although it is one of the two dominant paradigms in Vatican Council II, the Body metaphor is clearly linked to traditional concepts of filial and hierarchical relationships in the church. On the other hand, the People of God metaphor is a symbol of the change and renewal of the Vatican Council II era. Its focus is on "the people," a more democratic concept than body. As Dulles noted, the People of God model allows for greater distance between the church and the sacred. Not linked organically to the sacred, the church is composed of people who have individual freedom to choose to be both holy and sinful.[13] Both metaphors are communion models, and therefore they have sacred unifying characteristics, but the People of God allows for the possibility of movement away from the sacred.

John Paul II used these two metaphors consistently throughout his discourses during the 1987 visit to the United States. In fact, he rarely uses one without the other. The Body metaphor appeals to those church members who hold fast to the traditions and stability of hierarchical and organic relationships. The People metaphor appeals to those who wish to emphasize the inclusiveness and equality of the membership. In balancing these metaphors consistently, the pope continues the policy established by Vatican Council II of recognizing both views as legitimate ways of characterizing the church. If he emphasizes one over the other, it may signal that the pope favors either a complete restoration of the older tradition, or a total embrace of the newer model. This normally does not happen. In rare instances, when one metaphor is predominant, it appears to be an attempt to tailor meaning to the audience. For example, in Monterey, Pope John Paul II opens with the People of God model. He never uses the Body metaphor, but speaks of human activity in building the "reign" and "kingdom" of God.[14] The emphasis is on the human activity that discovers God's permeating presence and builds solidarity through noble work with others. God is present in creation and in the hearts of humans, but without the Body metaphor, the principle that bind humans to the Other and to each other is no longer as substantial and organically permanent. In fact, the speech focuses on the human element and responsibility of solidarity, an effort that without constant toil and effort can easily go awry.

There is good reason for John Paul II to concentrate on the People of God model for the Monterey audience. As part of the planned effort to appeal to all corners of the church populace, this site was chosen to reach those in the farming community. Although the church extended the invitation to both farm owners and workers, workers from the farms of the region were expected to comprise the majority of the audience. The pope's choices of symbols are aimed not only at these workers, but at those priests, religious, and laity who have aligned themselves with the causes of farm workers, supporting their rights, including their efforts to unionize the work force. It is a popular, anti-establishment cause, built upon freedoms of assembly and speech, and totally involved in the contemporary world. Choosing the People metaphor over the Body metaphor points the church outward to the world of those who serve farm workers, signaling to them that the pope supports not only their efforts but also their preference for a more updated definition of church.

The use of these two models of the church are also tailored to the messages within the speech. For example, in his address to the laity in San Francisco, Pope John Paul II uses the Body metaphor, as does the Vatican Council II documents on the church, to distinguish between priestly and lay roles. There are different functions, but all share equally in building up the same body. Lay members join in "collaboration and consultation" with the head of their local churches.[15] The Body metaphor allows discussion of a head and specific parts of the body that function on different levels and, at the same time, the differences do not interfere with the corporal and unifying principle. However, when the pope turns to discussing the laity's role to "become leaven, salt, and light" for the world, he switches to the people model. The stabilizing image of the Body no longer protects the laity as they face the "new challenges and new temptations." As "People of God" the laity are told not to "impose religious beliefs on others," but to defend the "most fundamental human rights and spiritual aspirations of every person" and "for the benefit of all people."[16] The People model allows for an open inclusive effort in constructing meaning.

In Pope John Paul II's talks to the youth in the United States, the Body model is absent, and the people image prevails. The Body image seems irrelevant to youth because they have been raised in a post–Vatican II era. In an age of fluid, interactive, electronic communication, the static, organic image of the church is part of the past. However, when the pope uses the People image with young people, he adds a unifying element that is familial. The individuals that make up the People of God are not "unrelated," but rather sons and daughters, brothers and sisters.[17] Youthful bonds to their parents and other family members have not yet been severed, and relation by blood, while not always comfortable, still makes sense.

Because the Body and People metaphors are intended to teach about the complexities of the church, the metaphor itself is sometimes not enough. A preacher often uses metaphoric extensions not only to extend the time needed to comprehend the complexity, but to control meaning by disciplining the interpretations of the audience. As Osborn and Ehninger note, these extensions serve "to make of the metaphor itself an argument in its own behalf."[18] For example, in his homily at Dodger Stadium in Los Angeles, John Paul II extends both the Body and People metaphors. Dodger Stadium was the central church event of the trip. As previously explained, it was the event to which all the

U.S. bishops were invited, along with representative priests and laity of the region. Because the dominant theme of the talk is the church and unity, it is not surprising that the pope takes the time to argue the two prevalent metaphors for the church, and to direct and control their meaning. As Jamieson noted, the Body metaphor inevitably leads to "diagnoses and prognoses" of its health.[19] For John Paul II, the church "has grown and *continues to grow.*" His emphasis is on continuity. There is no indication that the church has faltered, or will falter in the future. Growth is evaluated not only in localities and numbers, but in the ability of the church to "unfold and bear fruit" in "many places of the world" and among "many peoples and nations."[20]

The People metaphor leads to questions about the identification of these people and the diversity or commonness of the populace. In his homily at Dodger Stadium, John Paul II breaks down the boundary lines of the People of God and opens the church to "embrace" the "widest and richest variety." Not only is the church, or People of God, identified by their ethnic and national heritage, but Christ has multiple identities. He is "Anglo" and "Hispanic" and "Native American." The People of God from "all times and all places" have come together in an "awesome movement." The prognosis is optimistic, for the movement will reach its goal of "a *new unity* of humanity." As with a political movement, unity depends on the articulation of purposeful and reachable goals. In this case, the goal is not a far-off kingdom, but a new unity of humanity. The unifying factor of this movement of people, expressed as intimacy and communion between persons, is "animated" with a force or power derived from the sacred. Even though John Paul II consistently uses the People of God model to underscore "a diversity of human persons, of individuals," he modifies the centrifugal tendencies of the People metaphor by relying on symbols of intimacy and "communion" to direct these diverse individuals back toward unity and the sacred.[21]

In his speeches during the 1987 U.S. visit, John Paul II balances his use of the People and the Body metaphors. In the Dodger Stadium speech, John Paul II mixes and joins these two metaphors for the church. After describing the ethnic diversity of peoples and cultures, he adds that the church "with all her different members, remains the one Body of Christ." He explains the Vatican Council II's "teaching on the People of God" by reminding the audience that "People is at the same time the Body of Christ." Again, there is a concentrated effort to underscore continuity. The Body is "another image" and "another dimension" of unity. He attempts to resolve the differences of these two images of the church, which also represent the two tendencies in the church. In the end, the two metaphors are joined because they explain the same truth about unity, and that unity "does not come from us, but *from God*."[22] The pope uses human explanation in the form of metaphoric extension to resolve the two metaphors representing the opening and closing tendencies of the church. However, human analysis itself is open to interpretation. Ultimately, John Paul II reaches to the centripetal end of the normative dialectic by defining the unifying force as a norm from the sacred, thus legitimating his resolution of the opening-closing tendencies within the church.

Although both metaphors proceed from human experience to explain about the sacred, the People metaphor is grounded more in the secular experience of today's world. The Body metaphor is rooted in a long church tradition and has more sacred leanings. John Paul is obviously attempting to resolve the differences of the two perspectives within the church, but his use of the Body and People metaphors sometimes reinforces those tendencies. As in the Dodger Stadium homily, he uses the "whole Body" image in describing the relationship of the "Successor of Saint Peter" to the "local bishops" and the People model when talking about inculturation and evangelization.[23] In his meeting with bishops, the pope employs the body metaphor to underscore the organic and "vertical" dimension that explains the union of the universal with the particular churches. He uses the People metaphor to describe the church's pastoral efforts and witness of God's love in the world.[24] The two metaphors still move in different directions: in one, the sacred informs the secular; in the other, the secular informs the sacred. John Paul II needs to keep both tendencies within the church, and therefore he adjusts the appeal of his symbolic vocabulary accordingly.

Gift Metaphor: Centripetal Force with Centrifugal Undertones

A predominant metaphor in Pope John Paul II's discourse is that of gift giving and receiving,[25] a popular Christian theme which has many variations. Janice Peck described one variation used by televangelists as the "health and wealth gospel—or giving to get" in which "investments" in the Lord produce material and monetary returns.[26] The televangelist focus is pointed toward human action and the reciprocity of the reward. John Paul II's use of gift imagery has an opposite progression. Gift giving is a sacred activity. Because humans receive the gift, they become "debtors" and assume heavy responsibilities for appreciating, caring for, and sharing the gift. In fact, John Paul II's use of the gift metaphor constantly strikes out at the modern world's preoccupation with human achievement, "affluence and pleasure." The gift reestablishes the "proportion" that those in modern times have forgotten by underscoring the lavish, wonderful, and "undeserved generosity" bestowed on a human receiver.[27] John Paul II's gift metaphor contributes to the "tremendum" quality of the sacred and holy by keeping the audience awestruck by the greatness and all inclusiveness of God's gifts.[28]

For John Paul II, the U.S. audience is too proud of its human achievements. Modern Americans measure success by money and have lost an understanding of other measures of achievement. By describing the overwhelming proportion of God's gift, the pope is appealing to American understanding of greatness. However, John Paul II feels compelled to deflate American's pride and reminds Americans that they are "debtors" because "all that is in and around you," even "your existence," comes as a gift from God. The problem with the metaphoric theme is that the pope, having constructed barriers between humans and the sacred, cannot leave his audience separated, alone, and frustrated with their human inadequacies. Thus, he proposes a solution to the problem by suggesting that, even though we cannot possibly "repay a gift adequately," all gift receivers "must respond with a gift." And the only way is to empty oneself through a kind of love that "aims at imitating" the sacred act of giving.[29]

The pope's use of the gift metaphor rhetorically builds walls and chasms between two entities. Once the audience recognizes the barriers between the "debtor" humans and the awesome sacred giver, John Paul II proposes a solution. Ordinary everyday human activity cannot break down these barriers. The acquisitive, rational actions of human everyday life do not suffice. Instead, the pope calls for extraordinary action: total self-giving. Holiness is, therefore, not found in receiving and enjoying the abundance of God's gifts, but rather in giving up human claims to these gifts. Holiness is located in a sacred other, and the other can only be reached by employing extraordinary, and sacred imitating means.

In using the gift metaphor, John Paul II emphasizes the many and diverse gifts given freely by God to humans. He frequently refers to the variety or "flowering" of gifts that individuals must use for the whole community.[30] Before Vatican Council II, Catholics were familiar with the expression "the gift of faith." They learned about this gift of a one, true, and Catholic faith from the church in which the content of this faith had been permanently "deposited." The gift had a singular, objective, and static quality. After Vatican Council II, Catholic theologians spoke about faith as a living, ongoing process. The accent was placed on "personal freedom, inner appropriation, and active participation."[31] The way John Paul II uses the gift metaphor is consistent with these Council trends. Exchanging gifts creates meaning that is participatory in an ongoing relationship with God and the world. Gifts, given in a sign of intimacy and friendship, reflect personal conversations between those who give gifts. In a 1981 interview with André Frossard, John Paul II explained the definition of faith as "gift" by quoting the Council document, *Dei verbum*, "God . . . speaks to men as friends, and is conversant with them." The pope expanded on this description of God's gift as "a person-to-person gift," "a perfectly gratuitous free gift," and man's response, in giving of oneself is "the profoundest and most personal structure of faith."[32]

Clearly, John Paul II's use of the gift metaphor appeals to those in the church who support more "mystical" interpretations of one's relationship with the sacred. The gift metaphor is more sacred centered than incarnational. On the other hand, it is not devoid of incarnational elements, and it appeals to those who want to de-emphasize the external norms of the church and focus more on the interior, personal relationship between free, individual beings. On the surface, the gift metaphor appears as a centripetal force defining all in relationship to the sacred. However, for those church members who are apt to interpret signs in terms of pre– and post–Vatican Council II, the gift metaphor has centrifugal appeal.

Nevertheless, there are aspects even of this "personal and participatory" characterization of the gift metaphor which pose problems for some members of the church. For John Paul II, the ideal human response to God's gift is self-emptying. As Bellah et al. pointed out, Americans fear losing themselves in love. Because of the therapeutic emphasis on self-assertiveness, one's inner feelings and deeply personal views can be shared, but not to the point where one loses a sense of who one is. A person must assert one's individuality at all times.[33] The "old Catholic thinking—being a selfless person" interferes with developing a consciousness of one's self-interest.[34] Those who work as professional activists to "empower" the poor and the oppressed are suspicious that this self-effacing mentality functions socially to maintain the status quo. In adjusting to his audience, John Paul II does not speak of self-giving in his homily in Monterey where the audience contains farm workers and activists in the farm worker movement.

The strongest use of the gift metaphor as a self-giving, self-emptying response to God occurs in John Paul II's homily in Phoenix, where the trip planned to emphasize the health care efforts of the church. According to Bellah et al., those who are actively engaged in caring and being cared for are more likely to give of themselves for the sake of the community.[35] Nurses, counselors, social workers present in the Phoenix audience see themselves as "caring" professionals who work long hours, experience stress, generally receive inadequate pay, but who nevertheless are satisfied by having given of themselves to help and care for others. In this sense, they understand the pope's use of the gift metaphor.

Orientation toward the Millennium

Lakoff and Johnson used the term "orientational metaphor" to call attention to a type of metaphor that "organizes a whole system of concepts with respect to one another."[36] In John Paul II's rhetoric, two major orientational metaphors are apparent. The first is the forward moving, optimistic direction of the future. This "journey" and "movement" through time is characterized by "growth" and "building up" "from one generation to the next." There is a sense of a constantly bigger and better future ahead. The movement toward the future is unbroken and contains the breadth of a historical presence through time. Indeed, John Paul's use of a progressive futuristic theme is consonant with the symbolic worlds constructed by American culture. Throughout his speeches he uses contextual examples to praise the audience for its past "growth" and success, fully expecting that there will be these same opportunities in the future.[37] When the pope recalls for the audience the observable growth and successes of the church and projects a future based on the audience's current experience, this orientation, being set contextually, works centrifugally, opening the church to the local experience, and relying upon prior human experience for confirmation of its direction.

To mark the future, the pope sets a very precise time goal: the third millennium of Christianity. A few months after he was elected pope, John Paul II issued his first encyclical, *Redemptor Hominis*, in which he situated the beginning of his papacy at a moment "already very close to the year 2000."[38] In his speeches, his use of millennium has very clear apocalyptic overtones when he warns his American audience "on the eve of the third millennium of the Christian era, a part of the human family . . . is being specially tempted."[39] Scholars have noted that the persuasive appeal of apocalypticism increases during periods of crisis. Early Christians, faced with suffering and persecution, were often sustained by their belief in Christ's imminent second coming. During the Middle Ages and the Reformation, this belief, known as millenarianism because of adherents' conviction that Christ will establish an earthly kingdom lasting one thousand years, became popular among those populations most affected by social crises such as urban unemployment and rural poverty. At the last turn of the millennium, many Christians prepared anxiously for Christ's glorious reign to begin with the coming of the year 1000.[40]

Audiences tend to accept the apocalyptic visions of the rhetor when large numbers of them share a discontent with their present and an uneasiness about facing an uncertain future.[41] The pope articulates this uneasiness about a society where "God is forgotten."[42] According to Mixon and Hopkins, apocalyptic discourse is effective when audiences are ready to become "willing participants in the apocalyptic transaction."[43] This requires not only that the speaker use language to describe the anomie of the present and the vision of a millennium which replaces the crisis of the status quo, but that the audience share the view of the crisis and be ready to accept the speaker's view of the future. John Paul II's strongest apocalyptic language is used in discourses to church members. He expects that those members active in church ministries will agree that the church is facing increased competition from secularist ideologies. In the euphoria of the post–Vatican Council II era, there were high expectations that a flourishing church, renewed and open to the world, would be able to make significant inroads in transforming the world. The U.S. church believed that it could play a leading role in that worldwide effort because it had already worked out its model within a pluralistic political and cultural tradition. By 1980, those expectations had been scaled back and, in some sectors of the church, abandoned. The reasons for this loss of momentum differ depending on which side of the opening-closing continuum one favors, but most agree that there was a crisis of confidence within the American church. The church needed confidence-building and John Paul II's rhetoric aimed to help them identify the cause of their distress.

The nearness of the coming millennium is in itself a moment out of ordinary time. It is an opportunity for the pope to employ this extraordinary moment to articulate the "every time" nature of the church. The church's destiny is "of all ages," extending from one millennium to another.[44] The millennium as a measurement of time remains a mystery to American audiences whose understanding of history rarely extends beyond two to three hundred years. On the other hand, Americans are fascinated by John Paul II's use of the next millennium as a time to re-

call the Christian vision of a new age and a reassuring future for all who
"ask to walk in the paths of the living God."[45] The impending millennium becomes a mythic symbol, infusing the present with a future that
promises a utopia.

When John Paul II issues a rallying call for the church to "walk 'the
royal road' " on a pilgrimage toward a "vision" of glory and faith to the
"holy city," his words suggest strategies that have long been used in the
church by other popes.[46] For example, it became papal practice to proclaim a "holy year" every twenty-five years. During these "Jubilee"
years, Catholics made pilgrimages to holy shrines, and especially to
Rome where they received special blessings for their efforts. After the
Jubilee celebration in 1825, revolutions sweeping Europe caused the
practice to be suspended. In 1899, Leo XIII announced that a solemn
Jubilee would mark the turn of the century. As preparations and excitement for the event began to increase, Leo XIII added more elements to
the Jubilee year. The church would carry out a project to consecrate the
world to the Sacred Heart and special prayers and practices were written and promulgated to be recited and carried out in every church
throughout the world. During 1900, between the opening and closing
of the holy door of Saint Peter's Basilica, hundreds of thousands of pilgrims flocked to Rome for the holy year celebrations. Leo XIII called it
the "greatest act of my pontificate."[47] In a sense, these church festivities
at the turning of a century or of a millennium serve as antidotes to the
anxieties about the future which tend to erupt during these milestone
periods.

Like Leo XIII, John Paul II's millennium metaphor aims to reach
"entire nations and peoples." He articulates a vision of "true progress
of peoples" and a "future of humanity," so that "all of us, people of this
planet, *walk in faith* toward that same vision."[48] Redemption is seen as
a corporate, inclusive act. It involves "nations" and "peoples" walking
in the same direction toward the same goal. At a large, open, public
gathering in Detroit, John Paul II told the crowd that this apocalyptic
message is not just for the American church, or for Americans alone. It
is addressed to nations, including Americans, as part of a larger whole.
This universality of the apocalyptic message lifts the audience from its
differences and binds it to all peoples in a "new solidarity that knows no
frontiers" as this liminal moment when all "move toward the threshold
of the third millennium of Christianity."[49] John Paul has written of the
end of this millennium in terms of a time of "renewed vigor" for the effort to unite Christians, and he has referred to Poland's "millennial his-

tory" and its cultural source of "tolerance and openness" as testimony of his own deep-rooted ecumenical traditions.[50]

Amidst an age of anxiety and among a church that has lost a measure of its confidence, the pope's hopeful predictions of the new millennium are not contingent on individual conversions or any other human action. His reasons for hope are drawn from the fact that the church continues to proclaim the message that God "constantly remembers," even if humans tend to forget.[51] Success is assured because it is God's plan.

Being Americans, these church members are especially susceptible to visions of future hope and success. Indeed, Puritan adaptation of the religious apocalypticism had a profound effect on the strong faith in progress that is embedded in modern American culture.[52] By the time of the pope's 1987 visit, the American people had been courted by the rhetoric of Ronald Reagan, who reminded his audiences of their "rendezvous with destiny" as a chosen people, clearly warning them, however, of the possibility of betraying their covenant with God.[53]

Metaphors project multiple connotative meaning. The pope's use of "millennium" triggers the fundamentalist foreboding end of time. Those in the church who have a pessimistic view of the church's adaptation to the world hear the pope's confirmation of their fears. However, the pope's vision of the millennium contains a forward movement of diverse peoples walking together in solidarity. It has a futuristic, progressive ring that appeals to those church members who see themselves working in the world to construct "a third-millennium church" that is pluralistic and responsive to human social needs of peoples.[54] When the pope points to the "proclaiming" church in a causal relationship with the new millennium age, those in the audience who are active in church ministries identify themselves as cooperative agents in humanity's redemption. Even those audience members who are not active find themselves as witnesses of an historic event, where the pope, as head of a universal church, is physically present among the crowds of thousands, proclaiming that indeed God will not forget them. The enthusiasm of the crowd, the aura of the ceremony, all contribute to readiness of the audience to accept the pope's apocalyptic vision of a universal new millennium.

Orientation Inward toward the Core

A second directional symbol favored by Pope John Paul II is the metaphoric cluster of "depth." What is deep within is fundamental to humanity. The answers to difficult questions and the solutions to doubts can be found by moving inward to the depths, to the foundation, to the roots of one's being. It is in these depths that one finds the means of communicating with the Creator. "Only the human person is capable of releasing from the depths of his or her being" a voice that can communicate with the sacred. It is from these depths that the church "speaks her blessing." The words about these mysteries are so "profound" and "far down . . . into the history of man" that, as "the conversation becomes even deeper," it becomes possible for humans to encounter and understand mysteries. Because the depths act as a container, they shield humans from the vagaries of modern life and allow them to "purify" their beliefs so that they can feel, be moved, and be inspired.[55]

During his meeting with the American bishops in Los Angeles, John Paul II reminds his audience that the Vatican Council II's renewal of Catholic life is measured not in external structures but in "*deeper and more effective implementation* of the core vision." According to the pope, the problem is that many in the church have a "vivid sense" of the church's "horizontal dimension" through its visible service to the human family, but these church members experience "less deeply" the "vertical dimension" that links the church with the sacred.[56] John Paul II insists that in order to be called Christians, followers must "deepen" their communion with Christ, and the church must provide the means for them to do so. Inasmuch as the papal rhetoric relies heavily on the directional metaphor of depth to convey the core and rootedness of the relationship with the sacred, the employment of the depth metaphor has the effect of setting barriers between the secular and the sacred so that the "vertical dimension" can flourish.

John Paul II's use of the depth metaphor is consistent with the main theme of his theological and philosophical writings. His first encyclical, *Redemptor Hominis*, written soon after his election to the papacy, contains many ideas that he had begun to develop during his years at the university in Poland. There are two striking features about this encyclical which are related to his metaphoric choice. First, it contains a comprehensive vision of the whole of human experience, and this vision can only be understood through its historical and "original link with the divine source," the creation of humankind by God. Second, Christ as the Redeemer "penetrated" into the "mystery of man, which in biblical and nonbiblical language is expressed by the word 'heart.' " As John Paul II explains, "this tremendous mystery" of redemption is "at its deepest root" the heart of Christ.[57] As Williams observed, John Paul II's treatment of redemption is unique because he characterizes salvation as a satisfaction of God the Father's love that found its first human expression in the creation of the world and humankind.[58] In other words, the pope believes that love can be best approached by going to the root, or source of all love, by returning to the depths or root of human history.

Although the "depth" metaphor directs the audience to the depths of human history to reconnect with the sacred, the metaphor comes precariously close to portraying a spirituality that is "interior" and therefore individualized, lacking any need for externalized norms. Closed off and buried deep into one's spirituality, one can understand the sacred mysteries. If one encounters the sacred in the depths of one's being, it is hardly necessary for an institutional church to provide any guidance. The depth metaphor can work centrifugally, except the pope applies the same depth image to the church. In the "depths of the Church's memory" revelation about the sacred mysteries can be "stored."[59] In this sense, the depths of the church become the container where sacred meaning can be protected against the onslaughts of the secular culture.

The "depth" metaphor acts to close down meaning by closing off the self from external influences, but occasionally there are inconsistencies in the speech and use of this metaphor. In discussing the role of the church in helping Christians to "deepen" their faith, John Paul II talks of the "means" the church "employs" for this "task," namely a "systematic" and "carefully programmed study" that uses an "orderly" and "systematic presentation of all the essentials" to provide the "basis for sound judgments about the problems of life and society."[60] The centripetal pull of communion with the sacred in the "depths" is aided by a rationally planned and organized catechesis. The close encounter with the sacred is achieved by a contractual arrangement more consistent with the secular, scientifically based culture of the times. The pope articulates a social relationship of conversation with the sacred which occurs in the depths, shielded from the secular world. At the same time, the church finds its conversation very much affected by the world and its rational and scientific language. While insisting on the "purity" of faith, the pope acknowledges that the church resorts to using worldly means to accomplish the "task."

Recruiting for Conflict

John Paul II's rhetoric is permeated with images of struggle and conflict. The forward moving and assured future is also a "victory" that must be won by those who believe that grace is more "powerful" than sin. Followers of Christ are reminded of the "radical victory" of Christ's "triumph" on the cross. Battle lines are drawn between life and death, grace and sin, and Christians cannot "run away" from these struggles.

The church is seen "guarding" the human family and "directly oppos-ing the devil."[61] Priests, in a "silent army" and together with lay per-sons, work to "defend" life and human rights, and "protect" the family. Religious men and women are "in the front line of this never-ending struggle."[62] In battle, there will be heroes, such as the immigrant audi-ences who faced their lives in a new country with "heroism," and the la-ity whose "charity reaches heroic dimensions."[63]

Identifying an enemy and calling an audience to battle are well-used rhetorical devices to encourage and build unified action. [64] In the Bur-keian sense, John Paul II is aiming to congregate the church—and also those outside the church—by using metaphoric devices that segregate the church, and religion, from certain trends in secular culture.[65] Hu-manity must be defended and protected from a "rebellion" that acts to "threaten the existence of individuals, communities, and all society."[66] There are personal and corporate satisfactions for those who join in the struggle, namely, heroes will be recognized and given a salvific power. Because engagement in the conflict builds the church's reputation as a strong actor against a secular culture, these metaphoric clusters are em-ployed as antidotes against the growing belief that the fate of religion is inevitable.

The conflict metaphor in John Paul II's rhetoric also illustrates the sacred symbol and its potential. Conflict and struggle are associated with the negative human limitations that are known to humans through everyday experience. The holy should be the opposite—free from confrontation and conflict. Indeed, modern New Age religions seek peace, tranquillity, and pleasure. On the other hand, the pope, through his use of conflict metaphors, introduces a sacred character to this human experience of strife and confrontation. Once the conflict becomes ennobled with sacredness, it can be accepted and even em-braced. The image of a countercultural church in conflict with the sur-rounding secular culture is clothed in a supernatural character and therefore enhanced. Being in conflict with one's culture is no longer a sign of weakness, but a symbol of strength. This is the classic example of Christian inversion.

The conflict metaphors that build a separation between the sacred and secular appeal to those who see the process of accommodation with the secular culture as too risky for the church. To others, who support a church that is open and unafraid of the postmodern world, these con-flict metaphors raise suspicions that the church is turning back on its commitment to reach out to the world. Reintroducing the language of battle and conflict between the church and the world seems to negate the "civilization of love" to which Paul VI so often referred.

The rhetorical strategy of John Paul II acts to calm those suspicions by balancing metaphoric language of conflict with literal language of love and peace. John Paul II quotes from Paul VI, using his successor's "civilization of love" several times. John Paul II contends that this "merciful love calls for mutual understanding" and "ensures peace for ourselves and for the world." Even though there have been "tensions and conflicts," the audience is portrayed as "constantly moving toward reconciliation and harmony." Only rarely does John Paul II use metaphor against metaphor, juxtaposing a "spiritual sword" with "river of compassion" and "opposing" the devil by being a "channel" of mercy and love.[67] For the most part, the vocabularies of peace and reconciliation seem to be taken-for-granted, already understood concepts. The pope employs these literal terms to maintain the continuity with Vatican Council II's opening to the world. On the other hand, he uses the metaphor to reintroduce barriers between good and evil, distinguishing the church in "contradiction" to the world.

John Paul II also adapts his conflict metaphors to the audience. When speaking to groups outside the church, such as interreligious leaders, the pope rarely uses metaphors of conflict and concentrates instead on collaborative messages. The sparse hints of conflict are balanced immediately by peace and understanding messages. There is a "readiness to cooperate" and explore the "areas of convergence and divergence" in working out this "great battle for peace."[68] The rhetorical devices, such as conflict metaphors, that aim to put brakes on the church's accommodation to the world are not effective with these audiences. The groups represented hold varying views on the relationship of their churches with the secular world and, therefore, the pope looks to those symbols which will emphasize agreement, not disagreement.

Reid reminded us that a function of apocalyptic rhetoric is to identify and define the enemy.[69] John Paul II's use of conflict metaphors helps to visualize a conflict in which there is division between good and evil, but not complete separation of church and world. For example, John Paul II does not believe that scientific and technological progress are the enemies, for they are "a form of human cooperation in the creative work of God." However, like other observers of American culture, he contends that many Americans live in a culture marked by the most advanced progress and affluence, but they still are insecure, confused, and "very far from Love."[70] The problem, according to Pope John Paul II, is the God-forgetting spirit of the world prevalent in American ideologies and life styles. Rhetoric use of conflict metaphors sets barriers between the church and the world, but through metaphoric extensions, John Paul II defines and concentrates the battle, thereby rejecting a complete confrontation with all that is worldly.

IMAGERY: CHOICE OF WORDS

We expect religious speech to speak in high tones of moral norms and values. Do these norms command universal assent, or is there some acknowledgment of divergent views? In a rhetoric of belonging, the rhetor must "assert" the values and norms it wishes the audience to accept as beyond doubt and questioning. Religious rhetoric legitimates norms by giving them sacred character. By emanating from the sacred, or from the sacred's representatives, the norms cannot be challenged. Another rhetorical device is to separate the believers from the nonbelievers, asserting what we believe is right; what they believe is wrong. John Paul II uses both of these rhetorical tactics: legitimating norms with the sacred character, and building boundary lines between those who belong to the truth and those who do not. However, the pope's rhetoric is also filled with elements that signal a realization of a plurality of opinions.

Modifying a Pluralistic Discussion

When the pope speaks, audiences hear an array of modifiers that act to bolster words previously accepted as unconditional universals. A statement such as, "We must arrive at solutions that truly reflect both complete justice and mercy," allows for the possibility that there are forms of justice and mercy that may still be legitimate but not complete.[71] In other words, the church no longer can dominate the normative conversation by insisting that only one meaning of justice or mercy be the rule for discussion. John Paul II's use of such phrases as "authentically human," "true dignity," "true progress," and "authentic human progress"[72] acknowledges that his audience understands justice and mercy as human-based norms. Human dignity and progress are terms from rational humanism that have become agreed upon criteria in modern philosophical and political thought. By making distinctions as to what is "truly" or "authentically" human, the pope leads the audience to sacred normative meaning. In a sense, the pope is placing the church's "spin" on these secular-based terms. Even though distinctions are made and borders are drawn, by employing these terms and modifying them, the church is opening to the world of other thought and discussion. Instead of expecting audiences to respond to direct assertions of sacred character or the pressure of church belonging, the pope constructs meaning from criteria already accepted in the secular world.

In John Paul II's rhetorical strategy, modifiers act to tone down differences and work out compromises. For example, when the pope speaks on economic and social policy, he addresses audiences within the church who hold varying positions. On the one hand, there are those who rigorously support an unbridled free market economy as the best means of meeting the needs of all people, including the poor. At the other end of the spectrum are those who distrust and oppose those structures in society, including capitalist systems, which promote the fortunes of the rich to the detriment of the poorer members of society. John Paul II appeals to both points of view, but in moderation. He enunciates church policy that favors the "option for the poor" by insisting the church use its resources to promote the interests of the economically poor and politically marginalized. However, during his homily at Monterey, he does not commit the church to defending all interests of the poor, but rather their "legitimate interests." For example, he defended the church's action on behalf of illegal immigrants, but he did not condone the breaking of any laws. John Paul II, following a long tradition of social teaching by popes, has not condemned the free enterprise system and, in fact, has acknowledged some of its contributions. Nevertheless, at Monterey, the pope warned the audience of "exaggerated competition." By not condemning all competition, he leaves room for supporters of the free enterprise system to work out a moderated form of competition.[73] John Paul II introduces a rational character to the argument. There are gradations which require study and discussion to arrive at correct interpretations. These solutions are not literally handed down from the sacred, and therefore, there can be humanly constructed interpretations.

Throughout John Paul II's discourse, the word "authentic" is often employed to narrow interpretations of church teaching. "Authentic renewal" or "authentic catechesis" signals an interpretation that is fully approved and legitimated by the church.[74] Making sure that what is taught is true and authentic has always been a concern of the church. First and foremost, the church relies on apostolic succession to guarantee that authenticity. Believing that God through his Son entrusted to the apostles the task of handing on (orally or in written form) what God had revealed through Christ to humankind, the church depends on the successors of the apostles to accurately and faithfully guard and interpret the two forms of revelation: sacred scripture and tradition. Specifically, the teaching authority of the church resides in the bishops in communion with the Successor of Peter, or the pope. Catholic theology adds some complicated checks and balances. All teaching and authenticating is guided by the Holy Spirit, and the bishops can only teach what has been handed on to the church by God. Finally, there is the *sensus fidei*, or a sense of how the whole body of the faithful perceive the truth of God's revelation. If one considers the process by which truth is authenticated in the church, the word "authentic" carries great weight. Therefore, the pope's strategy is to point the argument toward the authority of the church and wed that message with his own credibility as authoritative speaker. However, the strategy itself raises questions about why John Paul II feels compelled to use such a weighty argument to persuade the faithful. Obviously, the strategy admits that within the church there exists other possible unapproved interpretations. As a result, the rhetoric becomes less assertive of what is and what is not a "catechesis" or "renewal," and instead focuses the discussion on what is the valid and approved version. Because John Paul II invests so much of the argument in his and other bishops' authority, he risks weakening his appeal to certain audiences. Arguments from authority have worked well in the past, but the concept of one-directional authority is eroding in Western society. More often, authority is worked out in dialogue.

In this regard, the pope feels compelled to use "true" and "authentic" to distinguish the "true nature of marriage" "as God established it" from current interpretations which regard divorce and adultery "as acceptable." The pope closes down meaning by portraying church authority and the God that established it as severely judgmental when he makes clear that he wants bishops to enforce the rules that prohibit divorced and remarried Catholics from receiving communion. However, even within papal speech, this "true nature" incorporates both open and closed dimensions, reflecting that the church is attempting to make sense to an audience that is confronted with changing lifestyles. Husbands and wives, parents and children are told to "forgive and accept forgiveness." Marriage cannot be treated as a contractual relationship which is seen "only in terms of justice" and "real and perceived injustices."[75] Single-parent families, divorced and separated couples who are in a "difficult situation" need "love, pastoral concern and practical help." John Paul II moves from the sacred ideal of married life as the centripetal glue that holds the church together to the pragmatic concerns of how to accommodate these people who are "striving to preserve their fidelity."[76]

Divorce rates among Catholics in the United States are the same as the rate for the general population. The church's process of annulling a marriage, that is, declaring a marriage to be null and void, was once a cumbersome process. Now it is carried out at the local diocesan level. As a result, the numbers of U.S. Catholics obtaining an annulment have increased. Just as the church has accommodated its process to the reality of failed marriage, papal rhetorical strategy no longer relies solely on sacred norms to combat divorce. For example, John Paul II argues that divorce is ineffective because the "brokenness" does not go away. The plight of children and disputes over property attest to the "ineffectiveness of divorce."[77] These appeals are grounded in rational reasoning and human empirical evidence, demonstrating that the character of John Paul II's arguments on divorce show some movement toward accommodation to the secular.

Authentic Feminism

Perhaps the most striking example of the pope's rhetorical intent to protect church norms from secular onslaught is his use of qualifiers with relationship to women's nature and role. When he speaks about "true feminine humanity" or the "authentic" plan for women's "true human advancement in the world,"[78] he is obviously distinguishing the church's view from other views of women's femininity. Of the many assaults on order that occurred in this century, feminism and its attacks on accepted cultural roles and patterns has and is continuing to break down barriers and reorder societies. By 1987 when John Paul II arrived in the United States, church members, including bishops, were beginning to believe that the church may have underestimated the importance of the feminist movement. Most women, including Catholic women, do not participate in the radical movements that portray a class struggle of subjugated females against the church's male rulers, but they strongly support feminist goals of equal opportunity and treatment.

In 1983, the NCCB decided to begin a process of writing a pastoral letter on women. Several dioceses began a consultative process, soliciting women's input. In 1985, twenty-five hundred women met in the Los Angeles archdiocese to voice their positions on the issue, and two years later, Archbishop Roger Mahoney issued his own pastoral letter. This letter, coming shortly before the pope's scheduled visit, took an accommodating view toward the changes in society that had brought about a recognition of the equality of men and women. The archbishop assumed that this recognition "must find new expression in our ecclesial life."[79]

On the other hand, John Paul II's arrival in the United States did little to further the discussion on women. There was little content on women specifically because planners did not include a separate meeting with religious women or any women's group. Furthermore, the pope's rhetorical strategy opted for continued tension, rather than resolution through accommodation. In his speeches, John Paul II attempts to demonstrate the church's defense of women's rights by insisting that women have "a dignity equal to men's dignity." However, rhetorically, John Paul II never allows the borders to fall between the genders. Women are discussed with "the personal dignity of women as women."[80] In other words, the pope refuses to erase or diminish references to gender distinctions. Gender differences and their complementarity have been important and relevant features in Catholic theology and symbolism. Christian tradition, which has continued traditions from its biblical past, has fostered and maintained a symbolic system that depends on a gender relationship, as for example, a feminine church is mystically wedded to a masculine God. Movements which aim to portray God as genderless, feminine, or even bisexual, are threatening to this tradition. However, many women, and men, who have become sensitized to women's objections to gender-loaded terms, are uncomfortable with the nuptial portrayal of Christ's redemptive relationship with the church. These masculine-feminine symbols represent an outdated view of sexuality because they are so dependent on the physiological description of male as source or fertilizing seed. In today's sexual relationship, the male partner is no longer considered the initiator; instead, equality and mutuality govern the sexual act.

Unmistakably, John Paul II's concept of "true" femininity does not include the priesthood. He repeats this position at the meeting with the bishops during the 1987 visit, but he softens his rhetorical stance by assuring his lay audience that women are "needed" and there is hope for their "fuller participation" in church activities.[81] He does not specify what that participation may be, and thus, it is open to interpretation. In John Paul II's rhetorical repertoire, women who are married have a clearer road to equality. As wives, women can act "in partnership" and as wives of married deacons, women can be "close collaborators" with their deacon husbands.[82] In his speech to the bishops, John Paul enunciates two principles governing consideration of women's issues: "the equal human dignity of women and their true feminine humanity."[83] Christine Gudorf contends that the equal principle is well supported by efforts in papal social teaching to favor equal rights in the political, economic, and social welfare realms. She claims that the true femininity principle is rooted in divine law, natural law, and hierarchical status. As a result, there is a "schizophrenic quality" to the teaching on women.[84] In fact, John Paul II's "authentic" femininity enunciates the church's preference for the "special and exalted roles fulfilled by women as wives, mothers, or consecrated women."[85] Of the three, motherhood is favored in his frequent reference to Mary as Mother of Christ.

John Paul II portrays Mary as "maternally present and sharing" in today's "many complicated problems." Through her "pilgrimage" she is an active and jubilant participant in the divine plan. It is to Mary that John Paul II sends women for the "secret" on how to fulfill their femininity. This Marian model involves obedience, compassion, and above all, suffering. For John Paul II, the view of Mary at the foot of the cross is the "perfect example" of how sorrow opens up the heart to love and compassion.[86] During his first trip to France, the pope argued that "Maternity is always pain—the love for which one pays with one's suffering."[87]

To those women in the audience who are participating more fully in the social, economic, and political life of their community and nation, the message on women's special suffering is difficult to accept. They have trouble reconciling their public roles with family roles in which they, as mothers, are supposed to excel in suffering, pain, and love. The rhetorical absence of male symbols in this special call to suffering and self-giving makes women suspicious. Women active in feminist causes have frequently voiced their concern with traditional Marian piety. They claim that these symbols have been shaped by celibate males, who, being hostile to women, idealize Mary in submissive roles so that women can be controlled and suppressed. Some advocate reconstructing the image of Mary so that she is no longer queen, or even mother, but rather "our sister in the struggle for survival and hope."[88]

There is no question that women in the United States have experienced enormous social change in the past thirty years. They are anxious about the growing weakness of family life and their own ability to sustain a balancing act between their professional and family roles, but most are not willing to give up the gains that they have made in the public arena. Nevertheless, as Bellah et al. contended, the family may have lost its power to tie the individual to the larger moral ecology, but Americans still regard it as one of their few "communities of memory."[89] The same is true for motherhood. It is difficult to imagine that an audience of mothers, young and old, would not relate in some way to John Paul II's portrayal of a mother's selfless devotion to her child. What they might question is that he neglects to talk about the selfless demands on fathers.[90] In a discussion of family issues during his visit to the United States in 1995, the pope changed tactics. He spoke about the obligations of fathers, rather than mothers. Undoubtedly, there have been accommodating adjustments in the church's position on women and men. John XXIII still spoke of a husband's authoritative leadership role in marriage, but John Paul II speaks of "partnership." Rather than schizophrenia, there is tension between the two principles of secular-driven equality and complementary difference based on natural law or divine creation. John Paul II's rhetorical strategies indicate some shifts in the definitive borders that separate these two realms, but gender complementarity of primary symbols in the church, such as the church itself, Mary, and even God the Father, are so much a part of Christian construction of the sacred that change is perceived as threatening to the concepts themselves. The difficulty of the church to strike the right balance on this issue may be related to the secular world's own confusion. Most women and men are still trying to sort out just where to place themselves on the equality-complementarity spectrum.

Using Codes to Appeal to Both Sides

In organizations and groups, certain vocabularies create special meaning. In the aftermath of Vatican Council II, the two tendencies within the church developed certain vocabularies that acted to "code" their positions on issues. These church members listening to the pope's speech look for those codes to signal agreement between the speaker and the audience. The use of "inculturation" and "multicultural" are terms that bind the rhetor to an audience appreciative of the proactive stance of a Vatican Council II church to understand and adopt diverse cultural elements into the practice of the church. The terms "voice of the poor" and "civilization of love" signal to the audience that John Paul II sees value in the church's efforts to serve the poor and bring about a just society. To show his identification with those who care about the environment, John Paul II uses the term "faithful stewardship," a term that also derives from Protestant vocabulary. The word "solidarity" triggers not only the worker movement, but John Paul II's special role in supporting the Polish workers in their effort to secure political freedom. "Collegiality" and "collaborate" when referring to the relationship of local bishops with the pope reaffirms the church's commitment to opening up the decision-making process of the church.

What may be surprising to many is that the pope often uses terms of sociology, not only in naming the ills of society, but in explaining the church's relationship to the world. For example, he acknowledges that the Sacrament of Reconciliation or Penance has some value as a means of "psychological liberation." He speaks about the role of communicators in "shaping the culture" of the world and relates self-giving to "human relations." Another code is that of nonsexist inclusive language. During the 1987 U.S. visit, John Paul II occasionally used "his or her," "he or she." In the homily at Dodger Stadium, women religious is placed before men in the sequence. These examples of code words demonstrate the rhetorical effort to incorporate the updated vocabularies of the church and the culture of the audience, particularly that sector of the audience who are supportive of the church's accommodation with the world.

At the same time, there are many who believe that those responsible for the church's pastoral life have been too prone to follow psychological theories that emphasize a "feel-good" holiness. They lament the fact that references to sin and eternal damnation are eliminated because people might be "burdened with undue anxiety."[91] Pope John Paul II treats the subject of sin, death, the devil, and eternal damnation in the personal lives of the audience. In his homily in San Antonio, Texas, he invites "all those who are listening" to recall their destiny, "eternal happiness of heaven, or the awful possibility of eternal punishment, eternal separation from God, in what the Christian tradition has called hell." He spends a considerable part of this homily discussing sin as "the death of the soul" and teaching the basics about the need to confess sins.[92] Throughout his homily, John Paul II interchanges the name for this sacrament, using the updated name, Sacrament of Reconciliation, as well as the older term, Sacrament of Penance. Even though he strikes a balance with the use of the two terms, John Paul II laments the "neglect" of the Sacrament of Penance. He states that "The Second Vatican Council never intended that this Sacrament of Penance be less practiced."[93]

Another group of code words that points to the need to slow accommodation with the world are those that indicate normative certitude. Those concerned with the church's failure to preach in absolutes want to hear signs verifying a fixed set of moral norms that cannot change. In his homily in San Antonio, John Paul II uses phrases such as "objective truths of faith," "firm and unchanged" and "certainty of teachings," but in all the other homilies these phrases are absent. On the other hand, he does pray that the Catholic audience will be strengthened in their "obedience" and their "fidelity" and extols those who have been "faithful to the Gospel and the law of God." John Paul II visualizes a body of Catholic norms that have a completeness: the Church proclaims "the whole of the Gospel message" and members must learn "*all of the essentials* of our Catholic faith." The pope's choice of "completeness" and "wholeness" imagery reinforces his directive to the bishops to "address" the problem of Catholics in the United States who are "selective" in their belief and observance of the church's moral teachings.[94]

REFERENCE: TESTIMONY AND CREDIBILITY

Testimony is supposed to add to a speaker's credibility. For the pope, who is perceived as exercising the "bully-est pulpit" in the world, credibility is constantly focused on the office of the papacy and the person who occupies it. Besides references from scripture, John Paul II quotes mostly from his own encyclicals and apostolic exhortations, and these references tend to reinforce his teaching authority. Because he has spoken on these matters before, there is no need to call upon others. In a sense, by quoting his own works rather than others', the pope is keeping himself on stage.[95]

This is not to say that he does not refer to other pontiffs. In fact, during the homilies in the 1987 visit, he quoted Pope Paul VI to signal some of the "opening" toward the world, such as incorporation of diverse cultures into evangelization, or the church's concern for the poor and needy. However, the quoted material selected from Paul VI shows how Paul VI has attempted to balance the opening and closing. For example, the passage on inculturation also warns about going too far so as to destroy universality. The passage quoted on the church's concern for temporal welfare of the poor also reminds the church that the Kingdom of God is not of this world and cannot be confused with earthly progress.[96] John Paul II uses a reference to John XXIII's encyclical, *Mater et Magistra*, in Monterey. Pope John XXIII has become a symbol of the opening in the church, much more so than Paul VI. This reference is found in the Monterey homily, where the audience's construction of meaning is largely formed by indicators of a more open position toward the secular world.

Other than his own writings, John Paul II most often quotes from Vatican Council II documents. For most Catholics, Vatican Council II is now accepted as a positive achievement in modern church history. Although there are still a range of interpretations on some subjects that were intentionally left ambiguous by the Council, reliance on Vatican Council documents has become standard practice in theological reflection and preaching. If there was an absence of quotations from the Council, it would signal a significant change. This is not the case. John

Paul II frequently increases the credibility of his arguments by aligning himself with Vatican Council II and its symbolism.

In his talks to the bishops, priests, religious, and laity, Pope John Paul II uses additional supporting material from his speeches and letters on pertinent subjects. This is very noticeable in his meeting with the bishops. The discourse is sprinkled with testimony from previous synods, *ad limina* visits, and papal correspondence involving the bishops. This type of testimony places emphasis on the governance of the church as an institution. Because it recalls for the audience of bishops the frequent and ongoing relationship with the pontiff, it gives an aura of systematization. Collegiality with the pope becomes layered with pronouncements, thereby losing the freshness of intimacy. By contrast, in his talk to the youth, Pope John Paul II uses church documents very rarely and instead relies on scripture and his own previous talks to young people.

Departures from quoting scripture, papal writings, and Council documents tend to stand out as unusual. For example, in his homily in New Orleans, the pope quotes from documents written by the Pontifical Commission on Justice and Peace, and from the U.S. bishops' pastoral message on the economy. This shows an appreciation and a papal approval for the work of his bishop colleagues, giving substance to the collegiality of bishops with the pope. John Paul II's occasional use of secular testimony contains material with prayer-like character: the inscription on the Statue of Liberty, passages from the U.S. Constitution and the United Nations, and lyrics from "America the Beautiful." The pope refrains from using other types of documentation from the secular world, even when commenting on modern trends. It is obvious that papal credibility is enhanced by authoritative sources from sacred otherness rather than human knowledge and experience. Furthermore, the pope's choice of references is a mark of the written tradition of papal speech. Working centripetally on itself, the citing of papal and other church sources reinforces concepts to assure strong links with the past and to enclose argument.

Jablonski, in her study of U.S. bishops' statements, noted that the bishops increased their use of scriptural quotations and refrained from quoting the pope. She reasoned that the bishops sought "hearers' assent on grounds other than those established by Church authority and tradition."[97] The pope continues to rely heavily on scriptural texts, which is consistent with the emphasis of the Vatican Council II. On the other hand, the pope does not shrink from using papal statements—

mostly his own. This suggests that the papacy's centralizing purpose is an important part of the rhetorical papal strategy.

SUMMARY: TEXTUAL SYMBOLS OF SACRED-SECULAR TENSION

Most of the metaphors in John Paul II's speech are archetypal in that they have been used and are understood across cultures and times. Generally built on biblical references and part of a long tradition of Jewish and Christian sermons, the pope's metaphoric choices remain in the sacred realm of church rather than world. Once in a while, the pope dares to apply "fresh" metaphors to illuminate known concepts. As Osborn and Ehninger noted, these "fresh" metaphors are usually controlled by contextual elements.[98] Certainly that is the case when John Paul II calls God the "Great Creditor," to describe how much humans owe to the sacred or when he describes priests as "artists" who can "inspire us" rather than the usual shepherds of pastoral work.[99] Unlike the archetypal metaphors, these metaphoric terms strike audiences with their contemporary newness.

Kathleen Jamieson concluded that to persuade church members to accept the tradition and authority of the church, popes use different and distinct metaphoric clusters "to transcend the inventional limitations imposed by one cluster by electing to communicate through a more apt one."[100] For John Paul II, the inventional limitations are related to where his audiences are located on the sacred-secular spectrum. By interchanging the church as Body with church as People of God, he broadens appeal and includes those favoring both the resistance and the accommodating postures. Because he tends to carefully balance the use of these two metaphors, he associates himself with a middle-ground interpretation of Vatican Council II. Moreover, he shows preference for the more updated symbol when addressing certain audiences, for example, the farm workers and the youth. In both cases, he is comfortable with the relationship that these audiences have with himself and the church. As with the Polish solidarity movement, John Paul II shows farm workers that he trusts the working poor's sense of unity with themselves and their God. The same is true for young people, in whom John Paul II puts his hope for the future.

His metaphoric choices also provoke tension and contrast. In these modern times, people who are alone and rootless express anxiety about the future. John Paul II's use of the millennium theme is reflective of the long tradition in the church of providing motivation and means to withstand crises. The pope's marathon visits throughout his papacy confer an immediacy on the mythic story of crisis and resolution that the millennium presents. Through the millennium theme and its promise of an assured future, the confrontation of earthly crisis leads to an understanding of the way towards the sacred. By contrast, in the depth metaphor, the sacred is approached by closing down contact with the everyday secular activity of the world. However, in the depth metaphor, John Paul II's use of the language of self accommodates to modern trends. By closing oneself off, one can hear the sacred and the sacred leads one back to the self and self-actualization.

The gift metaphor portrays a cosmos in which the sacred dominates all activity, but John Paul II's metaphoric extensions of the gift cluster supply interpretations that appeal to the mystical character of the sacred-human relationship. Illustrated by personal relationships rather than institutional or normative governance, these extensions of the gift metaphor accommodate to audiences influenced by the modern preoccupation with free, individual conscience. By contrast, the conflict metaphors are throwbacks to the classical means of drawing distinctions between the church and the world. They have been time-tested, even by modern political leaders. In this case, the pope names an array of enemies in order to make these distinctions meaningful to audiences with many points of view.

Papal speech recognizes and deals with the consequences of pluralistic culture. Because there is no longer audience agreement regarding some universal terms, as rhetor, the pope cannot effectively employ all embracing simple statements on what is true or what is human. He must find the precise term to speak meaningfully to a diverse world. Often this involves using terms in a modified form. By taking concepts that represent current thinking and placing a sacred "spin" on these terms, the pope's vocabulary uses the secular to inform about the sacred. At other times, his vocabulary of the sacred works out compromises, which tends to pull back the outer limits from their extreme points and allows the church to embrace the widest possible middle. However, the persistent use of "authentic" has the opposite effect. This strategy narrows interpretations to church-approved teachings. It is the sacred ordering of the secular world. Authentic feminism is a case where John Paul II's strategy provokes tension to protect sacred concepts from the world's confusion.

Code words have a triggering effect. John Paul II reintroduces words that had been abandoned, such as sin, devil, and hell. These recall an era in which there was less confusion about right and wrong. To some audiences they resonate deeply into past experiences. The pope also uses codes to signal solidarity with the poor, cultural diversity, and other updated versions of sacred vocabulary. Again, by using both types of code words, John Paul II opens wide the possible differing interpretations and provokes tension within them. Finally, the pope's overwhelming reliance on his own writings, which increases with his papacy, acts to enclose rhetorical argument. It is symptomatic of the Vatican's heavy dependence on written forms of communication and its preoccupation with consistency of tradition.

NOTES

1. Roderick P. Hart, *Modern Rhetorical Criticism* (Glenview, Illinois: Scott Foresman and Company, 1990), 213, 217.

2. George Lakoff and Mark Johnson, *Metaphors We Live By* (Chicago: University of Chicago Press, 1980), 5–9.

3. J. Vernon Jensen, "British Voices on the Eve of the American Revolution: Trapped by the Family Metaphor," *Quarterly Journal of Speech* 63 (February 1977): 43.

4. David Martin, *The Breaking of the Image* (Oxford: Basil Blackwell, 1980), 59, 127.

5. Peter L. Berger, *The Sacred Canopy: Elements of a Sociological Theory of Religion* (Garden City, New York: Doubleday, 1969), 86.

6. Janet Martin Soskice, *Metaphor and Religious Language* (Oxford: Oxford University Press, 1985), 158.

7. Robert Wuthnow, *Rediscovering the Sacred* (Grand Rapids, Michigan: William B. Eerdmans, 1992), 66–67.

8. Michael Osborn, "Archetypal Metaphor in Rhetoric: The Light Dark Family," *Quarterly Journal of Speech* LIII (April 1967): 126.

9. Kurt Ritter and David Henry, *Ronald Reagan: The Great Communicator* (Westport, Connecticut: Greenwood Press, 1992); Halford R. Ryan, *Franklin D. Roosevelt's Rhetorical Presidency* (Westport, Connecticut: Greenwood Press, 1988); Kathleen Jamieson, "The Metaphoric Cluster in the Rhetoric of Pope Paul VI and Edmund G. Brown, Jr.," *Quarterly Journal of Speech* 66 (1980): 51–72.

10. Northrop Frye, *Words With Power* (San Diego: Harcourt Brace Jovanovich, 1990), xv.

11. Janice Peck, *The Gods of Televangelism* (Cresskill, New Jersey: Hampton Press, 1993), 202–207.

12. Avery Dulles, *Models of the Church* (New York: Doubleday, 1987), 20.

13. Ibid., 53.

14. John Paul II, "Homily at Mass Celebrated at Laguna Seca," no. 3 in *The Pope Speaks to the American Church* (New York: HarperCollins, 1992), 298.

15. John Paul II, "Meeting with Members of the Laity," no. 5, in *The Pope Speaks*, 318.

16. John Paul II, "Meeting Laity," no. 7, in *The Pope Speaks*, 319–320.

17. John Paul II, "Youth Rally," no. 3, in *The Pope Speaks*, 183.

18. Michael M. Osborn and Douglas Ehninger, "The Metaphor in Public Address," *Speech Monographs* 29 (1962), 233.

19. Jamieson, "The Metaphoric Cluster," 57.

20. John Paul II, "Homily at Dodger Stadium," no. 2, in *The Pope Speaks*, 288.

21. Ibid., nos. 2, 4, 6, in *The Pope Speaks*, 288–291.

22. Ibid., nos. 4, 5, in *The Pope Speaks*, 290–291.

23. Ibid., nos. 7, 9, in *The Pope Speaks*, 291–293.

24. John Paul II, "Meeting with the American Bishops," nos. 1, 2, in *The Pope Speaks*, 267.

25. During the 1987 visit, the gift metaphor appeared in every Eucharistic homily except one; it also was used in meetings with priests, laity, Jewish leaders, and youth.

26. Peck, *The Gods of Televangelism*, 154.

27. John Paul II, "Homily in New Orleans," no. 5; "Homily in the Silverdome," no. 5; "Meeting with Ecumenical Leadership," no. 2; in *The Pope Speaks*, 160, 192–193, 356.

28. The tremendum quality of the holy includes an overpoweringness and awfulness, and is distinct from the mysterious nature of the holy. Rudolf Otto, *The Idea of the Holy,* trans. John W. Harvey (London: Oxford University Press, 1931), 12.

29. John Paul II, "Homily at New Orleans," no. 4, in *The Pope Speaks*, 191–192.

30. John Paul II, "Meeting with Members of the Laity," no. 5, in *The Pope Speaks*, 318.

31. Avery Dulles, *The Reshaping of Catholicism* (San Francisco: Harper and Row, 1988), 73.

32. André Frossard, *"Be Not Afraid!"* (New York: St. Martin's Press, 1984), 63–64. The gift metaphor has been used extensively by Pope John Paul II throughout his preaching career. For example, as cardinal, he gave a Lenten retreat to Pope Paul VI. One of his homilies was entitled "He Who Is Gift and the Source of All Giving." Karol Wojtyla, *Sign of Contradiction* (New York: Seabury Press, 1979), 53.

33. Robert N. Bellah, Richard Madsen, William M. Sullivan, Ann Swidler, and Steven M. Tipton, *Habits of the Heart* (Berkeley: University of California, 1985; reprint New York: Perennial Library, Harper and Row, 1986), 92–93.

34. Kenneth A. Briggs, *Holy Siege* (San Francisco: HarperCollins, 1992), 139.

35. Bellah et al., 194.

36. Lakoff and Johnson, *Metaphors We Live By*, 14.

37. John Paul II, "Homily at Westover Hills," nos. 8, 9; "Homily at Tamiami Park," no. 2; "Homily at Candlestick Park," no. 5; in *The Pope Speaks*, 150–151, 204–205, 323.

38. John Paul II, *Redemptor Hominis*, no. 1, in *Origins*, vol. 8, 40 (22 March 1979): 625.

39. John Paul II, "Homily at Laguna Seca," no. 2, in *The Pope Speaks*, 297.

40. J. P. Dolan, "Millenarianism," *Catholic Encyclopedia* (New York: McGraw Hill, 1967), 852–854.

41. Ronald F. Reid, "Apocalypticism and Typology: Rhetorical Dimensions of a Symbolic Reality," *Quarterly Journal of Speech* 69 (August 1983): 237.

42. John Paul II, "Homily at Laguna Seca," no. 2, in *The Pope Speaks*, 297.

43. Harold Mixon and Mary Frances Hopkins, "Apocalypticism in Secular Public Discourse: A Proposed Theory," *Central States Speech Journal* 39 (Fall/Winter 1988): 250.

44. John Paul II, "Homily at Dodger Stadium," no. 2, in *The Pope Speaks*, 288.

45. John Paul II, "Homily at Candlestick Park," no. 9, in *The Pope Speaks*, 326.

46. John Paul II, "Homily at Los Angeles Coliseum," no. 5; "Homily at Dodger Stadium," nos. 4, 10; in *The Pope Speaks*, 263, 290, 294.

47. William Kiefer, *Leo XIII: A Light from Heaven* (Milwaukee, Wisconsin: Bruce, 1961), 189–193.

48. John Paul II, "Homily at Candlestick Park," no. 9; "Homily at Dodger Stadium," no. 10; in *The Pope Speaks*, 294, 326.

49. John Paul II, "Address on Social Justice Issues," no. 8, in *The Pope Speaks*, 351.

50. John Paul II, *Crossing the Threshold of Hope* (New York: Alfred A. Knopf, 1994), 145. A number of authors have pointed out the possible influence of Polish messianism on John Paul II's thought. Many Polish messianic nationals were millennialists. Polish messianic poets who wrote of prophetic visions of a renewed Polish nation also extended reform and renewal to the church. A poet's prediction of a "Slavic pope" who would be the champion of working peoples of Eastern Europe has been used by many, including John Paul II, as a sign of destiny. It may be destiny that the first Polish pope is to lead the church into the next millennium. At the end of the first millennium, the church was led by the first German pope, and the first French pope saw the beginning of the second millennium. The latter, Silvester II, aided Emperor Otto III in his attempts to renew the Christian Roman empire. See Williams, *The Mind of John Paul II: Origins of His Thought and Action* (New

York: Seabury Press, 1981), 42–46; J.D.N. Kelly, *Oxford Dictionary of Popes* (Oxford: Oxford University Press, 1986), 134–137.

51. John Paul II, "Homily at Dodger Stadium," no. 10, in *The Pope Speaks*, 294.

52. Reid, "Apocalypticism and Topology," 234.

53. Ritter and Henry, *Ronald Reagan*, 26–28.

54. Penny Lernoux, *People of God* (New York: Viking, 1989), 410.

55. John Paul II, "Homily at Westover Hills," nos. 2, 4; "Homily at Arizona State University," nos. 3, 5; "Homily in Los Angeles Coliseum," nos. 1, 3, 7; in *The Pope Speaks*, 200–201, 244–245, 260, 261, 264.

56. John Paul II, "Meeting with American Bishops," nos. 1, 2, in *The Pope Speaks*, 267.

57. John Paul II, *Redemptor Hominis*, nos. 8–9, 630–631.

58. Williams, *The Mind of John Paul II*, 307.

59. John Paul II, "Homily at Candlestick Park," no. 6, in *The Pope Speaks*, 324.

60. Ibid., 323–324.

61. John Paul II, "Homily at Tamiami Park," no. 7; "Homily at Westover," no. 5; "Homily in Dodger Stadium," no. 9; in *The Pope Speaks*, 154, 202, 293–294.

62. John Paul II, "Address to Priests," no. 5; "Meeting with Men and Women Religious," no. 7; in *The Pope Speaks*, 139–140, 311.

63. John Paul II, "Homily at Tamiami Park," no. 6; "Meeting with Members of the Laity," no. 2; in *The Pope Speaks*, 153, 316.

64. See Halford R. Ryan, *Franklin D. Roosevelt's Rhetorical Presidency*, 81–85.

65. Kenneth Burke, *A Grammar of Motives* (New York: Prentice Hall, 1945), 370.

66. John Paul II, "Homily at Laguna Seca," no. 2, in *The Pope Speaks*, 297.

67. John Paul II, "Homily at New Orleans," no. 3; "Homily at Westover Hills," no. 7; "Homily in Los Angeles Coliseum," no. 5; "Homily in Dodger Stadium," no. 9; in *The Pope Speaks*, 191, 204, 263, 294.

68. John Paul II, "Meeting with Interreligious Leaders," nos. 2, 3, in *The Pope Speaks*, 285–286.

69. Ronald F. Reid, "Apocalypticism and Typology," 238–239.

70. John Paul II, "Homily at Tamiami Park," nos. 7, 8, in *The Pope Speaks*, 153, 155.

71. John Paul II, "Homily at New Orleans," no. 3, in *The Pope Speaks*, 191.

72. John Paul II, "Homily at Laguna Seca," no. 9; "Homily at Candlestick Park," no. 9; "Homily in Silverdome," no. 3; in *The Pope Speaks*, 301, 326, 354.

73. John Paul II, "Homily at Laguna Seca," nos. 4, 7, in *The Pope Speaks*, 299–300.

74. John Paul II, "Homily at Westover Hills," no 6; "Homily at Candlestick Park," no. 6; in *The Pope Speaks,* 202–203, 324.

75. John Paul II, "Homily at Tamiami Park," no. 7; "Homily at New Orleans," no. 3; in *The Pope Speaks,* 154, 190.

76. John Paul II, "Meeting with Members of the Laity," no. 3, in *The Pope Speaks,* 317.

77. John Paul II, "Homily at New Orleans," no. 3, in *The Pope Speaks,* 190.

78. John Paul II, "Meeting with the American Bishops," no. 13; "Act of Entrusting," no. 1, in *The Pope Speaks,* 277, 295.

79. Briggs, *Holy Siege,* 471.

80. John Paul II, "Meeting with Members of the Laity," no. 4; "Meeting with American Bishops," no. 13, in *The Pope Speaks.*

81. John Paul II, "Meeting with Members of the Laity," no. 4, in *The Pope Speaks,* 318.

82. John Paul II, "Meeting with the Members of the Laity," no. 4; "Meeting with the Deacons and Their Wives," no. 6, in *The Pope Speaks,* 318, 342.

83. John Paul II, "Meeting with the American Bishops," no. 13, in *The Pope Speaks,* 277.

84. Christine E. Gudorf, "Encountering the Other: The Modern Papacy on Women," *Social Compass* 36 (1989): 295–310.

85. John Paul II, "Meeting with the American Bishops," no. 13, in *The Pope Speaks,* 277.

86. John Paul II, "Homily at Westover Hills," no. 8; "Act of Entrusting," no. 1; "Homily in Los Angeles Coliseum," nos. 4, 5, in *The Pope Speaks,* 205, 262–263, 295.

87. John Paul II, "Homily at Saint-Denis, May 31," no. 2, in *France: Message of Peace, Trust, Love and Faith* (Boston: Daughters of St. Paul, 1980), 76.

88. Rosemary Radford Ruether, "Mary in U.S. Catholic Culture," *National Catholic Reporter* (10 February 1995): 15–17.

89. Bellah et al., 112.

90. Katherine Kersten, "What Do Women Want? A Conservative Feminist Manifesto," *Policy Review* (Spring 1991): 4–15.

91. George A. Kelly, *Keeping the Church Catholic with John Paul II* (New York: Doubleday, 1990), 245.

92. John Paul II, "Homily at Westover Hills," nos. 3, 5, 6, in *The Pope Speaks,* 201–203.

93. John Paul II, "Homily at Westover Hills," no. 6, in *The Pope Speaks,* 203.

94. John Paul II, "Homily at Westover Hills," no. 6; "Act of Entrusting," no. 3; "Homily at Tamiami Park," no. 6; "Homily at Candlestick

Park," nos. 6, 7; "Meeting with American Bishops," no. 5; in *The Pope Speaks*, 153, 202, 270, 296, 324–325.

95. Roderick Hart observes that elected officials avoid quoting others because it puts others on stage instead of themselves. Roderick Hart, *Modern Rhetorical Criticism*, 130.

96. John Paul II, "Homily in Dodger Stadium," no. 8; "Homily in Silverdome," no. 7; in *The Pope Speaks*, 292–293, 357.

97. Carol Jablonski, "Institutional Rhetoric and Radical Change: The Case of the Contemporary Roman Catholic Church in America" (Ph.D. dissertation, Purdue University, 1979).

98. Osborn and Ehninger, 233.

99. John Paul II, "Homily at New Orleans," no. 1; "Meeting with Priests," no. 7; in *The Pope Speaks*, 141, 189.

100. Kathleen Jamieson, "The Metaphoric Cluster," 63.

CHAPTER 7

Visits as Performance

For Kenneth Burke, a speaker must know how to arouse the desires of an audience. This entails an understanding and utilization of the symbolic shorthand descriptions with which audiences are familiar through experience with their cultural history. However, Burke knew that this familiarity and sameness was not enough to stimulate and prod audiences toward identification with the speaker. He understood the role of dramatic tension, where difference and strangeness along with the possibility of resolution and unity entice audiences to seek communion.[1] Kathleen Jamieson notes that John Paul II's "mastery of concise, dramatic symbols" gains the attention of the audience.[2] When the verbal message is visually synopsized by these brief symbols, the memorability of the message is increased. Jamieson aptly points out that the "moving synoptic moment has replaced the eloquent speech."[3] To build identification with today's audiences, speakers need to know how to concisely dramatize images.

Dramatizing images has long been a part of the tradition of the Catholic Church. The sacraments are visible signs by which the church fuses human life with sacred reality. The "drama" involves the mixing of two distinct realms: the human and the sacred. However, in order for the drama to intensify meaning, there must be a distinctive border between the two. Commentators and journalists frequently point to John Paul II's dramatic actions during his international trips as the most effective communicating tool of this papacy. They often place these actions in opposition to his message. The pope's sympathetic and warm gestures are in contrast to his preaching of strict adherence to unchanging moral rules. He is open to the modern world in his personal approach and use of modern communication technology. How he communicates softens the rigidity of what he actually says. This analysis may have some validity, but it is too simplistic. As the previous textual analysis demonstrates, papal speeches during the U.S. visit of 1987 construct a symbolic reality that resists and accommodates to the modern secularized world. The same applies to the performative character of the visits. For dramatic tension to exist, there must be an opening and a closing to the world.

TEXTUAL AND STRUCTURAL PERFORMANCE

The papal visit is more than a series of meetings and events with a very important personality. Its purpose is pastoral; it needs to be distinguished as religious and therefore different from other visits by secular personalities. The primary means of communicating the religious nature of the visit is the emphasis on liturgy. The Catholic Church considers the sacramental worship or liturgy to be the "summit toward which the activity of the Church is directed."[4] Vatican Council II documents on the church explain the importance of the entire church assembling and participating in the liturgy, especially the Eucharist, because the church "reveals herself most clearly when a full complement of God's holy people" actively participate in the liturgy with the bishops and priests.[5] According to Catholic theological doctrine, a sacrament is a sign that divine grace is present. At the Eucharist, the church, with its members bound together, present and participating, is a tangible, visible sign that Christ's redeeming grace is present and active. Inasmuch as the church achieves itself depending on how widely and intensively members participate in its sacramental life, the Eucharistic celebrations during the visits of John Paul II with their full capacity, rapt attention, and intense prayerful activity are special means for the church to reveal itself as a sacred sign. As mentioned previously, the Eucharistic celebration is the key event each day. Through the Eucharistic ritual, Catholics share in the suffering, death, and resurrection of Christ and they enter into the mystery of redemption. Participation in this re-creation confirms in an experiential way one's individual identity as a Christian and one's social identity as a member of the Catholic Church. Because it is an act of communicating with the sacred, the enactment of the ritual and its liturgical form become crucial components of the papal visit.

David Martin defines religion as a "set of spells" by which persons are "simultaneously bound forward by the spell and held in bondage."

Martin speaks of liturgy as a way in which religion holds up and protects images so that they can be recognized and remembered. The order of the liturgy, the repetitious chants and prayers are part of the act of remembering. It produces a community of memory through familiarity with the way of doing things. Moreover, liturgy is also a way to "transport" persons to "a new way."[6]

Ritual Mystery: Formality and Hierarchy

The liturgies during a papal visit are both familiar and unique. They are unique in that they are planned to be unrivaled spectacles. The setting, chosen to accommodate large numbers, conveys an aura of massiveness. At the altar, the centerpiece of this transformed space, John Paul II carries out the formulaic actions that most of the participants recognize and remember. There is a clearly defined hierarchical order to the physical form of the event. Cardinals, archbishops, and priests participating with him in the Eucharistic celebration move in procession to take their places at or near the altar. Marked by position and special garments, the priestly role is highlighted and separated from the rest of the community. Those serving the pope during the Mass (usually seminarians), as well as those chosen to read the scriptural texts and offer the gifts, are also given a privileged place. As the participants make their formal entry into the secular-made-sacred space, their distinguishing colors and garments, and their positions with relation to the central altar display the differentiation of tasks and the variety of levels of authority within the institutional church. This display defines for the crowds who are present and viewing through the mass media the hierarchical positions through which the church exercises order and authority. It is a style that celebrates past tradition, stability, and predictability in contrast to the fast moving, momentary world of the electronic age. For a few hours, time seems to stand still in a dream-like trance, forming moments of liminality where differences between the world of order and extraordinariness and the world of variability and ordinariness meet.

Each movement is timed and performed with near flawlessness. During the months preceding the trip, liturgists at the local dioceses have worked with the bishop and others on the pope's staff for liturgy. The scriptural readings are normally those prescribed by the daily liturgical calendar, but changes are sometimes made in order to emphasize a particular theme. Local variations occur in music and visual decorations, although even the musical and artistic forms are studied and approved on the basis of quality and appropriateness. During the ritual ceremony, a member of the Vatican's Office of Papal Liturgical Celebrations is always at the pope's side, guiding him with expert cues. In this way, the performance of John Paul II follows what Moore and Myerhoff observed as a preoccupation of ritual, that is, the precision of movement and form. Without any consideration of message, the ritual form acts to close down choice and indeterminacy.[7]

In the liturgical reforms of the Vatican Council II, laity were permitted to participate in the Mass, namely in performing the scriptural readings, offering the gifts and specific prayers of the faithful. Those individuals chosen to perform these functions, the types of gifts offered, and the locally created prayers of the faithful are parts of the Eucharistic liturgy that allow for variety and local choice. As a small relief from the rest of the liturgy, these are what David Martin calls "institutionalized spontaneity" which occurred as the church, adapting to the modern world, tried to allow for more individual expression.[8] For the papal liturgies, even these variations are planned in advance. There is room for local expression, but no chance for free spontaneity. The variations become deliberate symbolic choices precisely because they are designed to act as a bridge between the hierarchical differences that separate the priestly and lay roles. They break the tension for a brief moment, signaling the possibility of communion. At the same time, there is no unmasking or debunking of the hierarchical order. The crowd, in accepting the chosen few as their representatives, uphold the mystery created by difference so that they can feel the pleasure of resolving these differences even for those brief moments. They watch in delight as little children, married couples, farm workers, schoolteachers, people from diverse ethnic and racial backgrounds carry the offertory gifts to the altar, climb the steps, two by two, and kneel as courtiers before the throne. The crowd waits anxiously to see what will happen.[9] Very often the audience is rewarded by some small dramatic moment when the pope kisses the children or when a little boy hugs the pope. For those in the audience who are more familiar with the details of the liturgy, each choice can be weighed according to its significance. For example, Vatican and local planners are sensitive to the balance between men and women, particularly in performing the readings and prayers of the faithful. Their choices are also related to the composition of the audience.

The liturgical events during the papal visit celebrate the authoritativeness of prescribed codes. In David Martin's words, they are moments of familiarity and habit that encourage participants to commonly remember things. Because of its repetitive structure, liturgy can "allow the mind to stand outside for a moment." The steady rhythm of the liturgy during which the celebrant, in this case the pope, appears unhurried and deliberate captures and liberates because "boredom is the infrastructure of illumination."[10]

Liturgies during the papal visits are not opportunities to experiment with different forms. Participants need to participate and therefore want the familiar, but the familiar ceremony of chant, repetition, and prayer is expected to be magnified in the presence of the one who holds the highest office in their church. Attention is therefore given to presenting the very best choirs, readers, and visual elements, such as vestments and altar decorations. Contrasted with their parishes, the splendor of the celebration is unmatched in scale. As the ritual begins, priests, monsignors, bishops, archbishops, and cardinals process into the sacred place to position themselves in their proper order. Their movement is slow and precisely timed as they wait in attendance for the entry of the pope. Then the pope enters, sometimes carried in his popemobile. The vehicle winds through the crowd and John Paul II opens his arms and blesses those who are greeting him. People scream with joy, applaud, wave their hands, and some nearby try desperately to reach out and touch the figure of John Paul II. Approaching the altar area, the pope descends from the vehicle and slowly ascends the steps to the high sacred altar. In the language of Kenneth Burke, the pope is " 'ordained' with the properties of an absolute order" as the personification of a unified Catholic public. Being "magically endowed" by the crowd's attention, he transcends his nature as an individual and becomes an "impersonal motive."[11] He becomes less John Paul II and more "the pope" as a symbol of fixed order. Jamieson contended that Americans who have been "robbed of the rituals that once accompanied royalty" are drawn to the papal ceremony because it represents the oldest Western institution.[12] In their world of constant change and fleeting loyalties, these U.S. audiences accept the hierarchical mystery presented by the symbols of this ceremony because they want to belong, at least for a few hours, to the forgotten glory and majesty of a universal church. Duncan, writing about Kenneth Burke's theories, explained that human nature craves authority in order to create solidarity.[13] In the face of a fragmented and disorderly world, people flocking to the stadiums for the pope's Mass crave order and therefore are willing to take the risks associated with acting in attention toward the pope. David Martin contended that those who attend and give an "act of attention" in prayer are not expecting rational propositions. They go to church to "receive signs and signals" to alter their ordinary worlds of experience. The ascending movement to a high altar, the slow majestic rhythm, the distinguishing colors of priestly participants arranged in hierarchical order are designed to place distance between the ordinary and the extraordinary. For a society whose culture is immersed in democratic equality, these signs are very far from the everyday contemporary life. For some, the papal liturgical rite recalls the sights and sounds of a church past. For others, whose memory may be very faint, the possibility of a history and continuity of membership satisfies an unrealized desire. As David Martin wrote, liturgies "connect memory with expectation."[14] In giving homage to the sacredness and authenticity of liturgical tradition, the audience wraps itself in its own approval and becomes equally enhanced. Those who were there will boast to their neighbors, friends, and work mates of their presence at this historic moment. The event is extraordinary; they too are extraordinary.

David Martin also reminded the reader that the "spells" of religion are never pure, but must contain a mixture of text and context. The liturgy needs to be a sign that helps the community look a long way back and a long way forward. Therefore, there must be a balance between "memory and hope," "horizontal to vertical," "spontaneity and rule."[15] If the signs and spells that religion weaves become too reified, the congregation becomes alienated. The community must see some connection between this memory of a sacred and the experience of the present, and this connection or relationship will eventually lead to the hope of eternity. During the papal trips, John Paul II cannot only be a sign of the sacred, but he must be humanly present in order to be recognizable. David Martin named three modern changes that have "tampered with" the church's symbolic form. The first is an "intrusive moralism" in which sin is identical to social structuring. As noted previously, John Paul II's speech texts contain explicit references to the evil of certain social structures and these references are carefully balanced throughout the texts and overall visit. The others—the cult of spontaneity and obligatory communitarianism—can be found infiltrating papal performance.[16]

Spontaneity

As a relief from the heavily scripted events of the papal visit, the crowds look for some spontaneous moments from John Paul II. When they occur, the public reaction is immediate and positive. Journalists note these moments in their accounts and photographers capture them for their publications because spontaneity is supposed to reveal the true inner personality, free from the restraints of role-playing. Through experience, John Paul II has learned when those moments are most successful. He hardly ever allows spontaneity to break the rhythm of a ritual, for ritual form must close down choice. Instead, he tends to make unscripted remarks at the beginning or end of a ceremony or event. Journalists report how they pay special attention to the beginning and end of an event, specifically waiting for the pope to make some unplanned remark.

It is quite natural that a speaker will respond with impromptu remarks to an introduction or presentation. In New Orleans, when Archbishop Hannan told the pope that he should feel at home with the black Catholics in the United States, John Paul II motioned to one of his personal secretaries who is from Zaire and said, "I am at home with black Catholics in America, and even in the Vatican."[17] After Reverend Frank J. McNulty ended his presentation on the priesthood in the United States, John Paul II ad-libbed, "It's a long way to Tipperary." Some in the audience, including journalists, interpreted the pope's remark as a comment on the great difference of perspective between the American church and the Vatican on some of the issues presented by McNulty. Inasmuch as McNulty had raised the possibility that celibacy might be reconsidered, some interpreted these remarks to mean that the Vatican would resist these changes for a long time.[18] On the other hand, others who noticed that the pope gestured to his prepared text believe that the pope was simply joking about the long speech that he would deliver.[19] Because spontaneous remarks, especially those of comedy, are a relief from the formal and meticulously planned rituals and speeches, they provoke a mood of antistructure in which the limiting ties are loosened, creating a certain ambiguity and fluidness that provokes variety in interpretation.

John Paul II's unplanned remarks are usually in response to his audience, and they are often designed to elicit further response. In San Antonio, after a speech to seminarians, the crowd chanted in Spanish, "John Paul II, everyone loves you." The pope smiled and said that there were exceptions. Encouraged by his response to return expressions of even greater support, the seminarians applauded and cried, "Viva el Papa." The pope then commented, "I find myself in the United States, but I could easily think I am in Mexico."[20] After his talk to priests, religious, and lay leaders in the Los Angeles cathedral, someone called out a blessing on the pope. John Paul II thanked him, saying, "It is true that all popes and bishops need special blessings from the people of God."[21] Sometimes, John Paul II will add a phrase or comment at the end of an event to move from the formal to informal posture. The effect almost always provokes audience response. After speaking to Catholic elementary and high school educators, the pope said, "I have come here first as a student. So as a student I thank you for all that you have taught me this morning. I am anxious about what kind of notes (marks) I shall receive."[22] The crowd of educators broke out in applause. John Paul II connects with his audience through these unplanned remarks, engaging the audience in a direct conversation. The playful tone of his remarks, especially because the object of his humor is most often himself, disrobes him of his authoritative clothing, placing him on a more equal level with his audience. Duncan described this appeal of attention as a risk because the speaker wants to know if he or she is still loved, for "we seek reassurance from the other that our relationship still obtains."[23] In these instances, John Paul II's playful appeals to his audience provide that reassurance, and more.

There are events during the visits that call for unscripted impromptu remarks. At a visit to a hospital in Phoenix, John Paul II praised the work of hospital workers, speaking about their "evangelical mission." When visiting school children with Mrs. Reagan in Los Angeles, he informed them that he had no speech, but invited questions. There are also events that are planned as spontaneous visits. On some of his earlier trips, Father Tucci scouted out and designated places where the pope could make a more natural impromptu visit. For example, Tucci planned for the pope to visit a family's home in an African village. Unfortunately, Tucci found that when the authorities, or even the families knew in advance of the visit, the place would change considerably. The site was no longer the simple, natural setting. Villagers and government officials had transformed it into what they thought was a suitable place for the pope to visit. Tucci then began to search out sites on his own and no longer revealed to the local planners his intentions.[24] Considered important aspects of the visit, these spontaneous occasions allowed John Paul II to reach representatives of the local church and culture more naturally. They also assured media coverage. In a 1985 trip to Africa, the pope left his obligatory visit to the president of Togo and stopped at a thatch-roofed hut along his motorcade route. He listened to a woman tell how difficult it was for her to provide for her children. Journalists scrambled to take down the words as cameras clicked and whirred to obtain the image of a white-robed pope approaching the home of such simple and impoverished people. Vatican spokesman Navarro-Valls explained that this impromptu stop along the way was to make clear the fact that "wealth and poverty exist side by side in Africa."[25] This spontaneous moment was more than a relief from the formal portion of the trip; it had a purpose. As noted in the previous chapter, similar tactics were used by planners at the local archdiocese of New York when John Paul II made his first trip to the United States. When the papal schedule called for the pope to drive by one of New York's parishes, local planners lined the street with the handicapped, many in wheelchairs. The pope was so moved, he ordered his motorcade to stop so that he could personally greet them. For public figures, the art and practice of spontaneity is part of performance.

Occasionally, John Paul II will tinker with his prepared speech. In Miami, as he began to speak, the text referred to "this beautiful land of the sun." At that moment there was a clap of thunder from the threatening sky, and John Paul II added, "the sun must also mean rain."[26] Sometimes, the pope shortens his speeches to gain time, leaving out certain sections. These sections are always contained in the printed versions of the speech, but the absence of certain paragraphs is sometimes interpreted as a sign that the pope places less significance on the issue. Whether or not there is a clear motivation on the part of John Paul II, the absence of a paragraph or two can cause disappointment among audiences that favor those points that are dropped. For example, in his homily at the Eucharistic celebration in New Orleans, John Paul II dropped a paragraph in which he extended the obligation of forgiveness to the international debt question. Those interested in the issues of development and peace were undoubtedly disappointed that the pope was unable to deliver some poignant comments on human values during his talk in Miami. Being forced to end his talk when thunderstorms pounded the site with rain and lightning, the audience did not have a chance to hear his criticism of armament spending and dishonest business practices.

Spontaneity has been a part of John Paul II's style with two specific audience groups: the bishops and youth. The meetings with the bishops are closed to the public. Formal statements by the pope and bishops are published, but the free exchange that occurs when the pope answers questions or bishops make specific points remains private. In contrast, the meetings with youth are planned as public spectacles and are often widely covered by the media. Conversational exchange in meetings with youth became a tradition early in the pope's travels. A speech was written for the pope's meeting with the youth as part of his 1980 visit to France. As the young people from the various youth organizations prepared for the visit, they decided to submit questions to the pope. When these were sent to the Vatican only a few days before the visit, John Paul II decided to change his speech to respond directly to their twenty-one questions.[27] When he appeared before the fifty thousand young people present at a stadium in a Parisian park, he thanked them for organizing a "sorte de dialogue." John Paul II used their desire to speak with the pope as a reflection on the conversation that humans have with God through Christ. This word of God was not a "grand monologue" but a "dialogue incessant."[28]

Since this experience during the papal visit to France, youth groups have utilized the format of submitting questions, which are taken into account in preparing the written papal message. However, during the teleconference in Los Angeles, John Paul II, who had seen the questions in advance, responded in unscripted, impromptu fashion. A student on the teleconference hookup in St. Louis asked the pope why he had come to the United States at this time. John Paul II responded, "Perhaps it means that I should not come?" The audience shouted, "no."[29] During a visit to Krakow in 1987 John Paul II delivered a long improvised speech to young people. On that occasion, he told them that these improvisations were the only ones that originate deeply inside him.[30] When the conversation takes place deeper with the self, humans, unencumbered by the contextuality of the world, are in touch with the mysteries of life. The symbolic construction moves away from the world, but also toward self-actualization. In a sense, these spontaneous remarks are moments of liminality, for the rhetor is both in and out of his human condition, in touch with the self, and giving of self.

In Turner's description of liminality, to enter into these moments of neither here nor there, persons strip themselves of rank and role to develop "intense comradeship." For those communal bonds to be established, persons in the higher office must temper their pride with humility. In such a process, the opposites "constitute one another and are mutually indispensable."[31] The most poignant and frank presentations during the structured dialogues of the 1987 visit to the U.S. were those of Reverend Frank McNulty speaking on behalf of the priests, and Donna Hanson, speaking for the laity. Even though both used carefully worded phrases and a respectful tone, each raised troubling issues: celibacy and dissent on the part of the priests; collaboration in church ministries for the laity. After their speeches, John Paul II opened his arms to warmly embrace each of them. He spoke to each, and afterwards, both shared those private papal remarks with others, including journalists. To McNulty, John Paul II said, "You found good words."[32] To Hanson, he said, "Yours was a good talk."[33] Even though he may have expressed similar feelings to other presenters, the pope's praise for those who may have expressed views that contrasted with his teaching was fully noted by the American audience. His unscripted words and his spontaneous gesture of embrace imparted respect and esteem for the presenters. At the same time, these signaled a humble graciousness and patience on the pope's part. At that moment, the pope, the presenter, and the audience entered "a limbo of statuslessness" with relation to each other.[34] Hence, the structured dialogue was prevented from becoming a sign of human conflict and disagreement by this embrace of love and solidarity.

Shift towards Informality

David Martin's third example of modern changes that have seeped into the church's symbolic form is obligatory communitarianism. He pointed out that society has shifted from vertical to more horizontal relationships in which participation and democratization undermine the "lonely eminence of the speaker."[35] During the papal visits, John Paul II demonstrates that popes are also contributing to more informal horizontal relationships. John Paul II does not normally use a pulpit or lectern, only a microphone, thereby avoiding any barrier between him and the audience. He very often sits rather than stands to deliver his message. Although this sitting posture is a prerogative of rulers who speak from thrones, audiences unfamiliar with the nuances of royal symbol consider sitting as more a mark of informal, boardroom style than of formal speech delivery. Like his two predecessors, he has simplified the papal garments, preferring only his white cassock. John Paul II has made some small changes that present the pope in a slightly less formal attire than Paul VI. He wears simple unadorned soft maroon leather loafers on his feet instead of the more formal buckled shoes of Paul VI. In cold weather, John Paul is seen descending the airplane in a white overcoat instead of the ecclesiastical red cape. At meetings with the youth, he often tries on hats or plays with the props presented to him. In New Orleans, he tried, but failed, to put on a plumed Mardi Gras mask which had been given to him during the youth rally.[36]

David Martin contended that churches, as other institutions, have conducted an organized invasion into private space. Physical contact breaks the protective barriers so that people will begin to feel the coziness of fellowship.[37] In this fellowship, the emphasis is placed on the horizontal, face-to-face relationships. Because part of John Paul II's ceremonial style is to touch the crowd, his entrance and exit always include time to greet people face-to-face and come in contact with them physically. At least fifteen minutes at the beginning and end of a ceremony are needed for the pope to greet the crowd and a half hour is used for the sermon.[38] The pope, therefore, spends as much time in working the crowd as he does in speech giving.

John Paul II reaches with both hands to grasp the hands of the audience. He grabs the hand of a welcoming bishop, placing another hand on his shoulder. When children come forward to present him gifts, he places kisses on their heads, strokes their cheeks, and pats their hands. Even when tired, John Paul II will not eliminate these moments of contact with his constituents. A journalist, who was allowed to view the pope at close range for an entire day while he was in San Antonio, reported that the pope's aides tried to convince him to ride in the popemobile after the huge outdoor Mass at Westover. Despite the heat, he refused and walked out through the crowd. When the journalist asked the pope if he was tired, John Paul II answered, "I don't know."[39]

Using physical contact in performing one's leadership role can be tiresome business, but if the personal touch is to succeed, it has to be performed with enthusiasm and an aura of caring. Some observers contend that John Paul II's one-on-one performance does not receive high marks. He sometimes seems distracted by the next in line, giving the appearance that he is anxious to move on. His predecessor, Paul VI, was able to sustain intense face-to-face conversations. For example, Paul VI recognized journalists, recalled their names, and remembered details about the person's personal life.[40] John Paul II is not known for his "small talk." Driven to reach out to as many people as possible, his "touch-and-feel" performance is best before a crowd. Wilton Wynn, who covered four popes for *Time*, claimed that John Paul II's "show of warmth and humanity" is sometimes staged. When the pope seems to break through his security police to greet a person in a wheelchair, or a mother and her baby, the incident is not entirely spontaneous. Some of these actions have been worked out in advance.[41]

In writing of Franklin D. Roosevelt's rhetorical presidency, Halford Ryan contended that the president's grin was an important factor in sustaining the public's perception of his "warmth and sincerity." It did not matter whether this grin was "heartfelt or cultivated"; audiences perceived his good will toward them. Ryan concluded that President Roosevelt must have realized how his "buoyant appearance" would contrast with the dreariness of the depression.[42] John Paul II seems to gain energy when before a crowd. His spontaneous, playful moments before and after large ceremonies are techniques to break down the barriers that are so skillfully constructed through the ceremonial ritual. Even though he plays to the audience's need for structure, order, and authority, at distinct moments, he identifies with their expressive needs for disorder and familiarity. Describing being embraced by the pope, Reverend Frank McNulty said, "He was so warm. As I finished, he stood up and kind of opened his arms, and I went up and he gave me an embrace. That was a great feeling. I felt like he was embracing fifty-seven thousand of us."[43]

During the 1987 visit to the U.S., there were two moments that dramatically captured John Paul II's use of a touch-and-feel style. Inside Mission Dolores in San Francisco, fifty people with AIDS were among the elderly and sick gathered to meet the pope. As he worked through the crowd, John Paul II spotted four-year-old Brendan O'Rourke who had contracted AIDS through a blood transfusion. The pope took the boy, put him to his shoulder, and hugged him. The boy responded naturally, hugging the pope back and playing with the pope's ear. The second illustrative moment occurred in Los Angeles at the youth teleconference. Tony Melendez, an armless twenty-five-year-old musician, played a guitar with his toes and sang. When he finished, John Paul II rose from his place, jumped down from his high platform, and walked over to the stage where Melendez was seated. He reached forward to touch the youth's feet. Then the pope pulled him forward so that he could kiss him on the cheek. Astonished by this impromptu action of the pope, the crowd gasped and then burst into applause and screams of joy.

John Paul II leads the audience to a moment of liminality, when the audience is able to embrace all possibilities. As with the embrace of the lay and priest presenters, the pope removes himself from his rank and role to humbly take a sick baby in his arms, or reach at the feet of a severely handicapped young man. Only by making himself lesser can he raise the status of the sufferer. As equals, with barriers removed, each can experience the lowliness and the sacredness of suffering. John Paul II speaks often about the role of suffering and its value in understanding the mystery of redemption. In an interview with André Frossard, he told of his early embarrassment when confronted with the sick, "I was above all *intimidated* by human suffering." Then, through the invalid and bedridden who attested to their happiness, he began to appreciate that the existence of sin and physical evil is "a mystery greater than man, deeper than his heart."[44] The kissing of babies and visiting of the poor have become standard ways in political campaigns to demonstrate that the candidate can be trusted to help protect families and improve social conditions for the poor. John Paul II's demonstration of popular solidarity with those of lower status or physically suffering is not a promise to alleviate the world's evils. He reaches out to touch these people and his audience in order to give them courage to face and accept the unexplainable as an act of faith in the eternal plan of God.

The reaction of young people to John Paul II's expressive style continues to amaze observers. However, the youth are easily aroused by liminal experiences. Bernice Martin recalled that youth is a "precarious status." It is an in-between moment in the life cycle. One's identity as a youth, that is, between childhood and adult roles, allows and even "guarantees release from duties, responsibilities, certainties, and constrictions of past and future roles." However, liberation from the structure imposed by adult society is also linked to acceptance by their peers. Membership in the category of youth depends on their "choosing the same form of liberation as the rest of the peer group."[45] For youth culture, the act of employing antistructural symbols is essentially a group ritual.

The fascination of youth for John Paul II undoubtedly involves two areas. First, John Paul II has singled out youth and made them special. By holding separate meetings with them, he draws the attention of the adult world to their place and role in the church. According to a publication of the Pontifical Council of the Laity, John Paul II's dialogue with the youth in Paris was a turning point for French Catholic educators and parents. Suddenly, through the pope, they discovered their young people.[46] John Paul II speaks often about young people as the hope for the church. Unlike their adult counterparts whose sense of religious meaning has become so privatized as to fragment the church, youthful members are bound passionately to their peers. They can experience community, even if it is often in direct relation to the liberating forms they adopt.

Moreover, the pope enters their world of play. His planners allow popular forms considered by some as unusual for a religious motif. The teleconference in Los Angeles employed video technology to hookup the pope with gatherings of youth in other U.S. cities. The format resembled a call-in show, as designated young people took their turns to "video" their questions to the pope. Although not exactly as conversational as a talk show, the pope used a less formal tone in responding. It was talk, not speech. One youth remarked, "It was the next best thing to talking to God."[47] At times the teleconference's style seemed to be a cross between a talk show and a rock concert, especially when a master of ceremonies directed the "warm-up" activities that previewed the pope's entrance from behind a stage curtain.[48] At youth events, John Paul II sings along with his audience, taps his feet to the beat of a dance tune, tries on hats, repeats their slogans, leaps off his throne to join them. Françoise Champion, a French sociologist, remarked that a strong and dynamic pope who exhibits a smiling face, a kindly manner, and a robust sense of humor fits the expectations of young people because, in a youthful culture, Christianity means happiness, fulfillment, an enthusiastic optimism for the future. Solemnity is absent from these occasions. Planners make sure that the events contain what is important to youth: musical rhythm, bodily movement, and colors. These events, appealing to the festive spirit of young people, are ways of structuring "la sociabilité religieuse."[49] However, as Bernice Martin contended, the play of youth is not trivial. It can affirm order and disorder at the same time, and is often the vehicle for masking social change.[50] When John Paul II crosses the generational gap for a few moments with his youthful audiences, he engages in some of their taboo-breaking activity and legitimizes them. For any pope who is weighed down by the office of the papacy, this display of abandon and release makes the audience squeal with giddiness.

DRAMATIC PERSONA

Some critics contend that the pope's audiences do not listen to his words; after an event, they cannot even remember much of what he said. This is true for most speech making. Jamieson contends that in today's mass-mediated world, speakers have to be cognizant of the effects of a "memorable" picture.[51] Even before live audiences, speakers are evaluated by a public whose critical abilities have been affected by a mass media culture. Of course, this is not a new phenomenon. Physical appearance and movement were always part of a speaker's repertoire of persuasion. However, as the public's reliance on mass media has increased, the image projected through sight and sound has become more important in critical judgment.

John Paul II has often been described as strong and vigorous. His mildly athletic build was a contrast to his predecessors: the thin and ascetic Paul IV and the overweight John XXIII. In ceremonies, his energy was apparent as he sprang from and out of vehicles or thrones. With firm hands, he reached to grasp a hand or pat a shoulder. Very often, observers noticed the pope tapping a foot, and wondered if he was following the rhythm of music or just trying to release some of his physical energy. Even in his later years, he insists on keeping a grueling physical schedule, walking through a crowd instead of riding. He blesses scores of sick after a long ceremony and distributes communion to rows of Mass-goers. As one reporter remarked, he gives the impression of running a marathon.[52] The image of vitality and strength has been so much a part of John Paul II's papacy that the picture of an aging and physically struggling pope could present serious problems. When journalists use "frail," the public starts to conjure images of a faltering papacy.[53]

John Paul II uses a full range of facial expressions to communicate with his audiences. His long stillness as he gazes at a cross conveys a total concentration on the sacred. His face seems empty of expression, his lips are still, his eyes rarely move, as if he is listening intently to another world. The electronic media cannot deal with silence and stillness at the same time. Instead of viewing silence as an activity subject to interpretation, they treat it as a negative void that needs to be filled.[54] However, as David Martin claimed, the silence of prayer approaches the unspeakable sacred. Silence is the promise of plenitude.[55]

At times, John Paul II grimaces, shutting his eyes tightly, clenching his teeth and lips. His hands grip the arms of a chair or his staff. Observers wonder if he is in pain, or is it his way of bracing his body from the arduous ceremonial tasks he must endure. Because the audience is viewing these actions often within a majestic ceremonial setting where the sacred role of the rhetor is enhanced, they tend to interpret these expressions in lofty ways. The pope does not simply have a headache, but he is an imitator of Christ and therefore has entered into Christ's pain and suffering.

Perhaps John Paul II's greatest asset is his facial pleasantness. His rounded chin and cheeks give a naturalness to his slight smile. When he takes this posture, there are pronounced lines at the edges of his eyes and in his forehead, demonstrating that he is no stranger to showing his happy side. However, there are long periods of time when John Paul II's face shows a serious side. Some find that he appears distracted. They wonder if he is truly listening or paying attention. Holding his head still, his clear blue eyes tend to dart back and forth, giving the impression that he wants to see everything that is going on, not only in front of him, but to his right and left as well. Friends and close associates of the pope report that they sometimes feel the pope is not paying attention. They tell of meetings where John Paul II appears to be far away in other thoughts. However, at the end of the meeting, he is able to summarize exactly what had been discussed.[56]

Most popes have had years of practice in religious ceremony and ritual. As a priest, bishop, cardinal, and now pope, John Paul II handles the greeting and blessing of crowds with the usual open-arm stance. As with royal monarchs, popes are attentive to their "regal" posture. This usually entails holding themselves erect, moving with deliberate and graceful gestures and sitting still for long moments. John Paul II does all this, but not all the time. He sometimes fidgets on his throne, putting his elbow on the arm of the chair, and laying his head on his hand. Italian journalist Domenico Del Rio commented that he mixes the old gestures with the new; the new ones belong to the world of televised images.[57] He mimics the response of the crowds, throwing them an affectionate gesture, clapping with them. He shows the crowd that he can break the discipline of the heavy requirements of his office and relax in front of them. Because the planning for the visit emphasizes the extraordinary nature of the event, John Paul II moves through the ceremonies, amplifying the institutional role of the papacy in its splendor. At the same time, he knows how to effect dramatic contrast by breaking the rules of royal distance and decorum and becoming an ordinary human being who laughs and cajoles and has fun. In doing so, he cuts through the institutional structures to address the people directly.

The textual portion of John Paul II's visits is written, and largely read. In ritual ceremonies the pope is bound to the printed word of the prescribed prayers and scriptures. In speeches, he is bound to his own prepared words and those of his speech writers. Janice Peck spoke of the distinction in Protestant tradition between a "manuscript preacher" and a "spiritual preacher." She observed that a minister who uses a manuscript is a teacher whose sermons "follow the linear development demanded by written language."[58] This dependence on written form is linked to the pope's role as supreme teacher of the Catholic Church. In fact, even the noninfallible, ordinary teachings of the pope, as well as the teachings of bishops in matters of faith and morals, are authoritative in that Catholics are to receive these teachings as "safe and well-founded."[59] Because Catholic tradition holds that the Holy Spirit guides the church in these matters, the teaching of the pope is supposed to be an authentic voice and not just one opinion among many. When a pope preaches, he must be very careful not to misspeak. Furthermore, the pope, as the supreme administrative ruler of the Catholic Church, oversees the administrative workings of an institution of 945 million people. Scholars have noted that impromptu remarks of presidents can have serious repercussions when their words are misinterpreted or simply "senseless." [60] The same applies to popes. The words of a pope are very carefully studied for nuances by experts on a multitude of subjects throughout the world. Therefore, even when the pope writes his own speech, the Vatican's secretariat of state and the staff of writers must carefully edit it.

Finally, the character of a visit demands that the pope deliver a large number of speeches in a few days. These are televised and chronicled by journalists. As Jamieson noted, the broadcast age makes it difficult to give the same stump campaign speech at every stop. The live audiences may be different, but the media audiences are continuously following the campaigner from stop to stop. Also, presidents and politicians have been forced to use written scripts because of the time constraints of electronic media. They often need to fit their radio or televised speech into a prescribed time slot.[61] For the papal visits such as the visit to the U.S. in 1987, planners constructed the trip with the media in mind. They carefully varied groups and subject matter so that a different topic and audience would hold media attention. Also, the papal visit is tightly time-organized. For these reasons alone, the pope is constrained to follow written scripted texts in his sermons and talks.

Peck claimed that manuscript preaching is boring television. Unlike political rhetors who use a TelePrompTer to improve their naturalness, John Paul II simply reads his speeches with little attempt to make eye contact with his audience. Some observers wonder why John Paul II, who seems so magnetic in his ability to interact with crowds, does not use his acting background more effectively. Undoubtedly, the written tradition and the magnitude of the papal teaching role influence this style. Also, John Paul II's acting experience is somewhat unique in that it was gained in an experimental theater movement that de-emphasized props, costumes, and even movement. In order to focus on the meaning of words, actors used the voice for emphasis and tone.

John Paul II's speech delivery is characterized by his voice technique. Using a slow, deliberate rate, he varies his volume and pitch just slightly to underscore words and phrases, often repeating a word for emphasis. He hardly ever hesitates, even when delivering the speech in a language such as English, which he does not speak as fluently as Italian, or of course his native language, Polish. He gives a tiny hint of his need to work harder at pronouncing the words because his English speaking voice is slightly higher in pitch than his Italian or Polish voice. Overall, his voice, deeply baritone and well suited for amplification and electronic transmission, has a natural resonance that has been enhanced by years of practice. He knows how to speak into a microphone, spacing out his words and smoothing consonants to improve comprehension and avoid harsh sounds. The soothing effect of his voice enhances the dreamlike quality to the ritual. David Martin called this feeling a "waking dream" or "active stillness" that helps to place the mind in suspension, away from the everyday and ready to approach the sacred.[62]

MEDIATED FRAMING

Television is a powerful myth-maker. This is especially evident in live televised coverage of important current events. From the funeral rites of President Kennedy to the air raids during the Gulf War, television has demonstrated its ability to encourage the forging of communal shared sentiments among scores of individuals from all walks of life and parts of the globe.[63] This creation of identity and solidarity was once dominated by religious institutions which provided the pageantry and ceremony attended by crowds of people on special days of the year. Many believe that the mass media, especially the electronic media, has usurped this role of religion. As a result, society's holy icons are largely politicians, sports figures, and rock stars. To meet the media's challenge to the ritual role of religion, Goethals offers two approaches: the iconoclast and the iconofier.[64] John Paul II, in using his international visits to communicate, employs both approaches. He constantly challenges current cultural practices and beliefs in light of Christ's teachings. More importantly, his visits are constructed to be mediated, acting to "iconofy" a holy personality moving from site to site, preaching, touching, praying, and blessing. Through the media, viewers, listeners, and readers follow this series of extraordinary events, experiencing a pilgrimage of words, sounds, and images.

In this sense, the writers, editors, producers, commentators, and technicians select and organize elements to build a "preferred" set of meanings into a message, according to their needs and perceptions of reality.[65] Critics of religious coverage in the media contend that journalists and broadcasters have eliminated or diminished religion's role in the world of news and events.[66] This is evident in their tendency to evaluate the papal visit in political terms. David Shaw of the *Los Angeles Times* analyzed the U.S. press coverage of John Paul II and conceded that critics of the media may be right. First, the media tend to report on the sex-related strictures because editors know that sex sells. The media also have a propensity for sensationalism and conflict. Because the media tend to reduce everything to its simplest terms, the fine points of theological and philosophical nuances in John Paul II's speeches are overlooked. Finally, journalists and broadcasters are generally ignorant and sometimes hostile to religion. Shaw interviewed several colleagues, including Peter Steinfels, religious writer for the *New York Times*, who claimed that "the American media emphasize what they know best—sex and politics." Tim Rutten of the *Los Angeles Times* said that the American press is "anti-intellectual and intensely materialistic."

They are only interested in "the costume drama and . . . sex."[67] Nevertheless, Shaw noted that, despite the media's dearth of interest in religious news, the Catholic Church has gained an inordinate amount of time and space in U.S. newspapers and broadcast news coverage. Shaw attributed the media interest to the papacy and its current occupant, John Paul II, whose global media stature has been enhanced by his extensive trips.[68]

Stewart Hoover contended that the electronic church of televangelists articulates the personal crises of anomie experienced by its viewers.[69] John Paul II touches on many of these same personal crises themes and more. However, the wide spectrum as well as the depth of these issues is superficially reported through the media. Mediated framing of the papal trip tends to channel the message toward an interpretation that is limited to only a few subjects. In relation to the reality of the visit, the mediated narrative is fragmented. On one hand, for many Americans modern culture is fragmented. Because audiences interpret and frame media messages through their experiences, these fragmented messages may appear consistent with their own lives. On the other hand, the purpose of religious symbol is to provide comprehensive meaning to human experience. Whatever symbols that provoke and recall this sense of order have to be constructed and presented to allow for capsulation by the media and their audiences.

Breen and Corcoran have used the concept of myth to examine press and broadcast coverage of major events. They consider four functions of myth: (1) to provide a perceptual system of common social understanding, (2) to create heroic models for imitation, (3) to mediate conflict, and (4) to make history intelligible.[70] There is no doubt that the visits of John Paul II, especially the visit to the U.S. in 1987, capture media coverage and provide prime examples of the role of media in bringing together people from all over the United States and the world to share the unfolding of the pope's pilgrimage. The papal visit of 1987 attracted 18,700 accredited journalists, 44 percent more than his visit in 1979 and more than twice the number accredited to cover the Olympic Games in Los Angeles in 1984.[71]

Most of the television stations invited observers who were knowledgeable and articulate on the church, its ritual, and its teachings to assist their commentators in the broadcast. These experts, many of whom were priests, may have contributed to what some reviewers claimed was the media's soft approach. The media seemed to be "comfortable" with reporting on the pope. Inasmuch as it was difficult for any reporter to probe what the pope said for untruths and deliberate lies, journalists found their usual skepticism irrelevant. This reverent approach of broadcast presenters and commentators is characteristic of what Katz calls a "media event." Rather than a news report on conflict, the live broadcast of Pope John Paul II's visit is engaged in myth-making. The broadcaster is the master of ceremonies and also part of the ceremony.[72] Already recognized as a mythical hero, the media coverage tended to enhance the pope's mystical status.

During their television coverage of the papal visit, cameras focus on the pope as the lone figure for whom the crowds exist. No one else compares to him. If others are there with him, they play subordinate roles: to assist him, to give him gifts, to be blessed or touched by him, to tell him about the American church. When the pope is received by political leaders, or even leaders of other faiths, he is given an enormous amount of courtesy. There is a portrayal that John Paul II's visit cannot compare to any other celebrity visit. Even the media feel compelled to treat the pope differently. There are no press conferences, no direct interviews (except occasional question-and-answer sessions with those journalists traveling on the pope's plane), and no fielding of reporters' questions. The hero becomes a larger-than-life, mysterious character who seems oblivious to the rules and procedures of the secular mediated world. Only the television camera can move through security barriers and the crowds to catch an up-close glimpse of this figure. Inasmuch as the pope does not "tell all" about his own personhood, motives, and goals, journalists and broadcasters are challenged to interpret what they receive from sources, official and nonofficial alike. This sense of seeing the pope, but yet not seeing all, titillates viewers and readers, and amplifies this mysterious quality of the sacred other.

The media present the terms of the conflict. Journalists find the papacy fascinating because of its contrast with American democratic tradition. They structure the conflict as the Vatican against the American church, the pope's brand of Catholic Church against American secular culture. The terms seem loaded in favor of the "independent-minded" against the external head of a bureaucracy that is "stern" and "unyielding." There are predictions that John Paul II will find a "disobedient flock ready to challenge," as well as "angry confrontation." When the pope arrives, he is the underdog in the conflict, not expected to win. He uses his extraordinary personal abilities, his "charm" and his "presence," but does not shirk from his responsibilities to address the controversial issues. He is aided by the "pageantry," because the audiovisual elements of ceremony, emotion, music, and colors are captured and enhanced by the electronic media transmission. *Washington*

Post writers admitted that "it is hard to speak too critically of something wrapped in such overwhelming beauty."[73] Planners have done an effective job in presenting splendid settings of sacred space. Crowds materialize, although not to the extent that planners have predicted. The media begin to frame the conflict differently. Because the demonstrators are weak in numbers compared to the "adoring" crowds, the angry confrontations are placed on the periphery. Television cameras pick out a rapturous face and a tearful eye. Even the media's attention to the souvenir sellers tells viewers that the pope is good business. As the television camera switches from the pope to the audience, it frames the relationship of pope to people. This "rhetoric of image" is one of warm emotion rather than cool rationality.[74] The heroic pope seems to be winning the hearts of his live audiences. Viewers at home encode this "preferred reading" of the pope, not just at one event, but at multiple events as he moves from city to city. Nonetheless, the media keep alive the reports of pollsters and the opinion of experts that the American flock are "increasingly restive." Media commentators try to explain the discrepancies between what the media cameras have recorded for the millions of viewers and what was known about U.S. Catholics' opinions on moral teachings of the pope. They present the sacred-secular dialectic, but are unsure of the results. For example, the media expected that the "structured dialogues" of the U.S. visit would confirm an opinion that the church is indeed fragmented by conflicting opinions. When spokespersons for the representative groups, such as the laity and the priests, responded to the media about the warm embrace of John Paul II, giving the media little on which to base reports of dissent within the church, commentators and journalists concluded that the pope was not rejected by U.S. Catholics as predicted. Nevertheless, the media had played a significant role in constructing the narrative as a form of conflict.

SUMMARY: RITUAL AND RELIEF

Italian journalist Del Rio claimed that the pope governs the church through images, and this depends on the participation of the mass media.[75] The nontextual, nonverbal elements of John Paul II's performance form the visual and sensual images with which the electronic and print media work so effectively. First, the structure of the visit places spellbinding ritual at the center of its performance. Precisely timed, hierarchically arranged and splendid in form and color, the Eucharistic celebration transports audiences of participants and viewers to extraordinary space and time where, for a few hours, their fragmented and disorderly lives seem perfectly whole and fully united to the pope as the majestic symbol of sacred order.

In ritual, audiences are presented with an overload of sacred images, and in order to continue recognizing them, there must be some relief from the almost reified atmosphere. This relief comes fleetingly in spontaneous moments throughout the papal visit that reorder the position of rhetor and audience to create a short time frame of liminality. Shedding rank, pope and people become bound through unstructured equality, creating limitless possibilities for reconciling differences and resolving conflicts. The spontaneous moments when John Paul II embraced the lay and the priest presenters stripped away the previous layers of logical arguments, leaving only essential humanness, and that humanness, because it is the likeness of God, leads to the sacred.

Also in ritual, the sacred is held at a distance, high on an altar, and enclosed in bullet-proof glass. Used to informality and physical coziness, people crave a chance to touch and be touched by the pope. With a display of abandon and release, John Paul II complies by trying on hats, hugging babies, and singing songs. He is most at ease in this playful style with youthful audiences who react with giddiness when he crosses generational borders to engage in unlikely activities for a pope. His most poignant moments are when he reaches out to touch those whose sufferings attest to the moral or physical evils in the world. Not intending to offer them cures, he seeks to demonstrate how to enter into their suffering in order to have the courage to face and accept the unexplainable. His actions, gestures, and sometimes spontaneous words ask not for rational agreement or physical perfection, but a simple affirmation that there is a divine plan.

Despite the encumbrances of the papal office (mainly the written tradition and the heavy duty of supreme teacher), John Paul II uses his voice, physical stature, an array of facial expressions, and graceful gestures to increase the dramatic content of his performance. Sometimes these nonverbal actions are supportive of his deliberately solemn sacred vocabulary. Occasionally, a gesture, a wink, or even a sturdy workmanlike hand clasp provides hints of the pope's wholeness as a human being.

The majestic sights of ritual, spontaneous moments, the occasional informality, and timely gestures provide visual capsules that can be effectively used by the media. As Shaw indicated, there may indeed be a lack of background and cultural bias that affect the way the media construct their narrative of the church. However, many believe that John Paul II knows how to gain access and manage the direction of media coverage. In choosing sites and audiences, planners influence the themes of the visit. These themes, in turn, are treated textually by John Paul II as he adapts his address to the contextual and universal needs of his audiences. Undoubtedly, this preparation and execution of the papal visit affects the portrayal by the media. The example of the papal trip to the U.S. in 1987 demonstrates that the planning of the visit played a major role in the media coverage. Imagine if the media had concluded that the pope's visit was a failure. Local planners must indeed consider this possibility when making their decisions and carrying out their preparations.

In effect, the media's conclusion to their mythic narrative of the 1987 papal visit to the U.S. is accurate. Tension continues. However, there are differences in the television framing and the papal framing. The media's portrayal of conflict often centers on the internal church: the American church against the pope and the Vatican. For John Paul II, the conflict is between a God-centered moral order and a secular, hedonistic culture where God is absent. As long as the pope continues to construct sacred images, there will be continued tension. Some journalists grasped this message as they wrote their conclusions. The *Washington Post* concluded that the pope doesn't want to resolve the conflicts because "he sees himself not only as a symbol of peace, but of contradiction."[76] The *New York Times* wrote of a pope comforting Catholics as they deal with the "inevitable tests of faith" in sorting out the "worldly and the divine."[77] These were conclusions, and not lead paragraphs. Consequently, the headlines followed the story's emphasis: the American church against the pope. To some extent the media has helped to form John Paul II's new vocabulary of the sacred, but in other respects, they have been unable to accurately capsulize the essence of the sacred dimension.

NOTES

1. Kenneth Burke, *On Symbols and Society*, ed. Joseph R. Gusfield (Chicago: University of Chicago Press, 1989), 130; Hugh Dalziel Duncan, *Communication and Social Order* (New York: Bedminster Press, 1962), 117.

2. Kathleen Hall Jamieson, "Papal Rhetoric," *America*, 24 May 1980, 446.

3. Kathleen Hall Jamieson, *Eloquence in an Electronic Age* (New York: Oxford University Press, 1988), 117.

4. Vatican Council II, *Sacrosanctam concilium*, no. 10 in *Vatican Council II: The Conciliar and Post Conciliar Documents*, ed. Austin Flannery (Wilmington, Delaware: Scholarly Resources, 1975).

5. Ibid., 41.

6. David Martin, *The Breaking of the Image* (Oxford: Basil Blackwell, 1980), 82–84.

7. Sally F. Moore and Barbara G. Myerhoff, "Introduction: Secular Ritual: Forms and Meanings," in *Secular Ritual*, eds. Sally Moore and Barbara Myerhoff (Amsterdam: Van Gorcum, 1977), 18.

8. David Martin, *The Breaking of the Image*, 94.

9. Domenico Del Rio, an Italian journalist, described this courtier posture of the gift bearers and the silence of the crowd in an article about Pope John Paul II's 1982 visit to Spain in an article entitled, "Faithful in a Trance for Wojtyla Superstar," quoted in David Willey, *God's Politician: John Paul at the Vatican* (London: Faber and Faber, 1992), 198.

10. David Martin, *The Breaking of the Image*, 87–88.

11. Kenneth Burke, *A Rhetoric of Motives* (New York: Prentice-Hall, 1950), 277–278.

12. Jamieson, "Papal Rhetoric," 444.

13. Duncan, *Communication and Social Order*, 280.

14. David Martin, *The Breaking of the Image*, 89.

15. Ibid., 101.

16. Ibid., 91.

17. John Paul II, *Building Up the Body of Christ* (Washington, D.C.: National Catholic News Service, 1987), 32.

18. David Maraniss and Laura Sessions Stepp, "Pope Leaves Amid Contradictions, Affection," *Washington Post*, 20 September 1987.

19. Monsignor Robert Lynch, interview by author, 28 August 1992, Washington, D.C.

20. John Paul II, *Building Up the Body of Christ*, 46.

21. Ibid., 71.

22. Ibid., 32.

23. Duncan, *Communication and Social Order*, 280.

24. Reverend Roberto Tucci, S.J., interview by author, 13 February 1992, Rome, Italy.

25. Don A. Schanche, "John Paul II, CEO" *Los Angeles Times Magazine*, 13 September 1987.

26. John Paul II, *Building Up the Body of Christ*, 14.

27. Gérard Defois, archbishop of Sens, France, interview by author, 24 March 1993, Sens, France. John Paul II told the young people of his two speeches. The texts of both speeches, the one written in advance, and the one actually given, are included in compilations of his speeches during the papal visit to France in 1980. See John Paul II, *France, que fais-tu de ton baptême?* (Paris: Centurion, 1980); and John Paul II, *France: Message of Peace, Trust, Love, and Faith* (Boston: Daughters of St. Paul, 1980).

28. John Paul II, *France, que fais-tu de ton baptême?*, 166–167.

29. John Paul II, *Building Up the Body of Christ*, 71.

30. *L'Osservatore Romano*, 12 June 1987, 7.

31. Victor Turner, *The Ritual Process: Structure and Anti-Structure* (Chicago: Aldine, 1969), 95–97.

32. Cathleen Decker, "The Papal Visit: Speech to Pope Puts Priest in Spotlight, Creates Ripple," *Los Angeles Times*, 12 September 1987.

33. Kenneth A. Briggs, *Holy Siege* (San Francisco: HarperCollins, 1992), 554.

34. Turner, *The Ritual Process*, 97.

35. David Martin, *The Breaking of the Image*, 107.

36. John Paul II, *Building Up the Body of Christ*, 33.

37. David Martin, *The Breaking of the Image*, 95.

38. Reverend Robert Tucci, interview by author, 13 February 1992.

39. John Paul II, *Building Up the Body of Christ*, 47.

40. Valentina Alazraki, Mexican journalist, interview by author, 19 November 1992, Rome, Italy.

41. Wilton Wynn, *Keepers of the Keys* (New York: Random House, 1988), 142–143.

42. Halford R. Ryan, *Franklin D. Roosevelt's Rhetorical Presidency* (Westport, Connecticut: Greenwood Press, 1988), 15.

43. Decker, "The Papal Visit: Speech to Pope."

44. André Frossard, *"Be Not Afraid!"* (New York: St. Martin's Press, 1984), 83–85.

45. Bernice Martin, *A Sociology of Contemporary Cultural Change* (New York: St. Martin's Press, 1981), 140.

46. John Paul II, *Le Saint-Père parle aux jeunes: 1980–1985*, ed. Jean Claude Didelot (Vatican City: Conseil Pontifical pour les Laics, 1985), 5.

47. John Paul II, *Building Up the Body of Christ*, 71.

48. P. Pullella, interview by author, 18 November 1992, Rome, Italy.

49. Françoise Champion, "La rencontre des jeunes et du papé, une affirmation identitaire de la jeunesse catholique," in Jean Séguy et al., *Voyage de Jean-Paul II en France* (Paris: Les Editions du Cerf, 1988), 56–85.

50. Bernice Martin, *A Sociology*, 184.

51. Jamieson, *Eloquence*, 114–117.

52. John Paul II, *Building Up the Body of Christ*, 47.

53. There is already evidence that John Paul II's aging condition is becoming a theme in the mass media. During his visit to the United States in 1995, news articles spoke of his being "exhausted," "shaky," "slow and shuffling." See Celestine Bohlen, "Security, Formality, and Age Obscure Man of Wit," *New York Times*, 8 October 1995.

54. See Adam Jaworski, *The Power of Silence: Social and Pragmatic Perspectives* (Newbury Park, California: Sage, 1993), 78–79.

55. David Martin, *The Breaking of the Image*, 201–202.

56. Schanche, "John Paul II, CEO."

57. Domenico Del Rio, "Il grido di Wojtyla," in Domenico Del Rio and Luigi Accattoli, *Wojtyla: Il nuovo Mosè* (Milan: Arnoldo Mondadori Editore, 1988), 38.

58. Janice Peck, *The Gods of Televangelism* (Cresskill, New Jersey: Hampton Press, 1993), 122–123.

59. Patrick Granfield, *The Limits of the Papacy* (New York: Crossroad, 1987), 157. The Catholic Church makes the distinction between infallible and noninfallible teaching. In declaring an infallible teaching, the church gives a guarantee that the teaching is a truth revealed by God.

60. Jamieson, *Eloquence*, 174.

61. Ibid., 207.

62. David Martin, *The Breaking of the Image*, 87.

63. Gregor Goethals, "Media Mythologies," in *Religion and the Media*, ed. Chris Arthur (Cardiff: University of Wales Press, 1993), 26.

64. Ibid., 35.

65. Stuart Hall, "Encoding/Decoding," in *Culture, Media, Language* (London: Hutchinson, 1980), 134. See also Todd Gitlin, *The Whole World Is Watching, Mass Media in the Making and Unmaking of the New Left* (Berkeley: University of California Press, 1980), 7.

66. William E. Biernatzki, "Religion in the Mass Media," *Communication Research Trends* 15, no. 2 (1995): 3–15.

67. David Shaw, "Missing the Pope's Message: The Media's Ignorance of Religion and Their Zeal for Conflict Often Skew Coverage of John Paul II," *Los Angeles Times*, 16 April 1995.

68. David Shaw, "Activist Pope Puts Catholics at Front of Media Attention," *Los Angeles Times*, 18 April 1995.

69. Stewart Hoover, *Mass Media Religion* (Newbury Park, California: Sage, 1988), 243.

70. Myles Breen and Farrel Corcoran, "Myth in the Television Discourse," *Communication Monographs* 49 (June 1982): 128–131.

71. Jim Unsworth, "Oh Say, Did You See the TV Pope 'Pourri'?" *National Catholic Reporter*, 2 October 1987.

72. Elihu Katz, "Media Events: The Sense of Occasion," *Studies in Visual Communication* 6, 3 (1980): 85.

73. David Maraniss and Laura Sessions Stepp, "Pope Leaves," *Washington Post*, 20 September 1987.

74. Roger Silverstone, "Television, Rhetoric, and the Return of the Unconscious in Secondary Oral Culture," in *Media, Consciousness, and Culture*, eds. Bruce Gronbeck et al. (Newbury Park, California: Sage Publications, 1991), 154.

75. Del Rio, "Il grido di Wojtyla," 50.

76. Maraniss and Stepp, "Pope Leaves."

77. Ari L. Goldman, "Ideas and Trends: Can a Patriarchal Aura Close the Gap between a Pope and His Flock?" *New York Times*, 13 September 1987.

CHAPTER 8

Push and Pull
of Sacred and Secular

The international pastoral visit is John Paul II's distinct way of communicating to a church that is challenged by increasingly secularized cultures. As with any religious language, it deals with the interplay of opposites, coding the tension between what is human and what is above and beyond the human. Yet, through its planning process, its textual arrangement and performance, it recognizes the limits of diversity and fluidity that permeate the audience's experience, sustaining religious consciousness through a multileveled meaning structure that helps us to cope with the discrepancies between normative ideals and everyday practice. The papal visit is a new way of speaking about the sacred.

THE FLUIDITY OF SACRED-SECULAR BORDERS

The rhetorical strategy of John Paul II fluctuates with audiences, subjects, and settings as it weaves back and forth over a range of accommodating and resistance tendencies, thereby demonstrating how construction of a sacred cosmos cannot be held in check for very long at one point on the continuum. In fact, the papal visit employs a polysymbolic strategy that deliberately opens and closes to the secular world, and thus constructs a sacred cosmos of multimeanings. In other words, John Paul II attempts to return to a sacred image that is distinct and apart from the secular and, at the same time, he reaches across the borders to the secular world for symbols that cloud and shatter meaning with their opposing movement. The result is an ambiguity that embraces contrasting positions and appeals to audiences whose fluid lives roam through a myriad of symbolic identities.

The papal visit's rhetorical strategies that tend toward the resistance end of the spectrum are noticeable in five main areas: firming of permanent sacred norms, distinct ordering of personal roles, naming of evil to encourage communal identity and authenticity, promoting transcendent otherness, and representing the ideal community through a repertoire of social bonding symbols. With each set of resistance strategies, the papal rhetoric employs a reverse movement to reflect potentiality in the opposing direction: collaborative decision making and updated vocabulary, use of identity symbols that adapt to egalitarian and compartmentalized life, preference for contextuality and acceptance of pluralism, an easy familiarity with the ordinary, and a mixture of communicative techniques that reflect past scholastic traditions and adapt to newer organizational requirements.

Permanence and Durability

John Paul II's rhetoric stresses the durable nature of the sacred Other as prior to and the basis of all humanly constructed worlds, providing a permanent external referent to all human activity. His audiences are not asked to creatively discover the sacred in the individual recesses of their souls, but to collectively remember and reflect upon what has been given by God and what is in the memory of the church. Metaphorically, John Paul II emphasizes that the *nomos* proceeds from the sacred as from a gift giver and we, humans and debtors, must constantly look to return the gift. In this way the communicative relationship is fixed and cannot be reversed by humans. Time-tested metaphors, along with a multitude of historical references from the beginning of creation through the millennium to eternity, connect the audience in a permanent way to what is durable and beyond the here and now of their contextual lives.

At the same time, the papal visit is essentially a mechanism for collaborating with what is not durable and fixed. This collaboration begins within the church when barriers fall between the papacy, as the symbol of universal church, and the particular local churches. From the visit's beginnings, the Vatican insists on an invitational process signifying a two-directional relationship. Inviting the pope to experience their particular and contextual worlds, local churches provide significant input into the planning, execution, and even the textual composition of the visit. Consequently, the papacy is engaged in situations that it may not have sought within the confines of the Vatican walls, such as: reassuring demoralized priests; convincing restive laity; consoling victims of the newly discovered illness, AIDS; and handling the consequences of modern human failings, such as broken marriages. In effect, John Paul II relinquishes some control over sacred meaning by encountering the local church on its own ground of secularized culture. Thus, the papal visits are significant occasions for the local churches to take part in meaning construction.

Comparisons of locally prepared texts with final versions demonstrate how the papal versions are decidedly more "sacred" in that they use more sacred terms and often underscore arguments by relating the normative ultimately to Christ's words or the creative act of God. More importantly, the pope often avoids immediate causes in preference for longer-term, even eternal interpretation. Solving the current problems of immigrants may be laudable, but what matters most is the immigrant's steadfastness in the face of immense suffering. Sometimes, when the local church makes new demands on what "ought to be," Vatican final drafts respond with "authentic" reminders to distinguish what is "true" from the notions of other competing discourses. At other times, the visit's textual references co-opt secular terms, such as "feminism," by giving them an "authentic" and sacred character.

In this regard, the speeches of John Paul II are sprinkled with updated words and expressions that point to the church's opening to the world. From "collaboration" in decision making to the sacrament of penance as a "psychological liberation," John Paul II's vocabulary contains hints of the church's acceptance of the secular world's framework of a more equal, democratic, and self-fulfilling language that inevitably affects the human description of the sacred-human relationship.

Boundary Making

The visit demonstrates how John Paul II aims to restore boundary lines between sacred and secular functions and roles. Evident in both the planning and textual address of audiences, these strategies uphold what Burke contends is the mystery of hierarchical order that makes identification so desirable. With the bishops, John Paul II strikes an informal tone, structuring his speech by expressions of dialogue consistent with the need for popes to respect the bishops' collaborative role. His address to the priests is filled with an assumed "we" that encloses them in sacredness and isolates them from the secular world. With the laity, he takes the opposite tact. His mode of address maintains a distance between the lay audience and himself and this rhetorical distance reinforces his message that priest and lay remain different and mysterious to each other.

Despite the rhetorical insertion of boundary lines that uphold hierarchical order and distinction between the sacred and secular roles and functions, John Paul II addresses audiences and chooses imagery to conform to his audience's experience with change. Affected deeply by secularism and pluralism, church members lament the loss of order and certainty of the past, but they are now used to an expanded range of interpretation of sacred symbols. Thus, John Paul II follows Vatican Council II's compromise solution to church identity by balancing his use of dual forms of church metaphors: the Body of Christ to emphasize an organically binding image of the church and the People of God to characterize a more egalitarian, democratic church. Even though he tends to employ both metaphors, John Paul II selectively uses these metaphors to reinforce a particular audience's tendencies to favor a more open or more closed church.

The text of the 1987 U.S. visit also reveals that John Paul II's characterization of his audience's identity and role within the church may be influenced more by pragmatic considerations than by norms. By giving preference to the Body of Christ metaphor, educators and health workers are told to form their identity through an organic relationship with the sacred. The reasons appear to relate to church resources. The church has significant material and historical resources in the educational and medical field. Through his metaphoric use, John Paul II signals that the church needs to keep the functions and identity of those involved in education and health care more closely bound to the church's structure.

The papal visit's planning and structure act to restore boundary lines and uphold order between the sacred and secular roles and functions, but they also encourage movement in the opposite direction. Because the visit is designed to bring the pope to audiences in their particular settings, John Paul II often uses cultural variations to inform the audience of sacred identity. This intermingling of civic and religious historical and cultural references breaks down borders so that audiences feel a natural union of their sacred and secular lives. Sometimes the preparatory process of the visit encourages a secularization of identities. To convey a national character on the 1987 U.S. visit, planners organized events with specialized audiences to highlight different services, such as health care or education. Consequently, the rhetorical strategy of papal address to these audiences of narrowly defined services within the church leads the rhetor to accentuate audience identities that are over-specialized. Groups of educators, health care workers, communicators, and farm workers encourage church members to form their identity more by their association with a particular activity than by their hierarchically ordered functions in the church. As a result, a member of these specialized service groups sees himself or herself as a communicator or educator and not necessarily as a priest or lay person. In singling out these groups, the pope tends to support the compartmentalized life of modern society.

Naming Evils

A third way in which the papal visit's rhetorical strategy resists secular encroachment is to recognize the persistence of evil and the unique reputation of the church in withstanding that evil. Symbols of sin, Satan, and enemy are reintroduced as lurking outside the church but within culture. Military metaphors are used to discipline the armies of disciples who are called upon to resist these evils with heroic courage. These are classic rhetorical tools of disassociation that aim to convince like-minded people to put aside their own internal problems in order to build a strong united force against an external enemy. The borders between the church and the evils in secular culture are drawn not so much to enclose, protect, and close down meaning, nor to motivate the church members to conquer these evils in practical ways, but rather to engage the audience in restoring the church's reputation as a strong and united actor in the sacred-secular dialectic. The evils may be present outside the church, but the real crisis that John Paul II addresses rhetorically is the lack of confidence within the church. The pope's apocalyptic visions and his use of the coming millennium as a rallying call for the church tap into an uneasiness present in his audiences about an uncertain future. Disenchanted with the experimentation of the sixties and the seventies, people are ready for a more realistic rendering of the postmodern age. Thus, the rhetorical strategy is to use this uneasiness to gain the attention of the audience and motivate them towards congregation.

The naming of evils occurs consistently but within limits, and is usually confined to certain sections of papal speech. On the other hand, woven throughout the papal visits is an optimism that tends to counteract the countercultural and somewhat pessimistic renderings of the current secular age. In other words, John Paul II approaches the task of motivating his audience in dual directions. This optimism is drawn not only from the pope's frequent references to a sacred directed future, but also from a persistent tone that evokes his strong faith in human potentiality. John Paul II's constant use of contextual and historical examples point to his reliance on prior human experience to confirm the forward-moving direction of the church and culture. Contained in his speeches are themes and expressions related to his prior philosophical writings that express human dignity and self-actualization as profound mysteries of God's love. Most of all, John Paul II's use of self-references encourages audiences to view the papacy in modern human terms—equal to others, and speaking a language of self. By regularly employing the pronoun "I," the pope recognizes that his audiences no longer have a strong sense of a communal "we." Living in a pluralistic situation where allegiance is voluntary, these audiences need to be patiently courted through images of personal happiness and joy.

When John Paul II names the evils of the modern world, he includes a wide variety of moral and social ills to trigger recognition and identification in audiences at both ends of the accommodation-resistance spectrum. In other words, if there is not total agreement on every item of the papal agenda, a communal "we" is formed when audiences notice that the pope has at least named their particular priorities. In this regard, the papal rhetoric is symptomatic of the problem that institutions have in dealing with diversity. The inevitability of a more culturally diverse world led the church to adjust its universal mythic dimension by employing a new theological term, "inculturation," which aims to preserve and integrate one's culture into the sacred universality of the church. The visits of John Paul II are very effective in communicating the newly constructed mythical connection between the sacred universal and human contextuality because the pope approaches his audience as he is comfortable with himself: through a wholeness of person. The pope and his audiences are steeped in cultural peculiarities. These life experiences and cultural moldings do not have to be left behind or changed in order to construct a sacred identity. There is no question that John Paul II has an advantage over other immediate predecessors in communicating inculturation simply because he is the first non-Italian pope in modern times. He does not suppress his Polishness, but takes strategic advantage of it as he self-reveals about his own spiritual journey. He names people, and himself, by their multicultural contextuality, tapping into modern life's heightened sense of difference in order to construct a plausible "we" of the church.

The resistance strategy of naming evils aims to pull the church from the secular culture by tapping into the anxieties and instability of modern life, but the strategy doubles back to praise the human condition and passage in time in order to motivate church audiences to feel good about themselves and their potential. The pope encourages his audiences to look upon their secularized culture with suspicion and distaste, but on the other hand, the papal visit constantly demonstrates how John Paul II and his audiences are enthusiastically immersed in culture. The pope's call to be contextually countercultural illustrates how symbols can construct a unified "we" among an audience of diverse interests. For U.S. audiences sensitive to their pluralistic condition, the pope is faced with the problem of how to appear both openly ecumenical and decidedly confessional. He walks the fine line between the two, but the totality of the visit acts to shore up the church's exclusive position.

Majestic Contrast

From the start of the planning process, the visit is characterized as possessing a quality that distinguishes it from all other visits of important personalities. The political portions of the visit are assiduously controlled, while the spiritual functions become the heart of the visit. From the pretrip hype to the mobilization of national and local diocesan church resources, planning centers on how to present majestic contrast to the daily humdrum of everyday life. Both in performance and text, the visits invoke the sacred in dramatic tones of reverence. John Paul II prays respectfully and with the authority of his office, arranging the church in hierarchical order before an attentive but still distant and unknown God. His metaphors tend to keep his audiences awestruck by the "tremendum" quality of a great, all inclusive God toward whom the church walks in a "royal road" to reach the glorious vision of a "holy city" of pure community. The millennium has been an opportunity for John Paul II to reintroduce an element of fear, tapping into the apprehension people feel about an uncertain future. In other words, the way to holiness requires venturing into unknown and uncharted domains. Furthermore, John Paul II's textual themes and imagery are not simple, but complex, singling out the elements of life such as suffering and forgiveness as the mysterious workings of the sacred. Above all, the ritual performance during the visits presents audiences with a dream-time reality through its overload of intense splendor and perfect order. The pope becomes ordained with the properties of this extraordinary realm and, at least for a few hours, audiences are drawn from their everyday chaotic world into the glory and majesty of a sacred church.

In contrast to the ritual framing of the sacred where awesomeness distances sacred symbol from human everyday experience, John Paul II at times strips away the layers of mystery so that audiences can view the pope as human and therefore equal to the most common members of the audience. Textually, he treats ordinary human experience such as work, play, and family life. During certain moments of the visit, he acts the same as ordinary human beings; he laughs, sings, and tries on silly hats. Through these contrasting moments, John Paul II sheds his pontiffness to become a confidant, friend, and companion to the audience. Occasionally, the pope lapses into a more managerial tone of an organizational leader, asking for reports and follow-up. Although his references to the church's governing systems and mechanisms tend to increase the distance between the rhetor and the audience, the vocabulary of the bureaucratic and organizational structure is well known to the audience. In this regard, these instances of managerial talk make the church less special and "other," and more accommodating to the secular culture.

Intimate, Yet Rational Relationships

The fifth and final category of resistance strategies closely follows the operational framework in which symbols of an emotive, intimate, loving community are posed against the rational and contractual structures of social relationships found in the secularized culture. There are many examples of John Paul II's use of emotive communal signs, and these moments are now part of the audience's expectations. With an understanding of how religious faith is experienced on many levels, the church, no longer hampered by complete reliance on knowledge-based theological strategies, has revitalized its use of imagery and symbol. The papal visit is an excellent example of how the church communicates about the sacred through emotive symbol and imagery.

Nevertheless, there are two areas within the papal visit that indicate the influence of rationally based structures of social relationships. The first is a remnant of the neoscholastic tradition. The papacy has a long tradition of communicating in written form, and this written tradition, with its tendency toward logical arrangement, is a persistent strain in papal communication. Papal speech is necessarily authoritative, and therefore, there is an overconcern for papal talk to be part of the voluminous written record.

The second area shows a seepage into church culture of new forms of rational spirit, namely the efficient, managerial, technically pragmatic approach that is considered successful in creating and directing highly specialized and compartmentalized social systems. The reliance of the Vatican on the local churches to plan and execute the details of the visit can draw the church into a process largely dominated by methods of local governance. As was the case in the papal visit to the United States in 1987, the planning process encouraged cooperation among dioceses and parishes through a highly systematized national structure that operated under rules of democratic discussion and objective process. Moreover, planning of the visit is affected by its technical performance, namely the ability of portions of the visit to project synopsized moments that can be captured and mediated throughout the world. As a result, the papal visit became so professionally managed and systematically programmed that even some spontaneous moments were engineered.

To recall a sense of the sacred and to restore balance after a tumultuous period of accommodation, the papal visit shows a preference for rhetorical strategies that resist secularization. With each resistance movement there is a corresponding movement outward to the secularized world. This rhetorical strategy moves with audiences, responding and sorting out the ebb and flow of sacred symbols in peoples lives. Therefore, there is no exact midpoint of balance between sacred and secular symbol construction.

Audiences in the church are located at various points on the accommodating-resistance spectrum. Their experience of and reaction to social change and the effects of the social ecology on their grasp of the sacred varies. Also, audience groups and individuals are dealing with ongoing change, and they are searching for ways to cope with the crisis of meaning. The papal rhetorical strategies illustrate how the church's construction of a sacred cosmos responds to this fluidity by posing symbols that recreate the durable, ordered, socially binding, authentically other world of the sacred, and by constructing other symbols that overlap and reach in a contrary direction toward the collaborative, egalitarian, contractual, pluralistic, everyday lifestyles of a secularized culture. Even though the rhetorical strategies of John Paul II's papal visits show a preference for constructing borders between the sacred and the secular, his visits are polysymbolic, allowing a range of double meanings and interpretations that appeal to audiences who are affected in overt and subtle ways by their modern secular culture. Using David Martin's description, the sacred is known and unknown, limited and limitless. When we construct borders to give more precise meaning to the sacred, the image finds ways to break through these barriers because the sacred cannot be limited.[1] The only way we can express sacred character is through the double entendre language of ambiguity.

PERCEPTIONS OF PLAUSIBILITY

A sacred cosmos is maintained through plausibility structures. Pope John Paul II may appeal to the fluidity of his audiences by weaving elements of accommodating or resistance tactics into his symbol system, but his vocabulary of the sacred will have little appeal unless it is perceived as plausible. There are three ways that the papal visit shores up the church so as to maintain a sacred cosmos that appears believable to audiences: first, the visit helps the church to retain its massivity, even when reports indicate that the church's numbers are failing; second, the visit restores a mystical quality to the church that makes sense to those who have grown distrustful of the material world; and third, the visit highlights the church as a warm and compassionate community capable of healing the modern self's frightening solitude.

Berger observed that when churches ceased to be monopolies, they became subject to competition, and when they began to lose massivity, people ceased to believe in their reality systems.[2] The media often report on an upcoming papal visit by referring to polls and other quantifiable criteria that indicate the church's decline in numbers and support for its basic moral teachings. John Paul II does not attempt to answer these critics by citing numbers. Instead, his visits are designed to induce a perception of massivity among the faithful members that is both pervasive and intense.

With four trips a year, carefully scheduled so as not to favor one geographic area or cultural group, a global strategy portrays the church as everywhere throughout the world. The 1987 U.S. visit illustrates how, with networks fanning out into all parts of the country and into different service areas of the church as an institution, the papal visit can encourage members to develop a national consciousness. Many who participate begin to think of themselves not only in terms of their membership in a local parish or local school, but as "insiders" of a much larger national and global church negotiating with others a common understanding of their faith, its problems, and solutions.

Local and Vatican planners set their priorities on creating images of massivity. They examine the strengths and weakness of the local church institution and make site and setting decisions based on potential success rates. A key ingredient is an enthusiastic and emotional crowd for the main event of each day, a massive spiritual gathering of faithful members of the church. Organized in stadiums, open fields, and public grounds, these papal Eucharistic celebrations meet the American measure of grand scale and importance.

The crowded rituals also tend to increase the intensity of the event. Like parishioners being readied for a spiritual journey, church members at the site of the visit anticipate being persuaded. In a sense, they become malleable because they expect something extraordinary to happen to them. When they enter the crowded event to wait for the arrival of the pope, they have an immediate and direct awareness of a reality sustained by the thousands and sometimes hundreds of thousands of people who gather to see the pope and be part of a demonstration of their faith. As the pope passes through the crowd, some persons, moved to tears by their excitement, ignite the emotions of those seated nearby. This stirring embrace of John Paul II is infectious, and the response to the pope moves from a conglomeration of individual reactions isolated from each other to a unified movement of animation and joy. United with the pope and everyone assembled, people find it easy to believe the myth of oneness and universality of a diverse and worldwide church when it is experienced as real in such massive doses.

Of all the speeches given during the papal visits, John Paul II takes personal interest in the preparation of the homilies for the Eucharistic celebrations. His textual strategies often close and fix meaning on the sacred as something massive in time, space, and durability. In his homilies, he treats the church in a stream of history from the beginning of time to the beginnings of a nation and onward to a new millennium. With military metaphors, he moves the well-disciplined people from their individual homes and parishes to a crowded stadium and beyond, to counter the evils of a godless culture. John Paul II plays down internal differences and never admits any weakness in the church. Constantly quoting itself through citing other writings and addresses of John Paul II, papal speech appears unaffected by other voices and therefore durable.

Although not all the coverage is accurate or cast in a positive framework, the unusual amount of news coverage given to Catholicism and the pope during these visits gives the church an enormous legitimacy as an important referent in the construction of meaning. The possibility to reach many more people through the mass media is enhanced through the visits because John Paul II, no longer distant and hidden behind the Vatican walls, makes himself visible and encourages others to manifest themselves as visible members of the church. He and members of the local church externalize sacredness in contrast to the modern tendency to interiorize spiritual dimensions of one's identity. The television cameras increase the memorability of this externalization.

The second way that the visits create and maintain plausibility structures is by restoring a mystical quality to the church. People who become distrustful and frustrated with real-world solutions turn to more mystical answers to their problems. As Bernice Martin reminds us, the pursuit of ecstasy is really an attempt to escape the structure of human society. However, churches harness the mystical experiences to reinforce the structure of their sacred symbolic codes.[3] The majestic and awesome character of the papal visit lends itself to the kind of mythmaking that lifts people's spirits and provides relief from the insoluble problems of their human and earthly dimension. Like no other celebrity, the pope is often treated by the media as a larger-than-life, mysterious hero. This media coverage of the pope is not unrelated to the visit's planning and performance. With the enormous amount of courtesy accorded him, the pope arrives, but gives no press conferences nor personal interviews. He is present and compelling to the media, but he remains aloof. Since the pope does not "tell all" to the press, they must interpret what they receive from other sources. This sense of mystery titillates viewers and readers, for as Burke observed, mystery and the potential of bridging the gap between the known and unknown excites and motivates people toward greater union.[4]

With color, form, and pageantry, the large Eucharistic events provide a near-perfect rendering of the vertical or transcendent dimension of the sacred that is rarely seen in modern parish church settings. The pope, his Vatican liturgists, and the receiving church must make the ritual extraordinary, wrapping the ceremony in the very best that humans can offer, for only by being extraordinary can the church reclaim its prestige as the means of salvation. The elegant dignity of the ceremony, the attention to each detail, the precise timing, the order of procession, the solemn gestures and movements celebrate the church's ability to transport humans into the dream-time of sacred reality. Catholics present in the transformed stadiums and fields are led into an almost surreal world through audio and visual sensations of an ordered and dignified beauty. Soukup argued that imaging helps audiences move their understanding of moral norms from rules to "what ought one to do" in the future.[5] Nourished by these moments of intense imaging, the pope's audiences feel good about their church, are proud of their association, and consequently, are more open to the church as a moral communicator.

Many studies have pointed to the consequences of modern culture's emphasis on self-fulfillment and self-expression. Bellah et al. reports how people, even after reaching the pinnacles of professional and material success, are worried by their loneliness and inability to connect meaningfully with others.[6] Alone and frightened, they look for comfort and warmth from their religious institutions. Within and often in contrast to the majestic aura and pageantry of the papal visit, John Paul II employs strategies to communicate the warm and compassionate fabric of a Christian community. He achieves this textually in his imagery and address. Some of his greetings are especially affectionate. He singles out those who suffer, extolling them for their courage because the suffering members show how compassion can form a community. He counsels forgiveness, urging reconciliation within the family and the larger community. More powerful than his textual images are those synoptic moments when he reaches out in gesture and touch to those watching and viewing. A master in handling gesture, John Paul II allows his eyes and hands to linger on people, giving them time to make deep contact, even if for only a few seconds. With crowds, he not only shows patience, but enjoyment.

Looking back on the papal visit, most people remember a few intense moments when John Paul II dramatized publicly his messages of love and compassion. When he hugged the baby with AIDS or softly touched an elderly patient, John Paul II shed his papal mantle, emptying himself before the world to become more welcoming of all who are ill, troubled, and lonely. His embrace of the priest who hinted for changes in celibacy and his kind words to the lay representative asking for more responsibility were especially dramatic, not only because of the pope's disarming and inviting display of warmth, but also because of the reaction of the priest and lay person who confirmed their bonds of love and loyalty to the pope and the church. What makes these signs of compassion so effective is that, even if they are encouraged by adept planning, the pope makes them come alive as movements of the heart. These dramatic signs tell the audience that faith is not always reached on a safe and cautious route. Often, life's bumps, bruises, and disagreements can be opportunities for people to leave their frightening solitude and reach out to others in meaningful ways.

During his visits, John Paul II pays special attention to meetings with young people. He is especially warm and loving, expressing an unusual naturalness which is enthusiastically returned by his young audiences. Youth culture has been known for its assault on societal structures. Anxious to experiment, young people test the limits, leaping over the boundary lines to experience the thrill of unstructured living. John Paul II enters into his young audience's play, occasionally delighting them by partaking of their taboo-breaking activities, such as trying on hats and joining in their chants. Constantly emphasizing the role of young people in the future of the church, the pope draws out certain aspects of youth culture as principles for new and invigorated plausibility structures. Besides their zest for life, he alludes to their strong peer associations through which they confide in one another, building a common and close relationship.

The sacred meaning must be sustained by plausible structures. John Paul II's visits motivate the local church members to demonstrate their faith through their enthusiastic attendance at the communal gatherings. Affected by the sights, sounds, papal style, and imagery, these participants as members of the local church become the source of their own legitimacy. Their movement through these liminal moments gives the church its persuasive value. Without the television camera's capture of the rapt attention or silent prayerful moments of faces in the crowd, without the infectious emotion displayed by a people moved to tears, without the squeals of joy and ardent singing of young members of the audience, the visit's attempts to build and sustain meaning would lack plausibility. The papal visit is a new form of pageantry for the church. It serves to enhance the papacy as a visible sign of unity by using select tactics that amplify the celebrity status of John Paul II. Among today's audiences who long for some meaningful relationships, a celebrity pope who jumps off a stage to touch and connect with his audience in dramatic ways helps to make the Christian narrative of an all-powerful, loving, sacred Other more alive and real.

A NEW VOCABULARY OF THE SACRED

During the period of the church's accommodation to the world, Catholics lost touch with the old symbols of the sacred that used to order their world. In an attempt to address the confusion about the sacred, John Paul II returns to basic Christian messages, giving strong, clear, and factual definition to the sacred to counteract the vague and indistinct notions of sacred that resulted from unrestrained experimentation with religious thought. Furthermore, to restore the prestige of the church, he reestablishes the church's dependence on the external authority of God. These qualities of his rhetorical strategy represent the time-tested old ways of talking about the sacred. Yet, to address the crisis of meaning, he needs to speak in a new vocabulary that is more understandable to current human conditions and experience.

The overseas visit to local churches is this new form of sacred vocabulary. Using David Martin's framework of sacred image, the sacred symbol is full of double meanings, inversion, and complexities because it attempts to code what is known and not known. Most of all, the sacred symbol affects meaning through tension.[7] John Paul II introduces tension by approaching the sacred in opposing and contradictory ways. In other words, he attempts to reconstitute a sacred that is in keeping with traditional notions, but uses updated versions that, appearing at first to conflict with sacred meaning, invert and lead back to the sacred.

There are three ways that the visit of John Paul II uses new forms of expressing this tension of inversion that characterizes a vocabulary of the sacred. The first is his populist approach. The expressive revolution has cut deeply into the fabric of modern culture, weakening the authority of institutions, including the church. To develop trust, a speaker must demonstrate to the audience that there is no institutional barrier that lies between them and the rhetor. The direct address of the people by John Paul II is a deliberate attempt to appeal to those who distrust authority and want to affirm for themselves in a close and personal way their normative commitments. The obstacles preventing popes from developing this direct pope-to-people style are formidable. Representing the longest continuous line of succession in human history, popes are weighed down by the nearly two thousand-year tradition of the office. Part of that heritage is the strong written tradition of Vatican communicative policy which affects most papal strategies, including the papal visit. Also, the hierarchical composition of the church, in particular the collegial relationship of the pope to the bishops, interferes with the pope's ability to directly contact the people of the local church because collegiality demands that the papacy act in concert with all the bishops. Not withstanding all these impediments, John Paul II's visits to local churches include significant moments when the pope speaks directly to the people and gains their trust.

During the 1987 U.S. visit, the addition of "structured dialogues" afforded representatives of the laity, priests, deacons, religious men and women, as well as other specialists in the service of the church, an opportunity to speak to the pope without passing their reports through an intermediary. Even though the speeches were reviewed in advance, the process highlighted the group's ability to entrust one of their own to compose and deliver their message to the pope. The dialogue form increased the pope's populist posture with relation to the group because he became the patient and humble listener.

The most significant examples of the pope's populist style are found in his address to the large gatherings of church members, usually during each day's Eucharistic celebration. Using no intermediaries, John Paul II attends to the masses of people, his most important audience of each day, giving them preference, focusing on their needs and not those of an impersonal institutional structure. He works personally on the texts of speeches he delivers to them, but spends more time moving through the crowd than publicly addressing them through his homily. This movement through the crowd is accentuated because of the contrast with his majestic role in the ceremonial splendor of the ritual. In other words, he breaks through the barriers that he has helped to create between the awesome mysterious Other and ordinary human experience. Because of the contrast, his reaching out to people symbolizes the excitement of reconciling what was previously declared irreconcilable.

The pope, as head of the church, is a direct Successor of Peter and a symbol of the authority given to the apostles and especially to Peter, by Christ. The church's authority as an institution comes from God. However, John Paul II's populist style conveys a double sense of authority, that is, one that proceeds from an external Other, and one that rests with the people of the church. In Catholic theology, the term *sensus fidei*, refers to an objective communal instinct through which the whole church grasps the truth. The teaching on the *sensus fidei* links the faithful interdependently with the magisterium of the church and, at the same time, gives recognition to the intuitive ability of all believers to contribute to the church's understanding of the faith through living out the faith.[8] John Paul II claims that he travels to the local churches on pilgrimage to revivify the faith of individuals and the church as a community. In their work, Victor and Edith Turner illustrate how pilgrimages are manifestations of populist spirit; many were developed for and by the peasant classes, and these masses of believers often persevered in their adherence to popular shrines and holy places even when church and state authorities showed ambivalence and even hostility.[9] In this sense, John Paul II's visits to the local church are decidedly populist, attracting crowds of common folk who would not necessarily have the means to travel to Rome or Jerusalem. As they gather for the large-scale rituals in open fields and stadiums, these masses of people behave in ways that mix their popular forms with the more established rubrics of church ceremony. Their enthusiasm and support for these papal travels sometimes confounds and surprises those among the church's intellectual elite. In other words, like the pilgrimage, there is a certain capriciousness to the papal visit that resists the orderly ecclesiastical control.

A populist style persuades people that the rhetor is an ordinary person with the same human qualities as themselves. Unable to put forth photos of a biological family as many political candidates do, the pope kisses babies, hugs children, banters with his young audiences, and strokes the elderly to convey the image of a caring and approachable "uncle." Through his facial expressions, his wit, and his sense of timing, the audience see the pope as a "people" person who is open and responsive to those around him. Helping to boost his populist image are John Paul II's references to his personal past experiences as a laborer from a humble family and a priest in a communist-led country. When the pope alludes to his Polish heritage, audiences imagine those qualities that they admire: self-reliance, strength of character, and patriotism. There are also moments when John Paul recalls a song from his youth or a conversation during a vacation in the mountains, revealing his and the audience's playful and relaxed side. Audiences recognize themselves in these images of ordinariness. However, interwoven throughout these images of ordinariness is the knowledge and realization that John Paul II, as pope, is the symbol of sacred otherness. It is this extraordinary/ordinary coming together of images that makes his populist style so intense and exhilarating.

The second innovative strategy of the sacred symbol system constructed by the pastoral visits of John Paul II is the inclusion of a very personal and intimate language. The speaker must be able to articulate what is within his own self, and what is within the individuals in the audience whom the speaker is addressing. When this communication becomes a very personal conversation between a leader and the people, in which they are telling each other who they are, the audience and speaker feel that they know each other well because they have been able to share these intimate moments. John Paul II's intimate style is a significant change in papal rhetorical strategy. A simple change in the frequency of the personal pronoun "I" produced an enormous effect on the relationship of the pope to his audience because it became so much easier for the pope to reveal his own personal thoughts and experiences.

Spontaneous moments as a relief against the formal, scripted portions of the visits have become so much a part of John Paul II's style that the crowds at papal events watch anxiously for the pope to say or do something unplanned and unrehearsed. In tension with the precisely arranged ceremony, the pope's spontaneity appears as an affirmation that individual vitality and dynamism are not snuffed out by the heavy weight of the collective orderliness of a church recalling the sacred nomos. Those who are part of a culture so affected by the expressive needs of self-fulfillment and self-discovery cannot tolerate long periods of determined conformity. There has to be some outlet for the self and its peculiarity. In contrast to the known and predictable formulas of ritual, these spontaneous moments of John Paul II communicate an unadorned and unprotected self, who when stripped of papal trimmings is as multilayered, unpredictable, and profoundly unique as others in his audience. In other words, the construction of a sacred cosmos does not negate the individual existential self, but recognizes how the informal and personalized vocabulary of self-fulfilling individuals can inform the

collective recalling of the sacred by forming a church that is more intimate and approachable.

In describing the way Catholics have traditionally thought about
themselves, Jay Dolan explained that for Catholics, salvation, like sin,
was very personal. However, salvation was always achieved through the
church, and its external ritual and devotional practice. These external
rubrics of the church were expressed as duties extended from the
authority of God and mediated through the church, its pope, bishops,
and pastors. Dolan contended that the Catholic culture of that era pro-
moted salvation as an individual responsibility, but in sorting out the
way toward salvation, individual conscience was de-emphasized.[10] As
evident especially in his adoption of a more informal style of speaking
about himself, but also in certain choices of metaphors and use of updated terms, John Paul II's new vocabulary of the sacred speaks in a language that reaches out to those steeped in a culture that is preoccupied
with self. Although related to earlier traditions of individual salvation,
this vocabulary no longer rigidly expresses externally imposed duty. It
allows for self-exploration and self-expression not as an end in itself, but
as a means to confront humankind as a mystery leading to its sacred
source. The spontaneity of John Paul II symbolizes how humans can
approach the sacred because they are free to act and express themselves.
John Paul II explained this progression in his book, *Crossing the Threshold of Hope*, when he described human nature as "free and therefore *responsible*."[11] The same progression is apparent in pilgrimages. Turner
and Turner showed that pilgrims make individual voluntary decisions
to undertake their journeys to holy places.[12] Unlike certain rituals in the
church, these pilgrimages are not required for salvation.

The papal visits, more than other forms of papal communication,
stress the voluntary nature of the event through their "invitational" image. As an invited guest of the local church and the host country, John
Paul II's style of address follows the social rules of gratitude and politeness. When John Paul II criticizes, he does so using indirect terms.
Similar to pilgrimages, participation in these visits is not mandatory,
and therefore people are persuaded to participate through pretrip publicity extolling the celebratory, spectacle nature of this once-in-a-
lifetime event. Today, because voluntariness is a accepted code of a self-
determined populace, the church, as other social structures, has to
demonstrate that identification takes place freely and without obligation. John Paul II's use of self-references is a language of courtship.
More conversational in tone than the speech of his predecessors, and
less formal than other forms of papal communication, the visits open

the papacy to a certain risk-taking, that recognizes and encourages the dramatic tension between the self in dialogue with others. However, John Paul II uses a rhetorical strategy that casts this risk-taking in a confident mode, that is, he conveys a trust that freedom will eventually lead to the truth.

The third innovative strategy of John Paul II's vocabulary of the sacred is his revivification of the imaginative and emotive power of sacred images. This strategy is especially tested in John Paul II's special treatment of youthful audiences. As Bernice Martin noted, youth has an "interstitial" status between childhood and adulthood. Identity in this in-between status "guarantees release" from the strictures of their past and future roles. Therefore, youth culture was uniquely placed as a tightly defined in-group to smash taboos and expand the options of self-expression. In other words, youth culture employs to some degree an oppositional style.[13] In their natural and unrestrained enthusiasm, young people exhibit a sacredness which John Paul II imitates when he becomes more natural and less restrained in his emotions. A poignant example is his reaction to the armless singer at the youth rally in Los Angeles. Watching this young man play the guitar with his toes, the pope's face choked with emotion. When the young man finished, John Paul II, keeping his eyes on the performer, walked from where he was viewing the event, jumped off the edge of the stage and reached up to Melendez, touching his feet and motioning him to bend so that they could embrace. At that moment, the pope kissed Melendez on the forehead, and then the pope returned to his place, repeating the young man's name, "Tony! Tony!"[14] John Paul II had directed the attention and love of this audience of young people away from himself and to Tony, applauding him for his courage in searching for meaning in his life. In humbling himself as a mere admirer, John Paul II publicly and unhesitatingly displayed his own emotions, provoking the audience to do the same.

Emotions aid the inversion of sacred symbol. Humans may not intellectually comprehend the why of suffering, forgiveness, and love, but they can feel it. John Paul II often speaks about the youth as the hope of the church. These meetings between the pope and the youth, characterized by intense affection and enthusiasm, are strategies for imaging the future destiny of the church and its members. John Paul II portrays the youth as the "everyman" of the church. Secularism tries to structure life into compartments, but young people resist those structures. Knowing that the sacred cannot be contained into a logical arrangement, or intellectual argument, or even into a static institutionalized form, the youth are open to all possibilities of the sacred. In these meetings between the youth and John Paul II, the sacred can be fun, sorrowful, and frightening. Even the means of constructing the sacred are released from traditional limitations. In fact, during these events, some of the symbols of antistructure are employed to help construct sacred meaning: the strings of an electric guitar and the flashing images of a music video. The meetings with the youth during the papal visit demonstrate one of David Martin's contentions about the sacred symbol: it cannot be limited, but seeps out in search of unified space only to be stored again behind a new geography of partitions.[15]

Hoover speaks of the Protestant revival movements as being religions of the heart. Emotionalism encouraged by charismatic preachers was seen as a way to conversion that had little formal church structure requirements.[16] Catholicism's emphasis on ritual with its dependence on a priestly class and a body of intricate instructions is often cited as a marked contrast to the freewheeling style of evangelical Protestants. Nonetheless, Catholic ritual culture, especially devotional practice associated with saints, are "riddled with emotionalism and sentimentalism."[17] Religious processions and the popular reenactment of the Way of the Cross are carried on with a great deal of emotional display even today in southern European and Latin American cultures. In American Catholic culture, revival-type religion has played a major role in forming individual piety.[18] The parish mission movement of the nineteenth and early twentieth centuries emphasized a personal experience of conversion involving a sensing of the faith. Turner and Turner observed how Catholic theological abstractions are "fleshed out" by the imagery of saints and the reenactment of a narrative during pilgrimage. The images of saints recall that living Catholics can communicate with the saintly dead who are able to intercede with God on their behalf. Pilgrimages retell the stories of apparitions and miracles performed by the saints. These narratives are not always supported, and sometimes opposed by scientific rational criticism.[19] To a certain extent, the church has accommodated to rationalism of the modern age by de-emphasizing much of its imagery and narrative in favor of intellectual reflection. In Greeley's words, the contemporary church does not seem to understand the importance of a "culture that appeals to the senses."[20] During the visits, John Paul II's personal involvement in the bodily and sensual imaging of faith, along with a complex intellectual reflection on faith aims to build a vocabulary of the sacred that includes both heart and head.

The visits of John Paul II accentuate tension in order to construct a sacred cosmos. The tensions of contrast, inversion, double meaning, and paradox are intensified by introducing into a vocabulary of the sacred three innovative strategies of papal communication: a populist style, a language of existential self, and a revitalization of the imaginative and emotive power of sacred images. John Paul II, as pope and Successor to Peter, is the symbol of the authority given to the apostles and especially to Peter by Christ to uphold and preach church doctrine as "authentic" truth. During the visits, John Paul II uses the splendor and majesty of ritual to construct and maintain the distance that is necessary to maintain and legitimate authority. At the same time, he employs a rhetorical style that aims to erase the distance that separates pope from people. In other words, John Paul II effectively communicates the institutional authority of a hierarchically ordered church by seeking the trust of the ordinary people of the church who become the primary means of constructing the sacred cosmos. As David Martin reminded us, the sacred images express our frustration with our inability to make contradiction whole.[21] Traditional top-down authority does not fit with a populist style, but John Paul II's populist style is effective because it is so paradoxical.

Through forms of intimate address, moments of spontaneity, and attention to self-determination, John Paul II strategically demonstrates how human freedom and individuality contribute to the durability and plausibility of a sacred order in an age so affected by the expressive dimension. John Paul II's visits are filled with exhortations to listen and heed the Word of God that the church teaches. He pleads with his audience to acknowledge once again that a sacred Other has created all in this world, and as a result we humans are obligated to act in harmony with the sacred plan. The scenario developed by the pope casts the audience members as debtors in a fixed relationship to a giving God, and leaves little room for individual discernment. However, throughout the visits, John Paul II's open and spontaneous style and his respectful posture with regard to human freedom forms a language of self as a double meaning of the sacred. The self and its capacity for self-expression and self-determination are also creations of God, revealing that dichotomy and contradiction are resolved in a sacred vocabulary that has multimeanings and speaks in multisymbols. Moreover, the success of the papal visit is dependent on the audience being persuaded to participate in the celebration and to connect in some way with the pope. The papal visit and its ritual is not a duty, but a freely chosen, extraordinary opportunity to withdraw from the obligations of secular life in order to pursue the voluntariness of a sacred, social relationship. In other words, the new vocabulary of the papal visit turns meaning around: secular life is coercive and sacred life is associated with freedom.

One of the more important contributions that John Paul II makes to a new vocabulary of the sacred is the reinstatement of its dramatic, emotive character which recognizes the modern person's need to reclaim the expressive discovery of self as a sacred dimension. John Paul II uses his visits to search out and touch, both in mind and heart, as many people as he can. Knowing that he cannot reach these people directly through encyclicals, he turns to a vocabulary of the sacred that builds upon past church practice and capitalizes on the mediated experience of modern society. Medieval architects and Renaissance artists used cathedrals, sculpture, and frescoes to remind and teach about the sacred. Today, the media and their role in projecting images have replaced the architects and artists. Since people are living in an era when the dramatization of images is affecting if not replacing verbal argument, John Paul II's rhetorical strategy aims to recapture the visual stage of communication. Besides, images easily provoke the emotions, and emotions can sometimes help humans accept the sacred symbol's inversion as plausible. Suffering as a way toward salvation may be difficult to comprehend intellectually, but emotionally audiences can feel the power of cathartic experiences. In a sense, John Paul II's visits restore the emotive elements that were eclipsed by the rationalism of the modern age, but his new vocabulary reframes these emotions in two ways: (1) the emotive element does not cancel out the intellectual components of religious consciousness because the visit's vocabulary continues to contain complexity that stimulates intellectual reflection; and (2) the emotive factor is soft and gentle, and therefore more acceptable to those formed by the rationally organized world of symbols.

OBSERVATIONS

Relation to Other Discourses

Janice Peck concluded that those who preached resistance used new forms of communicating, namely television, as techniques that were subordinated to the message. Those who accommodated to the world treated television as "a site of symbolic production in its own right."[22] In other words, the framing had much to do with the message. My study of the rhetoric of John Paul II also concludes that as a new form of papal communication, the overseas pastoral visits frame the symbolic construction of the sacred in certain ways. As I have noted, the visits encourage a negotiation process between the papacy as universal symbol of church and the local churches in their particularity. The visits, because of their mediated and visual character, encourage dramatic production of the sacred symbol, making it possible for a pope to communicate the sacred dimensions of intimacy and emotion that would not be possible in other, more traditional forms of papal communication.

Peck also found clear distinctions between those who preached resistance and those who accommodated to the rational and consumer-driven lifestyles of modern culture. Marsha Witten, on the other hand, found more complex responses, in which accommodating responses dominated and resistance speech was mixed with accommodating talk. She proposed a reframing model of a middle-ground approach, but found little evidence of this category. My study proposes dialectic points of sacred-secular, resistance-accommodation indicators, but I did not expect to find clear distinctions nor middle-ground answers. I contend that John Paul II's strategy has to redraw borders between the sacred and secular because of the crisis produced by the erosion of these borders. However, I argue that a midpoint of balance is impossible for several reasons. First, unlike the composition of Protestant churches, whose individual parish elders and parishioners become important referents of a preacher's persuasiveness, the Catholic Church proclaims its universality and attempts to be universal in terms of its worldwide membership. A pope does not speak just to individual parishes nor even to the national local church, but to all churches at all times. Secondly, a pope must make sense to very diverse, contextualized audiences, even within the local church. Thus, John Paul II embraces a strategy that can be widely interpreted in both resistance and accommodating directions depending on the audience's character and situation. In other words, he preserves a tension between the two opposing directions, but he seeks no clear or static midpoint. He may tend toward a certain direction, but in some areas and with some audiences, he doubles back in the opposite direction, demonstrating a fluidity that is consonant with the ever-changing social systems of modern life. Finally, my conclusions point to the flaws of theoretical formulas that are too static. Religious language cannot be entirely clear nor can it reach an exact middle point because a sacred vocabulary is not grasped as a scientific, rational concept. It is communicated through paradox and ambiguity. To construct a sacred vocabulary, there must be a contrasting reference to the secular that exhibits tension. The tension between the two realms prevents pursuing only one end point to its extreme. It also tantalizes humans with the possibility of resolving these contrasts. This coding of how humans can glimpse the potentiality of unity and still live in difference is what makes the sacred image so powerful.

Kathleen Jamieson found that the papal encyclical as a genre shields the church from the changing world and impedes its address to contemporary men and women. As a consequence, she claims that the encyclical thwarts the institution's plausibility.[23] Jablonski has concluded that the pastoral letter of Catholic bishops as a genre functions to preserve institutional order and plausibility, especially when the bishops are introducing messages of change. She also noted that within the genre, bishops introduced new motivational arguments, moving away from compliance based on church authority and making appeals based on hope and love. By employing these expanded set of arguments, they diffused potential conflict within the church and enhanced their authority.[24] My conclusions contend that the papal visit is less constraining than the encyclical and other forms of written church communications, and therefore it allows for innovation and adaptation to time-bound situations. Instead of expanding sets of arguments, the visits allow the pope to change the form of communication so that he can appeal by infiltrating the realm of images. Plausibility is not judged on the logic of reasoning, but on the coherency of symbols. Commitment is related not so much to the authority of the institution or even the written word. Although the visit employs ample textual references to scripture, its primary call to renewal is achieved through textual and nontextual images that form a mythic narrative. In comparison to other forms of papal communication, such as written encyclicals and letters, the visit as a narrative is less definitive and illustrates how the sacred resists human definition.

Both Peck and Witten examined how churches draw on communicative resources to deal with the phenomenon of secularization. For Peck, these changes in society represent a crisis of meaning to which evangelical Protestants have responded by fusing elements of revivalism with the television medium, which in turn has, in some cases, transformed the methods of evangelism and affected the character of the evangelical belief system expressed through televangelism.[25] For Witten, modern secular culture has deeply affected religious speech, suggesting that even when preachers employ tactics of resistance, their speech is compromised by accommodating tendencies.[26] Witten and Peck demonstrate that differences exist within denominations even in the case of evangelical Protestantism, and that these differences confirm what Wuthnow asserted were important new alignments in society.[27]

There is a serious lack of similar studies of Catholic communicative strategies in response to the secularization problem. It appears obvious that Pope John Paul II through his style of communicating has achieved success in claiming the attention of millions of Catholics throughout the world. By examining his predominant form of communication, the papal pastoral visit, I have concluded that this communicative form constitutes a new vocabulary that is constructed in response to the crisis brought about by secularization. It is a new vocabulary in the tradition of revitalization movements in that it is designed to revive the ability of the church to maintain and construct sacred common meaning. The exciting freshness of the papal visit casts symbolic meaning within a new framework, but it also links this newer mode of communicating to the past and thus gives comforting assurance that the church can still provide a firm anchor against shifting opinions.

The development of the papal pastoral visit to overseas churches during the papacy of John Paul II is significant because it responded to a specific need. Vatican Council II was an attempt to update the church's official teachings with respect to the world and the enormous changes that had taken place in society. After the upheavals of change, there was a need to restore balance. The papal visit is neither an updating nor a reversal of those updating policies, but it is a new form of communicating. Like Hoover and Peck, who noticed how the technical means of religious communication can contribute to shaping meaning, the papal visit, as a new communicative form for the papacy, does not simply use modern technical means to transmit old messages, but rather draws the church into creating a new vocabulary of the sacred. The fact that a new language of the sacred was necessary demonstrates to what extent societal changes, namely secularism and pluralism, have affected religious meaning. My study has shown that, in terms of an accommodating-resistance continuum, the papal visit emphasizes the paradoxical nature of the sacred-secular relationship. I have demonstrated that there is no midpoint, but rather an adaptation to audiences and situation. In this regard, secularism and pluralism have fostered an idealization of diversity and individual freedom, making it impossible for a new religious language to be crafted to narrow segments or broad common denominators. Because the papal visit has a narrative dimension, it has the fluidity to adapt from site to site, audience to audience, constructing a mythic unity through its very personal story and image. In a sense, John Paul II engages secularism in order to combat its effects.

I believe that the papal visit as John Paul II's new form of papal communication will serve as an important benchmark in measuring future communicative efforts of popes, not so much as a mark of success, but rather as an indicator of the church's relationship with the culture of the times. In my study, I have only referred to some aspects of papal history to develop strains of continuance in order to understand the development of the papal visit as a means of speaking with the church. John Paul II's visits are both an outgrowth and an extension of the communicative strategies of three of his predecessors. Like Pius XII, he is comfortable with using all modern communicative means possible to reach the church and the world. Unlike Pius XII, John Paul II heads a church that has been deeply affected by the countercultural movements of the sixties and seventies. Like John XXIII, he employs a populist style, but unlike John XXIII, he speaks to a church that is tired of constant experimentation. John Paul II carries on Paul VI's international visits, benefiting from the structural organization given to these visits in their early development. However, John Paul II's visits are concerned with constructing new symbolic structures of the sacred and secular, and his audiences are primarily the church and then the world. My study examines a papal communicative form within a relatively short time frame to attempt to answer the question of secularization and the church's way of dealing with this phenomenon under certain historical and contextual conditions. A more exhaustive historical treatment and comparison could give further clues as to the resistance-accommodation posture of church leadership with respect to modern communicative developments over the long term.

Failings of John Paul II's Rhetorical Strategy

In my study, I have pointed out how John Paul II's rhetorical strategy constructs a new vocabulary of the sacred. A crucial element of that construction is the delineation of boundary lines between the sacred and the secular so that people can recognize the presence of a sacred Other in their lives. An important tactic to disentangling the sacred from the secular is to call attention to the persistence of evil. The attention given to an evil enemy is designed to motivate the church toward collective action. However, audiences will not be motivated if the enemy is not closely drawn, to give the impression that these evil forces are already at the gates. There are rhetorical weaknesses in John Paul II's attempt to identify the dangers threatening the church and society when the pope chooses terms such as consumerism and secularism. These terms of social science tend to objectify evil in ways that disconnect them from the people. In a sense, these terms are elements of a depopulist style, because their intellectualized forms make them distant from the everyday lives of ordinary people. Audiences acknowledge that consumerism is a problem, but because it is spoken about in cool scientific terms, it remains a topic for contemplation and discussion, but not necessarily a practical issue to be acted upon. For people to act, they need to see the threats as imminent and real as their frequent trips to the shopping malls.

My conclusions have contended that the visits promote a more awesome and transcendent sacred symbol by presenting majestic contrast to everyday life experience. The planning for a visit sets this distinctive tone. However, there is always a danger that efficiency and practicality may become more important than the purpose—that of communal construction of the sacred. As the visit unfolds, much time and effort are given to structuring and executing pragmatic event management elements of the trip. The compulsion to be fair and inclusive of every region and service area of the church can overload the visit and lose focus on what is really important. Instead of concentrating on the main ritual Eucharistic celebration and a few visually symbolic events that capture the enigmatic features of the sacred, the visit can become constrained by the specialized meetings with church members and other faiths. As I mentioned previously, the tendency to construct a sacred symbol according to compartmentalized service divisions in the church can add legitimacy to the already fragmented lives of our secularized culture.

Vocabularies that connect back to time-tested traditions provide anchors by which humans can order their lives as conditions change. However, vocabularies that are encased in forms that prevent any adaptation to new situations can become reified and unconnected to people's everyday experience. With time and experience, the papal visit develops set formats. The patterns of meetings, events, and their structural arrangement within a visit become elements of a genre with expectations that may be hard to change. One of the advantages that the visit has over the encyclical and other written forms of papal communication is that it is flexible enough to adapt to the changing conditions of the audience. With twenty years of experience and more than eighty overseas trips, some of which are repeated visits to the same country, planners both at the Vatican and the local level begin to rely heavily on what has been effective in past experience. There is a danger that the visit becomes so bounded that it no longer makes sense to those who have learned to live with fluidity.

Whether or not the visit is developing into a genre and what form this genre will take will only be evident when there is a change in papacy. A study that compares John Paul II's primary form of communicating with that of the next pope will be an important means of understanding possible changes in strategy and how these changes may be related to the context of changes in the church and society. For example, some have suggested that John Paul II's visits overemphasize the large-scale rituals. They contend that intimacy can best be established in smaller formats. However, John Paul II employs moments of intimacy within a large-scale public setting. I contend that, based on Berger's scheme of plausibility, John Paul II's strategy develops a perception of massivity which increases plausibility. In order to support a strategy that features smaller gatherings, critics would need to interpret plausibility in a different way. Wuthnow raised this issue when he wondered "what makes plausibility structure itself plausible."[28]

What the Rhetoric of John Paul II Means for the Church

My purpose is to examine John Paul II's rhetorical strategy in order to explain why he appears so enigmatic. I maintain that the way he communicates with the church, especially his enigmatic style, is a response to the problems the church encounters as it relates to the postmodern, secularized world. With Vatican Council II, the Catholic Church adjusted its symbols, discarding some of its old forms and reframing others to bring the sacred in closer proximity to the secular. The experiments that these changes unleashed shook the church, and members began to lose sight of Catholicism's sacred underpinnings. John Paul II's rhetorical strategy had to first address the church's symbol systems, deciding how to construct the relationship between the sacred and the secular, and how to place the church with relation to the world. By examining the planning, texts, and performance of the visit against the indicators of accommodating and resistance trends, I demonstrate that the visit of John Paul II as rhetorical symbol falls somewhere closer to the sacred resistance side of the spectrum. He accomplished this by helping his audiences appreciate the mystery and paradox of the sacred Other.

At the same time, in the text and performance of the papal visit, John Paul II twists and turns, and doubles back again between a resistance and accommodating mode. As John Paul II moves from audience to audience, he offers symbols that appeal to a wide interpretation of church. In other words, he deals with his audiences as they are located on this accommodating-resistance continuum, but he refuses to take a compromising middle-of-the-road approach to bring these tendencies together. In fact, the mixing and inversion of symbols within the same speech or event reflect the need to appeal to people who are exposed to the fluctuating positions and perspectives of their diverse and pluralistic world. It also highlights the difficult task of striving toward sacred ideals while making the pragmatic decisions of human life. The pope adjusts to this fluidity by accepting that the church not only has to live with tension, it has to find ways to make tension serve meaning. Accentuating tension, as long as resolution of tension is the ultimate goal, can be a positive means of expressing the sacred, for according to Burke, it is only in difference that we can experience the thrill of coming together.

I mentioned at the start of my study that there was a deepening chasm developing between the norms preached by the church and the tendency for church members to fail to live up to those norms. Local speech drafts have sometimes taken a "soft" approach to certain personal morality issues, evidently because many Catholics are not following church teaching in these areas. John Paul II sees no need to avoid these issues. In fact, he discusses them in a forthright manner, knowing that many will find his insistence on objectifiable criteria difficult. He is clear in his presentation of the essentials of Christian faith. On the other hand, he presents Christian faith as deeply complex and mysterious. Rather than make meaning plain, he asks people to stretch their intellect to struggle for insights. In this regard, his use of a language of self is designed to move his audiences toward a self-fulfillment that is far from easy. He presents the law to be followed and motivates those to follow the norms by using all his persuasive means—logic, psychology, poetry, and sheer personal energy, but when someone suffers or fails, he reaches out to touch and hug them, respecting them even to the point of lowering himself because they are human and sacred, sacred and human.

The papal visit allows the rhetor and audience to interact at multiple levels of human experience. However, unlike other symbolic systems in which it is possible for audiences to pick out bits and pieces from the different levels to form a conceptual whole that is reasonably consistent, religious symbol systems are inherently contradictory, simultaneously pointing in different directions. Employing a polysymbolic approach, John Paul II articulates the frustration of remembering the sacred norms and being immersed in the world. The effectiveness of the visits lies in the fact that meaning can be crafted through words and much more than words, leading the audiences to carry away memories of deep experiential liminal moments within which the disparities between the norms preached by the church and the pragmatic concerns of everyday life fade. The normative structure gives way to an unstructured feeling of oneness, and questions of faithful adherence or individual discernment no longer are important. After all, the visits are stories about stories in which audiences recognize themselves in a world of possibilities where the enigmatic fleetingly makes sense.

NOTES

1. David Martin, *The Breaking of the Image: A Sociology of Christian Theory and Practice* (Oxford: Basil Blackwell, 1980), 38.

2. Peter L. Berger, *The Sacred Canopy: Elements of a Sociological Theory of Religion* (Garden City, New York: Doubleday, 1969), 150.

3. Bernice Martin, *A Sociology of Contemporary Cultural Change* (New York: St. Martin's Press, 1981), 40, 220–221.

4. Hugh Dalziel Duncan, *Communication and Social Order* (New York: Bedminster Press, 1962), 117.

5. Paul A. Soukup, "The Church as Moral Communicator," in *Mass Media and the Moral Imagination*, eds. Philip J. Rossi and Paul A. Soukup (Kansas City, Missouri: Sheed and Ward, 1994), 202–203.

6. Robert N. Bellah, Richard Madsen, William M. Sullivan, Ann Swidler, and Steven M. Tipton, *Habits of the Heart: Individualism and Commitment in American Life* (Berkeley, California: University of California Press, 1985; New York: Perennial Library, Harper and Row, 1986), 284.

7. David Martin, *The Breaking of the Image*, 156–161.

8. Patrick Granfield, *The Limits of the Papacy: Authority and Autonomy in the Church* (New York: Crossroad Publishing, 1987), 140–147; Zoltan Alszeghy, "The Sensus Fidei and the Development of Dogma," in *Vatican II: Assessment and Perspectives*, ed. Rene Latourelle, vol. 1 (New York: Paulist Press, 1988) 138–156.

9. Victor Turner and Edith Turner, *Image and Pilgrimage in Christian Culture: Anthropological Perspectives* (New York: Columbia University Press, 1978), 30–32.

10. Jay P. Dolan, *The American Catholic Experience: A History from Colonial Times to the Present* (Garden City, New York: Doubleday, 1985), 231.

11. John Paul II, *Crossing the Threshold of Hope*, ed. Vittorio Messori (New York: Alfred A. Knopf, 1994), 180.

12. Turner and Turner, *Image and Pilgrimage*, 8–9.

13. Bernice Martin, *A Sociology*, 140, 150.

14. *The Pope's Visit to Los Angeles: Highlights from KTLA's Historic 24-Hour Coverage* (Channel 5, KTLA, Inc., 1987), videocassette.

15. David Martin, *The Breaking of the Image*, 38–40.

16. Stewart M. Hoover, *Mass Media Religion: The Social Sources of the Electronic Church* (Newbury Park, California: Sage, 1988), 45.

17. Dolan, *The American Catholic Experience*, 231.

18. Jay P. Dolan, *Catholic Revivalism: The American Experience 1830–1900* (Notre Dame, Indiana: Notre Dame University Press, 1978), xviii–xix.

19. Turner and Turner, *Image and Pilgrimage*, 204–211.

20. Andrew Greeley, *God in Popular Culture* (Chicago, Illinois: The Thomas More Press, 1988), 91.

21. David Martin, *The Breaking of the Image*, 126.

22. Janice Peck, *The Gods of Televangelism: The Crisis of Meaning and Appeal of Religious Television* (Cresskill, New Jersey: Hampton Press, 1993), 211.

23. Jamieson, "A Rhetorical-Critical Analysis of the Conflict over Humanae Vitae," Ph.D. dissertation, University of Wisconsin, 1972, 232–234.

24. Carol J. Jablonski, "*Aggiornamento* and the American Catholic Bishops: A Rhetoric of Institutional Continuity and Change," *Quarterly Journal of Speech* 75 (1989): 416–432; and "Promoting Radical Change in the Roman Catholic Church: Rhetorical Requirements, Problems, and Strategies of the American Bishops," *Central States Speech Journal* 31 (Winter 1980): 282–298.

25. Peck, *The Gods of Televangelism*, 228–231.

26. Marsha Witten, *All Is Forgiven: The Secular Message in American Protestantism* (Princeton: Princeton University Press, 1993), 136.

27. Robert Wuthnow, *The Struggle for America's Soul: Evangelicals, Liberals, and Secularism* (Grand Rapids, Michigan: William B. Eerdmans, 1989), 32–33.

28. Robert Wuthnow, *Rediscovering the Sacred: Perspectives on Religion in Contemporary Society* (Grand Rapids, Michigan: William B. Eerdmans, 1992), 29.

Appendix

	SACRED	*SECULAR*
Cultural Systems Level		
Nomos or Norms	defined by church as sacred community	defined by subjective feeling; external society
Institutions	traditional social units	changed lifestyles
Synthesizing Myth	universal	contextual
Social Systems Level		
Community Identity	holiness in sacred otherness	holiness in every day
Structure of Social Relationship	communitas	rational and contractual
External Church	emphasis on authentic	embrace of all belief
Personal Systems Level		
Status/Role		
Clergy; religious	return to sacred	inculturated; hyphenated
Laity	distinct	indistinct
Personal Identity	visible and separate	invisible and indistinct

Selected Bibliography

Accattoli, Luigi. "Notes and Comments: The Journeys of the Pope as Instruments of the 'Mission to the Nations.' " *Communio: International Catholic Review* 18, no. 3 (Fall 1991): 473–482.

Adler, Bill. *Pope Paul in the United States.* New York: Hawthorn Books, 1965.

Alazraki, Valentina. *Juan Pablo II: El Viajero de Dios.* Colonia del Valle, Mexico: Editorial Diana, 1990.

Alszeghy, Zoltan. "The Sensus Fidei and the Development of Dogma." In *Vatican II: Assessment and Perspectives,* ed. Rene Latourelle, vol. 1, 138–156. New York: Paulist Press, 1988.

L'Attività della Santa Sede nel 1965, 1980, 1985, 1987, 1991. Vatican City: Libreria Editrice Vaticana, 1966, 1981, 1986, 1988, 1992.

Bailey, F. G. *The Tactical Uses of Passion: An Essay on Power, Reason, and Reality.* Ithaca, New York: Cornell University Press, 1983.

Bellah, Robert N. *The Broken Covenant: American Civil Religion in Time of Trial.* New York: Seabury, 1975.

Bellah, Robert N., Richard Madsen, William M. Sullivan, Ann Swidler, and Steven M. Tipton. *Habits of the Heart: Individualism and Commitment in American Life.* Berkeley, California: University of California Press, 1985; reprint, New York: Perennial Library, Harper and Row, 1986.

Berger, Peter L. *The Sacred Canopy: Elements of a Sociological Theory of Religion.* Garden City, New York: Doubleday, 1969.

Biernatzki, William E. "Religion in the Mass Media." *Communication Research Trends* 15, no. 2 (1995): 3–15.

Black, Edwin. *Rhetorical Criticism: A Study of Method.* Madison, Wisconsin: University of Wisconsin Press, 1978.

———. "The Second Persona." *Quarterly Journal of Speech* 56 (April 1970): 109–119.

Blankenship, Jane. " 'Magic' and 'Mystery' in the Works of Kenneth Burke." In *The Legacy of Kenneth Burke,* eds. Herbert W. Simons and Trevor Melia. Madison, Wisconsin: University of Wisconsin Press, 1989.

Bohlen, Celestine. "Security, Formality, and Age Obscure Man of Wit." *New York Times,* 8 October 1995, 43.

Borgomeo, Pasquale. "In visita 'ad limina Ecclesiae.' "4 *L'Osservatore Romano,* 18 October 1988.

Breen, Myles, and Farrel Corcoran. "Myth in the Television Discourse." *Communication Monographs* 49 (June 1982): 127–136.

Briggs, Kenneth A. *Holy Siege: The Year That Shook Catholic America.* San Francisco: HarperCollins, 1992.

Brock, Bernard L., Robert L. Scott, and James W. Chesebro, eds. *Methods of Rhetorical Criticism: A Twentieth-Century Perspective.* Detroit: Wayne State University Press, 1989.

Brown, Richard Harvey. *Society As Text: Essays on Rhetoric, Reason, and Reality.* Chicago: University of Chicago Press, 1987.

Burke, Kenneth. *Counter-Statement.* Berkeley, California: University of California Press, 1968.

———. *A Grammar of Motives.* New York: Prentice-Hall, 1945.

———. *Language As Symbolic Action: Essays on Life, Literature, and Method.* Berkeley, California: University of California Press, 1966.

———. *On Symbols and Society.* Edited by Joseph R. Gusfield. Chicago: The University of Chicago Press, 1989.

———. *A Rhetoric of Motives.* New York: Prentice-Hall, 1950.

———. *The Rhetoric of Religion: Studies in Logology.* Berkeley, California: University of California Press, 1970.

Campbell, Karlyn Kohrs. *The Rhetorical Act.* Belmont, California: Wadsworth Publishing, 1982.

Carrier, Hervé. *Psico-sociologia dell'appartenenza religiosa.* Torino: Editrice Elle di Ci, 1988.

———. *The Social Doctrine of the Church Revisited.* Vatican City: Pontifical Council for Justice and Peace, 1990.

Catechism of the Catholic Church. Vatican City: Libreria Editrice Vaticana, 1994; English translation for the United States, United States Catholic Conference, 1994.

Champagne, Duane, ed. *The Native North American Almanac.* Washington, D.C.: Gale Research, 1994.

Champion, Françoise. "La rencontre des jeunes et du pape." In Jean Séguy, Danièle Hervieu-Léger, Françoise Champion, Martine Cohen, Patrice Berger, André Julliard, Jacques Sutter, Jean Baubérot, Agnès Rochefort-Turquin, and Renaud Sainsaulieu, *Voyage de Jean-Paul II en France,* 56–85. Paris: Les Editions du Cerf, 1988.

Chandler, Russell. "The Papal Visit: Exchange of Ideas with John Paul Are Staged with Care." *Los Angeles Times*, 15 September 1987.

———. "Pope's Visit: A Tug of War: Church Leaders Vie for Extra Time, Attention." *Los Angeles Times*, 22 February 1987.

Cheney, George. "The Rhetoric of Identification and the Study of Organizational Communication." *Quarterly Journal of Speech* 69 (1983): 143–158.

———. *Rhetoric in an Organizational Society: Managing Multiple Identities.* Columbia, South Carolina: University of South Carolina Press, 1991.

Coffee, Raymond. "Among Americans, It Seems, the Pope Is Losing the Game." *Chicago Tribune*, 20 September 1987.

Cohen, Richard. "They Should Have Criticized the Pope." *Washington Post*, 15 September 1987.

Coleman, John. *The Evolution of Dutch Catholicism, 1958–1974.* California: University of California Press, 1978.

Cook, Michael J. "The Bible and Catholic-Jewish Relations." In *Twenty Years of Jewish Catholic Relations*, ed. Eugene Fisher, 109–124. New York: Paulist Press, 1986.

Corcoran, Paul E. *Political Language and Rhetoric.* Austin, Texas: University of Texas, 1979.

Crossan, John Dominic. *The Dark Interval: Towards a Theology of Story.* Niles, Illinois: Argus Communications, 1975.

Decker, Cathleen. "The Papal Visit: Dodger Stadium Mass Gives Immigrants a Night of Joy." *Los Angeles Times*, 17 September 1987.

———. "The Papal Visit: Speech to Pope Puts Priest in Spotlight, Creates Ripple." *Los Angeles Times*, 12 September 1987.

Del Rio, Domenico, and Luigi Accattoli. *Wojtyla: Il nuovo Mosè.* Milan: Arnoldo Mondadori Editore, 1988.

de Montclos, Christine. *Les Voyages de Jean-Paul II: Dimensions sociales et politiques.* Paris: Editions du Centurion, 1990.

Dobbelaere, Karel. "Secularization Theories and Sociological Paradigms: A Reformulation of the Private-Public Dichotomy and the Problem of Societal Integration." *Sociological Analysis* 46 (1985): 377–387.

———. "Some Trends in European Sociology of Religion: The Secularization Debate." *Sociological Analysis* 48, no. 2 (1987): 107–137.

Dolan, Jay P. *The American Catholic Experience: A History from Colonial Times to the Present.* Garden City, New York: Doubleday, 1985.

———. *Catholic Revivalism: The American Experience 1830–1900.* Notre Dame, Indiana: Notre Dame University Press, 1978.

———. "Millenarianism." In *Catholic Encyclopedia*, 852–854. New York: McGraw Hill, 1967.

Duffy, Bernard K., and Halford R. Ryan. *American Orators of the Twentieth Century: Critical Studies and Sources.* Westport, Connecticut: Greenwood Press, 1987.

Dulles, Avery. "The Church is Communications." *Catholic Mind* 69 (October 1971): 6–16.

———. *Models of the Church.* New York: Doubleday, 1987.

———. *The Reshaping of Catholicism: Current Challenges in the Theology of Church.* San Francisco: Harper and Row, 1988.

———. "Vatican II and Communications." In *Vatican II: Assessment and Perspectives,* ed. René Latourelle, vol. 3, 528–547. New York: Paulist Press, 1989.

Duncan, Hugh Dalziel. "Axiomatic Propositions." In *Drama in Life,* eds. James. E. Combs and Michael W. Mansfield. New York: Hastings House, 1976.

———. *Communication and Social Order.* New York: Bedminster Press, 1962.

Eilers, Franz-Joseph. *Church and Social Communications: Basic Documents.* Manila: Logos Publications, 1993.

Fisher, Eugene J. "Reflections on the Thirtieth Anniversary of *Nostra Aetate.*" *Pace* 25 (January 1996): 9–25.

Fisher, Walter R. *Human Communication As Narration: Towards a Philosophy of Reason, Value, and Action.* Columbia, South Carolina: University of South Carolina Press, 1987.

Flannery, Austin, ed. *Vatican Council II: The Conciliar and Post Conciliar Documents.* Wilmington, Delaware: Scholarly Resources, 1975.

Frossard, André. *"Be Not Afraid!"* New York: St. Martin's Press, 1984.

Frye, Northrop. *Words With Power.* San Diego: Harcourt Brace Jovanovich, 1990.

Gallup, George, Jr., and Jim Castelli. *The American Catholic People: Their Beliefs, Practices, and Values.* Garden City, New York: Doubleday, 1987.

Geertz, Clifford. "Blurred Genres: The Reconfiguration of Social Thought." *American Scholar* 49 (1980): 165–179.

———. *The Interpretation of Cultures.* New York: Basic Books, 1973.

Gitlin, Todd. *The Whole World is Watching, Mass Media in the Making and Unmaking of the New Left.* Berkeley: University of California Press, 1980.

Goethals, Gregor. "The Expressive Face of Culture: Mass Media and the Shape of the Human Moral Environment-1." In *Mass Media and the Moral Imagination,* eds. Philip J. Rossi and Paul A. Soukup, 11–24. Kansas City, Missouri: Sheed and Ward, 1994.

———. "Media Mythologies." In *Religion and the Media,* ed. Chris Arthur, 25–39. Cardiff: University of Wales Press, 1993.

———. "Symbolic Forms of Communication." In *The Church and Communication,* ed. Patrick Granfield. Kansas City, Missouri: Sheed and Ward, 1994.

Goldman, Ari L. "Ideas and Trends: Can a Patriarchal Aura Close the Gap between a Pope and His Flock?" *New York Times*, 13 September 1987.

Granfield, Patrick. *The Limits of the Papacy: Authority and Autonomy in the Church*. New York: Crossroad Publishing, 1987.

———, ed. *The Church and Communication*. Kansas City, Missouri: Sheed & Ward, 1994.

Gray, Paul. "Empire of the Spirit." *Time*, 26 December 1994/2 January 1995, 53–57.

Greeley, Andrew M. *The Catholic Myth: The Behavior and Beliefs of American Catholics*. New York: Charles Scribner's, 1990.

———. *God in Popular Culture*. Chicago, Illinois: The Thomas More Press, 1988.

Griffin, Leland. "A Dramatistic Theory of the Rhetoric of Movements." In *Critical Responses to Kenneth Burke*, ed. William Rueckert, 456–473. Minneapolis: University of Minneapolis Press, 1969.

Gronbeck, Bruce E. "Electric Rhetoric: The Changing Forms of American Political Discourse." Paper based on lectures at Hayward Conference on Rhetorical Criticism, California State University-Hayward, 1989.

———. "Ronald Reagan's Enactment of the Presidency in His 1981 Inaugural Address." In *Form, Genre, and the Study of Political Discourse*, eds. Herbert W. Simons and Aram A. Aghazarian, 226–245. Columbia, South Carolina: South Carolina Press, 1986.

Grootaers, Jan. *De Vatican II à Jean-Paul II: le grand tournant de l'Eglise catholique*. Paris: Le Centurion, 1981.

Gudorf, Christine E. "Encountering the Other: The Modern Papacy on Women." *Social Compass* 36 (1989): 295–310.

Guizzardi, Gustavo. *La Narrazione del Charisma: I Viaggi di Giovanni Paulo II in televisione*. Torino: ERI/RAI, 1986.

———. "Religion in the Television Era." *Social Compass* 36 (1989): 337–353.

Hall, Stuart. "Encoding/Decoding." In *Culture, Media, Language*, 128–138. London: Hutchinson, 1980.

Hargrove, Barbara. "The Church, the Family, and the Modernization Process." In *Families and Religion: Conflict and Change in Modern Society*, eds. William V. D'Antonio and Joan Aldous, 21–48. Beverly Hills: Sage Publications, 1983.

Hart, Roderick P. *Modern Rhetorical Criticism*. Glenview, Illinois: Scott Foresman, 1990.

———. *Verbal Style and the Presidency: A Computer-Based Analysis*. Orlando, Florida: Academic Press, 1984.

Hebblethwaite, Peter. *In the Vatican*. Oxford: Oxford University Press, 1986.

——. *John XXIII, Pope of the Council*. London: Geoffrey Chapman, 1984.
——. *Paul VI: The First Modern Pope*. New York: Paulist Press, 1993.
——. *The Year of Three Popes*. London: William Collins, 1978.
Holmes, J. Derek. *The Papacy in the Modern World*. New York: Crossroad Publishing Co., 1981.
Hoover, Stewart M. *Mass Media Religion: The Social Sources of the Electronic Church*. Newbury Park, California: Sage Publications, 1988.
Jablonski, Carol J. "*Aggiornamento* and the American Catholic Bishops: A Rhetoric of Institutional Continuity and Change." *Quarterly Journal of Speech* 75 (1989): 416–432.
——. "Institutional Rhetoric and Radical Change: The Case of the Contemporary Roman Catholic Church in America." Ph.D. dissertation, Purdue University, 1979.
——. "Promoting Radical Change in the Roman Catholic Church: Rhetorical Requirements, Problems and Strategies of the American Bishops." *Central States Speech Journal* 31 (1980): 282–289.
Jamieson, Kathleen. "Antecedent Genre As Rhetorical Constraint." *Quarterly Journal of Speech* 61 (December 1975): 406–415.
——. *Eloquence in an Electronic Age: The Transformation of Political Speechmaking*. New York: Oxford University Press, 1988.
——. "The Metaphoric Cluster in the Rhetoric of Pope Paul VI and Edmund G. Brown, Jr." *Quarterly Journal of Speech* 66 (1980): 51–72.
——. "Papal Rhetoric." *America*, 24 May 1980, 444–446.
——. "A Rhetorical-Critical Analysis of the Conflict over *Humanae Vitae*." Ph.D. dissertation, University of Wisconsin, 1972.
Jaworski, Adam. *The Power of Silence: Social and Pragmatic Perspectives*. Newbury Park, California: Sage, 1993.
Jensen, J. Vernon. "British Voices on the Eve of the American Revolution: Trapped by the Family Metaphor." *Quarterly Journal of Speech* 63 (February 1977): 43–50.
John XXIII. *Princeps Pastorum: Encyclical Letter on the Missions, 28 November 1959*. Washington, D.C.: National Catholic Welfare Conference, 1959.
John Paul II. *Building Up the Body of Christ: Pastoral Visit to the United States*. Edited by National Catholic News Service. Washington, D.C.: National Catholic News Service, 1987.
——. *Crossing the Threshold of Hope*. Edited by Vittorio Messori. New York: Alfred A. Knopf, 1994.
——. *France: Message of Peace, Trust, Love, and Faith*. Boston: Daughters of St. Paul, 1980.
——. *France, que fais-tu de ton baptême?* Paris: Le Centurion, 1980.
——. *Insegnamenti di Giovanni Paolo II*, vol. III. Vatican City: Vatican Polyglot Press, 1980.

———. *The Pope Speaks to the American Church: John Paul II's Homilies, Speeches, and Letters to Catholics in the United States.* New York: HarperCollins, 1992.

———. *Redemptor Hominis.* In *Origins*, vol. 8, no. 40 (22 March 1979).

———. *Redemptoris Missio.* In *Origins*, vol. 20, no. 34 (31 January 1991).

———. *Le Saint-Père parle aux jeunes: 1980–1985.* Edited by Jean Claude Didelot. Vatican City: Conseil Pontifical pour les Laics, 1985.

———. *Unity in the Work of Service.* Washington, D.C.: United States Catholic Conference, 1987.

———. Video tape recordings of visits. Africa, 8–10 August 1985; Brazil, 12–21 October 1991. Centro Televisivo Vaticano, Vatican City.

Johnson, Paul. *Pope John Paul II and the Catholic Restoration.* New York: St. Martin's Press, 1981.

Katz, Elihu. "Media Events: The Sense of Occasion." *Studies in Visual Communication* 6, 3 (1980): 84–89.

Kelly, George A. *Keeping the Church Catholic with John Paul II.* New York: Doubleday, 1990.

Kelly, J.D.N. *Oxford Dictionary of Popes.* Oxford: Oxford University Press, 1986.

Kersten, Katherine. "What Do Women Want? A Conservative Feminist Manifesto." *Policy Review* (Spring 1991): 4–15.

Kiefer, William. *Leo XIII: A Light from Heaven.* Milwaukee, Wisconsin: Bruce, 1961.

Klenicki, Leon, and Richard John Neuhaus. *Believing Today: Jew and Christian in Conversation.* Grand Rapids, Michigan: William B. Eerdmans Publishing Company, 1989.

Lakoff, George, and Mark Johnson. *Metaphors We Live By.* Chicago: University of Chicago Press, 1980.

L'Attività della Santa Sede. Vatican City: Vatican Polyglot Press, 1965, 1980, 1985, 1987, 1991.

Lemieux, Raymond. "Charisme, mass-media et religion populaire: Le voyage du Pape au Canada." *Social Compass* XXXIV, 1 (1987): 18–19.

Leo XIII. *Rerum Novarum.* In *The Papal Encyclicals 1878–1903*, ed. Claudia Carlen, vol. 3. Wilmington, North Carolina: McGrath Publishing Company, 1981.

Lernoux, Penny. *People of God.* New York: Viking, 1989.

Luckmann, Thomas. "Shrinking Transcendence, Expanding Religion?" *Sociological Analysis* 50 (1990): 127–138.

Luzbetak, Louis J. *The Church and Cultures: New Perspectives in Missiological Anthropology.* Maryknoll, New York: Orbis Books, 1988.

MacKenzie, W.J.M. *Political Identity.* New York: St. Martin's Press, 1978.

Maraniss, David, and Laura Sessions Stepp. "Pope Leaves Amid Contradictions, Affection." *Washington Post*, 20 September 1987.

Martin, Bernice. *A Sociology of Contemporary Cultural Change*. New York: St. Martin's Press, 1981.

Martin, David. *The Breaking of the Image: A Sociology of Christian Theory and Practice*. Oxford: Basil Blackwell, 1980.

McBrien, Richard P. *Catholicism*. Minneapolis: Winston Press, 1980.

———. "The Hard-Line Pontiff." *Notre Dame Magazine* (Spring 1987): 27–29.

McLoughlin, William. *Revivals, Awakenings, and Reform*. Chicago: University of Chicago, 1978.

Mixon, Harold, and Mary Frances Hopkins. "Apocalypticism in Secular Public Discourse: A Proposed Theory." *Central States Speech Journal* 39 (Fall/Winter 1988): 244–257.

Moore, Sally F., and Barbara G. Myerhoff. "Introduction: Secular Ritual: Forms and Meanings." In *Secular Ritual*, eds. Sally Moore and Barbara Myerhoff, 3–24. Amsterdam: Van Gorcum, 1977.

Morley, Hugh. *The Pope and the Press*. Notre Dame, Indiana: University of Notre Dame, 1968.

Murphy, Francis X. *The Papacy Today*. London: Weidenfeld and Nicolson, 1981.

National Opinion Research Center. *The Catholic Priest in the United States*. Washington, D.C., 1972.

Neuhaus, Richard John. *The Naked Public Square: Religion and Democracy in America*, 2d ed. Grand Rapids, Michigan: William B. Eerdmans Publishing Company, 1984.

Niebuhr, H. Richard. *Christ and Culture*. New York: Harper and Brothers, 1951.

Orfei, Ruggero. "I viaggi del papa e i loro riflessi internazionali." *La Comunità Internazionale* 26 (1981): 5–19.

Osborn, Michael. "Archetypal Metaphor in Rhetoric: The Light Dark Family." *Quarterly Journal of Speech* 53 (April 1967): 115–126.

Osborn, Michael M., and Douglas Ehninger. "The Metaphor in Public Address." *Speech Monographs* 29 (1962): 223–234.

Otto, Rudolf. *The Idea of the Holy*. Trans. John W. Harvey. London: Oxford University Press, 1931.

Packard, Jerrold M. *Peter's Kingdom: Inside the Papal City*. New York: Charles Scribner's Sons, 1985.

Pearson, Michael Vincent. "Audience Adaptation and Argument in John Paul II's American Speeches—October 1979: A Textual Analysis." Ph.D. dissertation, Temple University, 1987.

Peck, Janice. *The Gods of Televangelism: The Crisis of Meaning and Appeal of Religious Television*. Cresskill, New Jersey: Hampton Press, 1993.

———. "Religious Television and the Creation of Meaning: A Study of Evangelical Programming." Ph.D. dissertation, Simon Fraser University, 1988.

Pope's Visit to Los Angeles: Highlights from KTLA's Historic 24-Hour Coverage. Channel 5, KTLA Inc., 1987. Videocassette.

Quinn, John R. "Toward an Understanding of the Letter on the Pastoral Care of Homosexual Persons." *America,* 7 February 1987, 92–93.

Reese, Thomas J. *A Flock of Shepherds: The National Conference of Catholic Bishops.* Kansas City, Missouri: Sheed and Ward, 1992.

———. *Inside the Vatican: The Politics and Organization of the Catholic Church.* Cambridge, Massachusetts: Harvard University Press, 1996.

Reid, Ronald F. "Apocalypticism and Typology: Rhetorical Dimensions of a Symbolic Reality." *Quarterly Journal of Speech* 69 (August 1983): 229–248.

Ritter, Kurt. "American Political Rhetoric and the Jeremiad Tradition: Presidential Nomination Acceptance Addresses, 1960–1976." *Central States Speech Journal* 31 (1980): 155–171.

Ritter, Kurt, and David Henry. *Ronald Reagan: The Great Communicator.* Westport, Connecticut: Greenwood Press, 1992.

Roper Center for Public Opinion Research. University of Connecticut, Public Opinion Polls, December 1979 and October 1981. Public Opinion Online, US Roper 80–1, RO 3; US Roper 8110, R 3.

———. *Survey on Sex, Profanity, and Violence.* Storrs, Connecticut: University of Connecticut, 20 April–3 May 1981.

Rudin, A. James. "The Dramatic Impact of *Nostra Aetate.*" In *Twenty Years of Jewish Catholic Relations,* ed. Eugene Fisher, 9–18. New York: Paulist Press, 1986.

Ruether, Rosemary Radford. "Mary in U.S. Catholic Culture." *National Catholic Reporter,* 10 February 1995.

Ryan, Halford R. *Franklin D. Roosevelt's Rhetorical Presidency.* Westport, Connecticut: Greenwood Press, 1988.

———. *Harry Emerson Fosdick: Persuasive Preacher.* Westport, Connecticut: Greenwood Press, 1989.

Salvini, Gianpaolo. "I viaggi di Giovanni Paolo II, annunzio itinerante del vangelo e 'segno' per il nostro tempo." *Civiltà Cattolica* IV(1985): 545–557.

Sanford, David. "The Pope's Groupies." *Harpers,* December 1979, 86–89.

Schanche, Don A. "Pope John Paul II: CEO." *Los Angeles Times Magazine,* 13 September 1987.

Schanche, Don A., and Russell Chandler. "The Papal Visit; Speeches May Discomfort Some Americans; Pope's Call to U.S.—Behave Responsibly." *Los Angeles Times,* 6 September 1987.

Schmitz, Kenneth L. "Modernity Meets Tradition: The Philosophical Originality of Karol Wojtyla." *Crisis* (April 1994): 30–36.

Shaw, David. "Activist Pope Puts Catholics at Front of Media Attention." *Los Angeles Times,* 18 April 1995.

———. "Coverage of UN Conference Shows Vatican Media Savvy." *Los Angeles Times*, 17 April 1995.

———. "Missing the Pope's Message: The Media's Ignorance of Religion and Their Zeal for Conflict Often Skew Coverage of John Paul II." *Los Angeles Times*, 16 April 1995.

Silverstone, Roger. *The Message of Television Myth and Narrative in Contemporary Culture.* London: Heinemann Educational Books, 1981.

———. "Television, Rhetoric, and the Return of the Unconscious in Secondary Oral Culture." In *Media, Consciousness, and Culture*, eds. Bruce Gronbeck, Thomas J. Farrell, and Paul A. Soukup, 147–159. Newbury Park, California: Sage Publications, 1991.

Simons, Herbert W. "Requirements, Problems, and Strategies: A Theory of Persuasion for Social Movements." *Quarterly Journal of Speech* 56 (February 1970): 1–11.

Simons, Herbert W., and Trevor Melia, eds. *The Legacy of Kenneth Burke.* Madison, Wisconsin: University of Wisconsin Press, 1989.

Solomon, Martha. "Redemptive Rhetoric: The Continuity Motif in the Rhetoric of Right to Life." *Central States Speech Journal* 31 (Spring 1980): 52–62.

Soskice, Janet Martin. *Metaphor and Religious Language.* Oxford: Oxford University Press, 1985.

Soukup, Paul A. "The Church as Moral Communicator." In *Mass Media and the Moral Imagination*, eds. Philip J. Rossi and Paul A. Soukup. Kansas City, Missouri: Sheed and Ward, 1994.

Spicer, Edward H. *The Cycles of Conquest: The Impact of Spain, Mexico, and the United States on the Indians of the Southwest, 1533–1960.* Tucson: University of Arizona, 1962.

Statistical Yearbook of the Church. Vatican City: Vatican Polyglot Press, 1995.

Swanson, Jon Charles. "The Rhetoric of Evangelization: A Study of Pragmatic Constraints on Organizational Systems of Rhetoric." Ph.D. dissertation, University of Texas, 1989.

Szulc, Tad. *John Paul II: The Biography.* New York: Scribner, 1995.

Thimmesch, Nick. "On the Secular Press." In *The Pastoral Vision of John Paul II*, ed. Joan Bland, 165–174. Chicago: Franciscan Herald Press, 1982.

Tompkins, Phillip K., Jeanne Y. Fisher, Dominic A. Infante, and Elaine L. Tompkins. "Kenneth Burke and the Inherent Characteristics of Formal Organizations: A Field Study." *Speech Monographs* 42 (June 1975): 135–142.

Tucci, Roberto. "Come gli Apostoli Pietro e Paolo, pellegrino verso i santuari viventi del Popolo di Dio." *L'Osservatore Romano*, 16 October 1985.

Tulis, Jeffrey K. *The Rhetorical Presidency.* Princeton, New Jersey: Princeton University Press, 1987.

Turner, Victor. *The Ritual Process: Structure and Anti-Structure.* Chicago: Aldine, 1969.

Turner, Victor, and Edith Turner. *Image and Pilgrimage in Christian Culture: Anthropological Perspectives.* New York: Columbia University Press, 1978.

Unsworth, Jim. "Oh Say, Did You See the TV Pope 'Pourri'?" *National Catholic Reporter,* 2 October 1987.

Vallier, Ivan. *Catholicism, Social Control, and Modernization in Latin America.* Santa Cruz, California: University of California, 1970.

Varacelli, Joseph A. *The Catholic and Politics in Post-World War II America: A Sociological Analysis.* St. Louis, Missouri: Society of Catholic Social Scientists, 1995.

Versaldi, Giuseppe. "Priestly Celibacy from the Canonical and Psychological Points of View." In *Vatican II: Assessments and Perspectives,* ed. Rene Latourelle, vol. 3, 131–157. New York: Paulist Press, 1989.

Washington Post-ABC News National Survey. *Washington Post,* 4 October 1995.

White, Robert A. "The New Communications Emerging in the Church." *The Way Supplement: Communication, Media, and Spirituality* 57 (Autumn 1986): 4–25.

Willey, David. *God's Politician: John Paul at the Vatican.* London: Faber and Faber, 1992.

Williams, George Huntston. *The Mind of John Paul II: Origins of His Thought and Action.* New York: Seabury Press, 1981.

Wilson, Bryan. *Religion in Sociological Perspective.* Oxford: Oxford University Press, 1982.

Witten, Marsha G. *All Is Forgiven: The Secular Message in American Protestantism.* Princeton: Princeton University Press, 1993.

Wojtyla, Karol. *The Collected Plays and Writings on Theater.* Edited by Boleslaw Taborski. Berkeley: University of California Press, 1987.

———. *Sign of Contradiction.* New York: Seabury Press, 1979.

Woznicki, Andrew N. *A Christian Humanism: Karol Wojtyla's Existential Personalism.* New Britain, Connecticut: Mariel Publications, 1980.

Wuthnow, Robert. *Meaning and Moral Order: Explorations in Cultural Analysis.* Berkeley: University of California Press, 1987.

———. *Producing the Sacred: An Essay on Public Religion.* Urbana, Illinois: University of Illinois Press, 1994.

———. *Rediscovering the Sacred: Perspectives on Religion in Contemporary Society.* Grand Rapids, Michigan: William B. Eerdmans, 1992.

———. *The Struggle for America's Soul: Evangelicals, Liberals, and Secularism.* Grand Rapids, Michigan: William B. Eerdmans, 1989.

———, ed. *Vocabularies of Public Life: Empirical Essays in Symbolic Structures.* London: Routledge, 1992.

Wuthnow, Robert, James Davidson Hunter, Albert Bergesen, and Edith Kurzweil. *Cultural Analysis: The Work of Peter L. Berger, Mary Douglas, Michel Foucault, and Jürgen Habermas.* Boston: Routledge & Kegan Paul, 1984.

Wynn, Wilton. *Keepers of the Keys.* New York: Random House, 1988.

Zahn, Gordon. *War, Conscience, and Dissent.* New York: Hawthorn Books, 1967.

INTERVIEWS

Alazraki, Valentina, Mexican journalist. Interview by author, 19 November 1992, Rome, Italy.

Defois, Gérard, archbishop of Sens, France. Interview by author, 24 March 1993, Sens, France.

Falez, Steve, former advisor to Paul VI on international visits and ambassador of Slovenia to the Holy See. Interview with author, 11 November 1992, Rome, Italy.

Foley, Archbishop John, prefect of the Council for Social Communications. Interview with author, 7 June 1990, Vatican City.

Harvey, Monsignor James M., secretariat of state of the Vatican. Interview by author, 21 November 1992, Vatican City.

Justo, Archbishop Mullor Garcia, papal nuncio to Lithuania. Interview with author, 4 January 1994, Vilnius, Lithuania.

Laghi, Pio Cardinal, prefect of the Congregation for Catholic Education. Interview by author, 21 September 1992, Rome, Italy.

Lynch, Monsignor Robert, general secretary, National Conference of Catholic Bishops. Interview by author, 28 August 1992, Washington, D.C.

Pullella, P., journalist with Reuters. Interview by author, 18 November 1992, Rome, Italy.

Rigali, Archbishop Justin, Congregation for Bishops. Interview by author, October 1992, Vatican City.

Shakespeare, Frank, former U.S. ambassador to Holy See. Interview by author, 16 May 1995, Washington, D.C.

Shaw, Russell, vice president, Knights of Columbus. Interview by author, 8 August 1992, Washington, D.C.

Szoka, Cardinal Edmund, president of the Prefecture of Economic Affairs. Interview by author, 8 November 1992, Rome Italy.

Travis, John, Catholic News Service. Interview by author, 28 October 1992, Rome, Italy.

Tucci, Reverend Robert, S.J., president of the Coordinating Committee of Vatican Radio. Interview by author, 13 February 1992, Vatican City.

Velloso, Gilberto C. Paranhos, ambassador of Brazil to the Holy See. Interview by author, 5 November 1992, Rome, Italy.

UNPUBLISHED SPEECH DRAFTS CONSULTED

Shaw, Russell. Drafts of proposed John Paul II speeches for 1987 U.S. papal visit composed while serving as press secretary to the National Conference of Catholic Bishops:

- Homily, Los Angeles, 16 September 1987
- Homily, New Orleans, 12 September 1987
- Remarks at Our Lady of Guadalupe Parish, San Antonio, 13 September 1987
- Remarks to Interreligious Leaders, Los Angeles, 16 September 1987
- Remarks on Departure, Detroit, 19 September 1987
- Remarks upon Arrival, 10 September 1987
- To Permanent Deacons and Their Wives, Detroit, 19 September 1987

National Conference of Catholic Bishops, Office of General Secretary. Drafts of proposed John Paul II speeches for the 1987 U.S. papal visit submitted to the NCCB:

- Address on the Ministry of Higher Education, New Orleans, 12 September 1997
- Address at the Youth Rally, Superdome, New Orleans, 12 September 1987
- Communication and the Media, 15 September 1987
- Papal Discourse to the Laity, San Francisco, 18 September 1987

Index

Accattoli, Luigi, 86, 87, 115
Ad limina, 55, 64, 123, 127, 165
African Americans, 60, 80
Agca, Mehmet Ali, 47
AIDS, 84, 91, 187, 205, 215
Alazraki, Valentina, 38, 48, 200 n.40
Anti-Defamation League, 110
Antone, Alfretta, 109
Apocalypticism, 148, 151

Barth, Karl, 115
Bellah, Robert, 19, 20, 21, 101–102, 113, 131, 147–148, 161, 214
Benedict XV, 3
Berger, Peter, 18–19, 24, 58, 120, 212, 230
Black, Edwin, 99
Breen, Myles, 194
Briggs, Kenneth A., 66, 73
Burke, Kenneth, 26, 108, 112, 118, 121, 135 n.62, 175, 179, 205, 214, 231

Casey, James V., 59

Castro, Fidel, 79
Catholic Charities, 59
Centrifugal tendencies, 8, 67, 73, 140, 144, 145, 147, 153
Centripetal tendencies, 67, 90, 104, 145, 147, 153, 158
Champion, Françoise, 189
Cheney, George, 53, 60, 63, 71, 76, 135 n.50
Chirac, Jacques, 56
Collegiality, 7, 32, 44, 64, 123, 165, 217
Collor de Mello, Fernando, 56
Communism, 43, 47, 89
Contextuality, 128, 184, 204, 208, 228; of audience, 102, 103, 110, 111, 131, 148, 198; local church, 70, 71, 73, 204; of metaphors, 166; papal visit, 14, 26, 57; sacred and, 13
Corcoran, Farrel, 194
Curia, 35-36, 39, 54
Curran, Charles, 38, 83

Deaconate, 72–73

Del Rio, Domenico, 191, 196, 199 n.9

de Montclos, Christine, 78

Deskur, André-Marie, 45

Dialogue, 62, 86, 109, 221; with audience 102, 104, 110, 114, 129; and authority, 158; with bishops, 205; of church and communism, 47–48; of church and world, 4, 18, 33; ecumenical, 127; with Jews, 130; structural, 63, 67, 83, 89, 91, 106, 185, 217; with youth, 184, 188

Diversity, 22, 168, 203, 227; of American culture, 70, 91, 102; in church, 19, 53, 144, 208; of church and world, 24, 118; ethnic, 72, 81; multicultural, 102, 162; and Polish background of John Paul II, 9

Dobbelaere, Karel, 17

Dolan, Jay, 11, 21, 220

Douglas, Mary, 24

Dulles, Avery, 19, 33, 114, 141

Duncan, Hugh Dalziel, 99, 102, 106, 108, 110, 111, 112, 121–122, 126, 129, 179, 182

Dutch Church, 6–7, 35

Ecumenism, 19, 119, 127, 151, 209

Ehninger, Douglas, 143, 166

Encyclical, 27, 226, 229; *Mater et Magistra*, 164; *Miranda Prorsus*, 49; *Redemptor Hominis*, 46, 148, 152; *Redemptoris Missio*, 49; *Rerum Novarum*, 2–3; *Vigilanti Cura*, 49

Equality, 126; of church membership, 104, 111, 142; and modernity, 180; of pope with audience, 101, 124, 197; and women, 159–160, 162

Evangelicalism, 13, 22, 23, 145, 222, 226

Evangelization, 31, 32, 49, 51, 77, 145, 164

Expressive revolution, 7, 8, 12, 20, 23, 100, 219, 223–224

Feminism, 159–162, 167, 205

Foley, John, 38

Frossard, André, 12, 147, 169 n.32, 187

Frye, Northrop, 140

Fundamentalism, 11, 12, 20, 116, 130, 151

Garvey, Helen M., 66

Geertz, Clifford, 24

Giscard d'Estaing, Valery, 56

Goethals, Gregor, 81, 87, 193

Greeley, Andrew, 222

Gronbeck, Bruce E., 89, 132 n.2

Gudorf, Christine, 160

Hannan, Philip, 181

Hanson, Donna, 66, 111, 184

Hart, Roderick, 73, 128–129, 137 n.115, 139, 173 n.95

Hebblethwaite, Peter, 34, 39–40, 46

Hierarchy, 101, 104, 129, 177–178, 179–180, 205–206, 209

Hispanic American, 79, 114

Holocaust, 74, 110

Homosexuality, 84

Hoover, Stewart, 20, 22, 23, 194, 222, 227

Hopkins, Mary Frances, 149

Hughes, Patrick S., 66

Immigration, 76, 79, 105, 128, 157, 205

Inculturation, 19, 72, 145, 162, 164, 208

Jablonski, Carol, 27, 72, 165, 226

Jamieson, Kathleen, 22, 27, 39–40, 123–124, 132 nn.8, 9, 144, 166, 175, 179, 189, 192, 226

Jews: address by John Paul II, 100, 119, 130; in background of John Paul II, 46; meeting with John Paul II, 80, 91, 110; *Nostra Aetate*, 75; relations with Vatican, 74–77

John XXIII, 3–4, 34, 37, 141, 162, 164, 189, 228; and Vatican Council II, 37, 141; and women, 162

John Paul I, 6, 9, 120

John Paul II: *The Acting Person*, 43, 44; assassination attempt on, 47; *Crossing the Threshold of Hope*, 220; early papacy, 44–48; visit to Africa (1985), 182; visit to Brazil (1991), 56, 57–58, 64, 65, 69, 78; visit to Fatima (1982), 47; visit to France (1980), 56, 68, 69, 86, 161, 183–184; visit to Mexico (1979), 45; visit to Nicaragua (1983), 56, 87; visit to Poland (1979), 45; visit to Poland (1987), 184; visit to Senegal, 57; visit to Thailand, 57; visit to U.S. (1979), 40, 59, 60, 62, 68, 183, 188, 194; visit to U.S. (1993), 62; visit to U.S. (1995), 56, 162. *See also* Wojtyla, Karol

Johnson, Mark, 148

Justice and Peace, Pontifical Commission for, 165

Katz, Elihu, 195

Keeler, William, 74

Kelly, Thomas, 58

Kennedy, John F., 193

Klaperman, Gilbert, 74

Klenicki, Leon, 110

Laity, 104, 105, 128, 129, 142, 154, 205; papal meeting with, 72, 73, 79, 165, 184, 196, 217; in planning visit, 57, 65–66, 86; Pontifical Council of the, 188; position in church, 8, 111, 129; relations with clergy, 70, 110, 143; Vatican Council II, 4, 112, 178; in world, 33, 111, 143

Lakoff, George, 148

Lefebvre, Marcel, 6

Leo XIII, 2, 36, 150

Liberation theology, 45

Liminality, 19–20, 21–22, 177, 184, 187, 197

Local church: collaboration with papacy, 204–205, 225; and media, 37, 48, 213; parish, 14, 32–33, 50; planning visit, 55, 57–66, 78–79, 210–211; speech drafting, 66–74, 82, 85, 90–91

Los Angeles Times, 87, 88

Lynch, Robert, 88

Mahoney, Roger, 64, 159

Marcinkus, Paul, 34

Marconi, Guglielmo, 37

Martin, Bernice, 19–20, 21–22, 24, 100, 188, 189, 213–214, 221

Martin, David, 20, 24, 78, 176–180, 185, 190, 192, 211, 216, 222, 223

Marxism, 42

Massivity, 19, 22, 26, 58, 120, 212, 230

May, John L., 74

McBride, Alfred, 66

McNulty, Frank, 66, 106–108, 181, 184, 187

Media: coverage of John Paul II, 1, 9–10, 214; framing, 198, 216, 224; journalists and Paul VI, 34, 120, 186; as papal image creators, 47–48, 51, 87–88, 189–190, 192; press coverage of papal visit, 65–66, 76, 83, 195, 198, 212, 213; press relations of Vatican, 4, 35, 37–39, 48, 50; and religion, 40, 84, 193–194, 197; strategy, 87, 88, 90; televangelism, 226; television coverage of papal visit, 45, 88–90, 91, 182, 195–196; Vatican policy on, 48–49; and youth, 183

Meese, Edwin, 76

Melendez, Tony, 187, 221

Metaphor: Body of Christ, 141–145, 206; of conflict, 153–156; of gift, 145–148; of orientation, 148–153; People of God, 7, 32, 54, 77, 82, 107, 117, 141–145, 166, 206; and religious meaning, 139–140, 143, 166–167

Mixon, Harold, 149

Moore, Sally, 178

Mussolini, Benito, 36, 37

Myerhoff, Barbara, 178

Myth, 115, 140, 198, 213; television as myth-maker, 193, 194, 195

National Conference of Catholic Bishops: and demonstrations, 84–86; and diversity, 82; and Jews, 74; National Advisory Committee, 111; papal speeches, 66–67, 69; planning papal visits, 58–64, 79, 83; and women, 159

Native American, 80, 82, 91, 108–109, 130, 144

Navarro-Valls, Joaquin, 38–39, 76, 88, 182

NCCB. *See* National Conference of Catholic Bishops

New York Times, 193, 198

Norms: and everyday behavior, 23, 203, 206, 214, 231; external, 147, 153; institutional, 72, 73, 120, 129–130, 159, 167; and modernity, 6–9, 10–11, 13, 217; objective, 117, 163; sacred, 70, 91, 104, 113, 131, 145, 156, 159, 204, 205; sexual, 83

O'Rourke, Brendan, 187

Orthodox Church, 5, 34, 60

Osborn, Michael M., 143, 166

L'Osservatore Romano, 3, 36–37

Paul VI, 5–6, 9, 40; communicative style of, 112, 120, 186; compared with John Paul II, 54, 155, 164, 185; and laicization of priests, 7; and media, 10, 37–38, 87, 186; papal visits of, 4–5, 34–35, 50, 228; and social communications, 49

Pearson, Michael Vincent, 101, 132 n.7

Peck, Janice, 20, 22, 23, 115, 145, 191, 192, 224–225, 226, 227

Phenomenology, 24, 42

Pilgrimage, 40; and holy year, 150; and narrative, 222; papal visits as, 34, 50, 54, 77, 78, 88, 193, 194; and populism, 218; voluntary, 21, 220

Pius XI, 3, 8, 37, 49, 76

Pius XII, 3, 5, 37, 49, 76, 120, 141, 228

Plausibility, 90, 223, 224, 226; conclusions about, 211–216, 230; and formation of community, 112, 130, 208; planning and, 58, 86; theory of 18–19, 53; thesis of papal visit, 13, 22, 23, 26, 27

Pluralism, 4, 17, 63, 70, 204, 206, 227

Poland: cultural background of John Paul II, 9, 41–44, 46, 152, 208, 219; papal visits to, 45–46, 47–48, 50; Polish American, 60–61; Polish language, 68, 192; Polish Solidarity, 162, 166

Populism, 4, 20, 21, 217, 218, 223, 228

Priesthood: and celibacy, 7, 83, 106, 108, 181; and deacons, 72; and identity, 166, 205; and laicization, 5, 7; and laity, 111; and media, 194, 196; meeting with priests, 65–66, 105, 106–108, 181, 184; ordination to, 10; papal address of priests, 110–112, 118, 124–125, 130; and planning papal visits, 65, 83, 122; and theological dissent, 83, 106; and ritual, 177, 179, 222; and women, 160

Protestantism, 11, 22, 27, 60, 114, 115, 116, 162, 191, 222, 225

Quinn, John, 84

Reagan, Nancy, 56, 182
Reagan, Ronald, 47, 151
Reese, Thomas, 58
Reid, Ronald, 155
Rigali, Justin, 40, 68, 76
Ritual, 19, 87, 178, 181, 186, 192, 197, 209; Catholic, 220, 222; Eucharistic celebration, 85, 90, 113, 176, 179, 196, 229; and media, 193, 194; Native American, 109; popes and, 190; secular, 81; and setting, 78, 89, 214; and text, 191; at Vatican, 40; of youth, 188
Roosevelt, Franklin, 88, 186
Rudin, James, 75
Ryan, Halford R., 29 n.34, 88

Secularization: accommodation and resistance to, 211; Christian response to, 11–12, 17–18, 27, 226–228; and church members, 206; in John Paul II speech, 117; and priesthood, 106; in U.S. culture, 25

Self: in dialogue with others, 102, 221; and intimacy, 114, 124–126, 219–220; language of self-fulfillment, 20–21, 205, 214, 231; and objective reality, 116; papal self-reference, 119–129, 131, 208, 220; philosophical study of self by John Paul II, 42; self-actualization, 167, 184, 208, 220, 223; self-determination, 109, 147, 223; self-giving, 147, 161–162; and social bonds, 121

Sensus fidei, 38, 158, 218

Serra, Junipero, 80

Shakespeare, Frank, 76, 95 n.70

Shaw, Russell, 66, 67, 89, 93 n.42, 94 n.55

Social Communications: Commission for, 45, 49; *Communio et Progressio*, 49; Pontifical Council on, 38

Solidarity: of bishops, 123; and love, 84, 185, 187; and millennium, 150–151; and order, 179; Polish, 162, 166; with poor, 142, 168; and role of religion, 193

Soukup, Paul A., 214

Spicer, Edward H., 109

Steinfels, Peter, 193

Symbolism: of audiences, 84–85, 90; of contrast, 131, 203–204, 209, 219, 229; cultural change, 11, 188, 206, 211, 222, 230; of family, 101; and gender, 160–162; of inversion, 105,

154, 216, 221, 224, 230; and
John XXIII, 164; and methodology, 25, 26; of order, 194,
196–197, 223; and papacy, 6,
44, 90, 91, 100, 179; and Paul
VI, 5; sacred, 20–23, 24, 87–88,
231; of setting, 59, 62, 78–82;
visual, 175, 210, 225, 226
Szoka, Edmund, 61, 62, 64, 93
nn.26, 27
Szulc, Tad, 42, 43, 45

Taub, Samuel, 66
Thomism, 3, 42
Time, 1, 9, 38, 186
Tucci, Roberto, 54, 57, 65, 92 n.8,
182
Turner, Edith, 21, 22, 24, 218,
220, 222
Turner, Victor, 21, 22, 24, 184,
218, 220, 222
Tutas, Stephen, 66

United Nations, 5, 34, 38, 40, 68,
165
Universality: and church organization, 32, 35, 71; and contextual,
71, 128, 164, 198; and inclusiveness, 115, 130, 150, 225;
and local church, 55, 59, 68, 90,
91, 145, 204, of meaning, 156,
167, as myth, 208, 213; and order, 179; and papacy, 61, 77,
121, 127, 151, 204, 224

Vallier, Ivan, 3, 14 n.2
Vatican Council, First, 2
Vatican Council II: and accommodation to world, 12, 18, 116,
149, 155, 227, 230; ambiguities
of, 5–6, 152, 164; characteriza-

tion of church by, 141–144,
166, 176, 206; characterization
of faith by, 146–147; as church
norm, 70, 164; and communications, 31, 32, 35, 37, 49; and inculturation, 71–72, 162; and
Jews, 75; and John XXIII, 4;
and laity, 111, 112, 178; on national episcopal conferences, 55;
and Paul VI, 4; on pope and
bishops, 74, 123; and preaching,
140; Wojtyla at, 42–43; and
youth, 143
Vatican Radio, 3, 36, 37, 65
Voice of America, 37

Waldheim, Kurt, 74, 76, 110
Walesa, Lech, 47
Washington Post, 90, 195–196, 198
Waxman, Mordecai, 74, 110
Williams, George Huntston, 41,
46, 152, 170 n.50
Witten, Marsha, 22, 114, 225, 226
Wojtyla, Karol, 41–44, 52 n.24, 54,
56, 169 n.32. *See also* John Paul
II
Wuthnow, Robert, 11, 13, 17,
26–27, 103, 125, 140, 226, 230
Wynn, Wilton, 6, 38, 186
Wyszynski, Stefan, 44

Youth: address of 101; emotive
power and, 221; informality
with, 183–184, 185, 187–189,
215; intimacy with, 119, 125;
meeting with pope, 63, 64, 70;
and social change, 22; and testimony, 165; and updated vocabulary, 143, 166; Wojtyla and, 43

About the Author

MARGARET B. MELADY is the President of the American University of Rome, Italy. She has a rich background in university administration and teaching, corporate management, and global communications. She is the author of studies in international culture and communication, and has been a consultant to domestic and foreign clients for a Washington-based public affairs firm.